T0304104

The Korean Labor Market After the 1997 Economic Crisis

Korea recovered from the 2007 world financial crisis more rapidly than most advanced economies. Why? Because a decade earlier Korea had been a victim of the Asian financial crisis and Washington Consensus economic policies that created great economic and social pain. Korea had learned from that experience that it is better to preserve jobs in a crisis than to allow market forces to displace huge numbers of workers.

Korea's concern about employment and the labor market reflects the fact labor played an exceptional role in Korea's transformation from an impoverished agricultural land to a developed country. The Korean road to economic success is through investing in the skills of people. It rests on a well-functioning labor markets and labor institutions. The Asian financial crisis of 1997 led to many changes in the economy and in policies, some of which succeeded and others of which did not, but all of which taught the country how better to address the 2007 crisis and "great recession".

For economists, policy-makers, and historians who want to learn how the Korean labor market dealt with the 1997 financial crisis and how this informed future policies, this volume provides a succinct summary of what Korean experts know and how they view the problems the country must overcome to continue its journey to the top rungs of economic success. The book is filled with institutional detail and statistics to enlighten scholars, and with critiques of policy and potential solutions from labor specialists. It provides a guide to the data on Korean workers and firms that can inform future research work.

Joonmo Cho is Professor of Economics at Sungkyunkwan University, Korea.

Richard B. Freeman is Professor of Economics at Harvard University, USA.

Jae-Ho Keum is a Researcher at the Korea Labor Institute.

Sunwoong Kim is Professor of Economics at the University of Wisconsin, Milwaukee, USA.

Routledge studies in the modern world economy

The Korean Labor Market
After the 1997 Economic Crisis

Edited by Joonmo Cho,
Richard B. Freeman, Jae-Ho Keum and
Sunwoong Kim

 Routledge
Taylor & Francis Group

LONDON AND NEW YORK

First published 2012
by Routledge
2 Park Square, Milton Park, Abingdon, Oxon OX14 4RN

Simultaneously published in the USA and Canada
by Routledge
711 Third Avenue, New York, NY 10017

Routledge is an imprint of the Taylor & Francis Group, an informa business

British Library Cataloguing in Publication Data
A catalogue record for this book is available from the British Library

Library of Congress Cataloging in Publication Data
The Korean labor market after the 1997 economic crisis/edited by Joonmo Cho ... [et al.].
    p. cm.
    1. Labor–Korea (South) 2. Financial crises–Korea (South) 3. Korea (South)–Economic conditions–1988– I. Cho, Joonmo.
    HD5828.A6K645 2011
    331.12095195–dc23

                                                            2011033810

ISBN: 978-0-415-59209-3 (hbk)
ISBN: 978-0-203-12801-5 (ebk)

Typeset in Times New Roman
by Wearset Ltd, Boldon, Tyne and Wear

Contents

Figures

Tables

Contributors

Chang Kyun Chae is Research Fellow of the Korea Research Institute for Vocational Education and Training (KRIVET), Seoul and has worked on labor economics and economics of education. He is a member of the employment forum run by the Ministry of Employment and Labor, and the Public Announcement Committee of Education Institutions Information run by the Ministry of Education, Science and Technology, Korea.

Joonmo Cho is Professor of Economics and Provost of Academic Affairs at Sungkyunkwan University in Seoul. His research covers many topics in labor economics including law and labor relations, industrial relations, and wage differentials. He has published papers in scholarly journals such as the *International Review of Law and Economics*, *Southern Economic Journal*, *International Labor Review*, and *Public Choice*.

Richard B. Freeman holds the Herbert Ascherman Chair in Economics at Harvard University. He is currently serving as Faculty co-Director of the Labor and Worklife Program at the Harvard Law School. He directs the National Bureau of Economic Research/Sloan Science Engineering Workforce Projects, and is Senior Research Fellow in Labour Markets at the London School of Economics' Center for Economic Performance.

Jai-Joon Hur is Senior Research Fellow of the Korea Labor Institute. He has worked on the impact of macroeconomic shocks, such as technological progress, FTA, and migration regulation, on the labor market and improvement of the social insurance system. He is actively participating in advisory groups for high government officials. His work experience and activities include Senior Economist at the World Bank and ILO consultant.

Jaeseong Lee is Research Fellow at the Human Resource Development Center at Sungkyunkwan University, Seoul, South Korea. His research interests are labor relations and the dual labor market.

Kyuyong Lee is Research Fellow of the Korea Labor Institute. He has worked on the labor issues of foreign workers and immigration policy.

Young Lee is Professor of Economics at the College of Economics and Finance, Hanyang University, Seoul, Korea and has worked on economic issues related to taxes, corporate finance, economic growth, and education. He was a research fellow at the IRIS center at University of Maryland and the Korea Development Institute before joining Hanyang University in 2002.

Jae-Ho Keum is Senior Research Fellow of the Korea Labor Institute. He directed the Korea Work Place Innovation Center and the Labor Insurance Research Center of the Institute. His major research area is dynamic changes of job stability and dual labor market.

Hyewon Kim is Assistant Professor of Korea National University of Education in Korea. He has worked on labor economics, social enterprise, and human resource development issues of the disadvantaged and female.

Sunwoong Kim is Professor of Economics at the University of Wisconsin, Milwaukee. He worked on Korean labor market and human resource issues for more than ten years. He is the co-editor of *International Economic Journal*.

Cheolsung Park is Professor of Economics at College of Economics and Finance, Hanyang University, Seoul, Korea and has worked on economic issues related to labor market, education, and family for more than a decade. He had been a Fulbright scholar and a faculty member at National University of Singapore before joining Hanyang University in 2009.

Ki Seong Park is Professor of Economics at Sungshin Women's University in Seoul, Korea and has worked on human capital, labor market, and economic growth.

Donggyun Shin is Professor of Economics, Kyung Hee University. His primary areas of expertise are cyclical fluctuations of the labor market, earnings volatility, and the income distribution. He is currently leading a government-sponsored research team which specializes in income polarization and social conflicts.

Kwangho Woo is a Research Fellow at Human Resource Development Center at Sungkyunkwan University, Seoul, South Korea. His research interests are labor economics and applied micro-econometrics.

Abbreviations

3D	Difficult, dangerous, and dirty
A&HCI	Arts and Humanities Citation Index
ALMP	Active labor market policies
BSSBE	*Basic Statistical Survey of Business Establishment*
BSSWS	*Basic Statistical Survey of Wage Structure*
CPS	*Current Population Survey*
EAPS	*Economically Active Population Survey*
EGR	Esteban, Gradin and Ray
EPL	Employment protection legislation
GOMS	*Graduates Occupational Mobility Survey*
GRDP	Gross regional domestic product
GSP	Gross state product
HIES	*Household Income and Expenditure Survey*
HRM	Human resource management
ICT	Information and communication technology
IT	Information technology
KEDI	Korean Educational Development Institute
KLI	Korea Labor Institute
KLIPS	*Korean Labor and Income Panel Study*
KLRC	Korean Labor Relations Commission
KSCO	Korean Standard Classification of Occupations
KSIC	Korean Standard Industry Classification
MLSS	*Monthly Labor Statistics Survey*
MOU	Memorandum of understanding
NAWRU	Non-accelerating wage rate of unemployment
NEET	Not in education, employment or training
NLYS	*National Longitudinal Survey of Youth*
NSO	National Statistical Office
OJL	On-the-job learning
OWS	*Occupational Wage Survey*
PES	Public employment service
SCI	Science Citation Index
SKKU	Sungkyunkwan University

SMBA	Small and Medium Business Administration
SME	Small and medium-sized enterprise
SSCI	Social Science Citation index
STLD	*Survey on Trends of Labor Demand*
UIW	University Information Web
YES	*Youth Employment Survey*
YPS	*Youth Panel Survey*

1 Introduction

Richard B. Freeman and Sunwoong Kim

The collapse of the US subprime mortgage market in 2007 generated financial panic and economic crisis in countries throughout the world. Korea was no exception. The annual GDP growth rate which exceeded 5 percent in the years preceding the crisis dropped by 3.2 percent in the fourth quarter of 2007 and declined further by 4.0 percent in the first quarter of 2008. The immediate impact of the crisis was greater in Korea than in many other countries because more than 40 percent of Korea's GDP comes from exports, making it highly vulnerable to global economic conditions.

To the surprise of many analysts Korea bounced back from the crisis remarkably quickly. While the economies of most OECD countries contracted for five- to eight-quarters after the onset of the recession, the Korean economy returned to a positive growth in the third quarter of 2009, after only three-quarters of decline. Thereafter, Korea accelerated to a very strong recovery of 6.3 percent in the fourth quarter of 2009 and 8.4 percent in the first quarter of 2010.

How did Korea manage such a quick recovery? In part because it had learnt from its recent history both how to respond and how not to respond to a sudden sharp decline. Only a decade earlier, in 1997–1998, Korea had experienced the devastating financial panic and economic crisis that afflicted many Asian nations. The foreign exchange crisis that started in Thailand in the summer of 1997 quickly spread to other Asian nations, including Korea. While the international bailout program coordinated by the IMF eventually extinguished the flame of the panic, the conditions the IMF placed on the Korean economy had huge costs that Koreans remembered and sought to avoid in the 2008–2009 crisis.

The 1997 crisis generated fundamental changes in the Korean economy. The scale and scope of the changes rivaled the economic changes that followed the democratization of the Korean political system in 1987. The advent of democracy in 1987 greatly strengthened the power of workers in the market. It produced a huge rise in real wages accompanying rapid economic growth, an increase in union membership and power – though no more than one in five workers ever joined the union movement – and diverse pro-worker legislation. The higher wages and cost of labor brought with it some economic problems, among other things: inflation, shifts of employment from manufacturing to the service sector, and militant labor relations.

The economic crisis of 1997, on the other hand, greatly weakened the position of workers. Although the crisis was in the financial markets, labor bore much of the brunt of the fall in real GDP. Unemployment increased greatly. Real wages fell in the year of the crisis and increased less rapidly after the crisis than they had increased before. Unions were weakened. After 1997 Korea had a more dualistic labor market with greater income inequality and a sharp division between regular and other workers. The crisis showed that the model of growth through export manufacture could not sustain the country to the next rung of economic development. Even when Korea recovered from the crisis, the labor market remained under considerable stress, with a larger share of workers in nonstandard jobs, falling employment in large manufacturing, and a developing mismatch between the "non-regular" or "non-standard" jobs (see definitions below) on offer in the service sector and the increasingly university-educated younger entrants to the job market with skills beyond those used in traditional services.

The 1997 crisis notwithstanding, by the onset of the twenty-first century Korea was one of the world's highly advanced economies, at the top of the second rung of high income OECD countries. Excluding small states, Korea ranked twenty-seventh in the world in per capita income in purchasing power parity terms.[1] Korean firms such as Samsung, Hyundai, and LG were world class in manufacturing. The United Nations Human Development Index placed Korea twenty-sixth in the world in its measure of development that goes beyond income per head.[2] Indicative of where Korea is headed, more than 80 percent of all young Koreans are in university or enrolled in at least some form of post-secondary education.

The transformation of Korea from an impoverished agricultural land to a developed country that is among the most human capital intensive in the world is one of the great growth stories of the twentieth century. Half a century ago, Korea was an economic disaster. The country had little natural resources. More than two-thirds of workers were poorly educated peasant farmers. The Korean War had ravaged its infrastructure. Japan had ruled Korea from 1910 to 1945, during which time it operated a colonial economic system designed for the needs of Japan, using resources for the Japanese military machine rather than for Korean economic development. After the Korean War, the country had to deal with the communist threat of more-industrialized North Korea. It overcame devastation and grew under the military protection of the United States with effective economic development policies.

Labor played an exceptional role in Korea's growth success – in large part because the country has little beyond its people as economic resources. During the years of the strong developmental state between the early 1960s and late 1980s, the government suppressed the unions and supported the chaebol conglomerates in their efforts to keep wages down and profits high with the purpose of maintaining a high rate of investment. Koreans worked more hours than any other people in the world during this period. Both government and individuals invested heavily in education, producing a huge expansion of college education in the 1980s. But the country treated the female half of the population poorly in the job market. The contribution of labor to Korean development makes it critical that researchers concerned with the Korean road to economic success understand the functioning of the Korean labor market and labor institutions, and that policy analysts and policy-makers monitor the operation of the labor market and seek ways to improve its functioning.

This volume brings together chapters by leading Korean labor researchers on some of the problems that face the labor market in the post-crisis period. The project was first initiated when Richard Freeman was visiting Korea in 2004 to deliver a keynote speech at the international conference on "Flexibility and Performance: International Perspectives on Labor Market Institution." While the conference was not exclusively on Korea, the conference organizer Sunwoong Kim and conference participants from one of the key sponsors, the Korea Labor Institute (KLI), felt that a monograph on the Korean labor market evaluating the labor market performances and examining the major challenges ahead would be useful. Under the leadership of Sunwoong Kim and Jae-Ho Keum, then research director of KLI, the KLI commissioned the authors to write papers on Korea's major labor market issues. The monograph was published by KLI in Korea under the title of "Beyond Flexibility." This book is an updated and revised version of the monograph. There are several substantial changes in the revision. Five of ten chapters (excluding the introduction) are totally new, and the remaining six chapters are thoroughly updated and revised from the KLI volume. Some contributors are affiliated with KLI and others are in academia. All are active researchers in the Korean labor market.

For historians, economists, and policy-makers who want to learn how the Korean labor market dealt with democratization and financial crisis, this volume provides a succinct summary of what we know. For those who want to understand the challenges that face a successful developing country on its way to the top rungs of economic progress, the book lays out Korea's problems and the types of policy solutions that may help resolve them. For researchers, the book provides a guide to the data on Korean workers and firms that can inform their own work. The Appendix describes key data sets that are used in this volume, and how to acquire them.

In this introduction we summarize some of the major findings in the book. We lay out the changes that have brought the Korean labor market from a period of extraordinary economic boom to the less heady economic world that followed the 1997 financial crisis and the institutional and policy responses to the changing labor market and economic realities. We conclude with a discussion of the lessons of past experience and the Korea's key future challenges.

Before we start it would be useful to lay out the definitions commonly used in Korean data regarding the labor force status or employment status of a worker. Korean data classify workers in the following way:

1   Working

    A   Wage worker

        i   Permanent (with a contract no less than a year)

        ii   Temporary (with a contract no less than a month and less than a year)

        iii   Daily work (with a contract less than a month)

    B   Non-wage worker

        i   Employer

        ii   Self-employed

        iii   Unpaid family worker

2   Unemployed (work less than an hour and has looked for a job during the last week)

3   Not in the labor force

As a substantial number of workers are in non-regular or non-standard employment, Korean statistics contain detailed classifications of these types of work:

1   Employment contract with indefinite period

    A   Continuation of employment expected

    B   No commitment of the continuation of employment

2   With fixed-term employment contract

    A   Possibility of renewal

        i   Contract period with no less than a year

        ii   Contract period with less than a year

    B   No possibility of renewal

3   Atypical or alternative employment

    A   Part time

    B   Agency worker (hired by an employment agency but supervised by a workplace supervisor)

    C   Contract worker (hired by an employment agency and supervised by the agency)

    D   Independent contractor

    E   Daily worker

    F   In-house worker

Based on these categories, research and policy analysts define non-standard or non-regular workers in two ways. The narrower definition adopted by the government in 2002 includes (2.A.ii) and (3). The broader definition favored by many labor activists and some researchers includes (1.B) and (2) and (3). It classifies a markedly higher proportion of the workforce in non-standard jobs. Both measures show that the proportion of the workforce outside the formal sector trended upward in the 2000s.

This book is composed of three sections. The first section contains five chapters that deal with the most important issues of the Korean labor market since the financial crisis of 1997. In addition to the historical overview of the post-crisis Korean labor market, it examines the pressing labor issues of improving opportunities for female workers, raising productivity in the service sector, reducing social polarization and the disadvantages faced by non-regular workers. The second section focuses on the increasing supply of college-educated workers. With a rapid expansion of higher education for the last two decades, more than 80 percent of high school graduates enroll in higher education institutions in Korea. The resultant sharp increase of the supply of college graduates created an enormous challenge in the labor market, with great competition among graduates for securing professional jobs. In addition to the two chapters on youth employment, this section includes a chapter on the market for university professors, who play a major role in research and the education of college students. The last section deals with other labor policy issues including the social safety network, the use of migrant workers and the vocational training system. In the following we discuss each chapter in more detail.

I The major issues in the Korean labor market after the crisis

Following the advent of democratization in Korea in 1987, the labor market experienced a huge boom that created abundant jobs and doubled the real wages of Korean workers in the decade that followed. Unions grew rapidly. The government introduced diverse legislation to improve labor standards. Income inequality fell substantially; in part because the supply of the highly educated workers grew, which limited wage increases for highly skilled workers, and in part because unions negotiated large pay increases for blue collar workers. Then the Asian financial crisis struck in 1997, raising unemployment, lowering the employment population rate, and leading the government to favor greater "flexibility" for firms to deal with the economic crisis. The post-crisis reform in corporate, financial, public and labor sectors began the process of transforming an industrial structure that was heavily reliant on the accumulation of capital and labor to one that would rely more on technological innovations. In the labor market, the crisis showed the limits of job protection policies. Job retention rates fell for all demographic and industry or occupation groups between 1995–1997 and 1997–1999, particularly for those with irregular jobs. During the ensuing recovery, job retention recovered for all but workers with 0–2 years of tenure (Chapter 2).

Historically, the Korean labor market has also been dualistic. High job retention and low mobility exist among workers in the large conglomerates and unionized firms. However, among the workers in small firms and temporary workers, job retention was low and mobility was high. Job tenure dropped in the age categories 45–49 and 50–54 because some 80 percent of Korean employees were covered by mandatory retirement around that age span and most retired from their regular job (see KLI survey referred to in Chapter 2). This contrasts to rising job tenure with age in other advanced countries. The OECD's measure of the strictness of employment protection legislation places Korea in the middle of advanced countries, with considerable protection for regular employees but with firms free to dismiss workers overall.

Between 1980 and 2000, the industrial composition of employment changed more rapidly in Korea than in other OECD countries due to the rapid shift of employment to services, particularly to low wage personal services, and hotel and restaurants. Given the huge productivity gap that developed in the 1990s between manufacturing and services, the shift portends a much lower growth of aggregate productivity unless service productivity increases. Indicative of the dualistic nature of the Korean economy, in 2003, manufacturing productivity in Korea was comparable to that in Spain, but service sector productivity in Korea was just 60 percent that in Spain. Similarly, while manufacturing sector productivity was twice as high in Korea than in Mexico, service sector productivity was just 10 percent higher in Korea than in Mexico (Chapter 3).

During Korea's growth spurt, manufacturing was the leading contributor to growth, with heavy industries and the chemical sector increasing output and exports even after the financial crisis. Productivity in manufacturing increased very rapidly. Between 1990 and 2004, it went from being below productivity in services to twice services' productivity. The rapid increase in manufacturing productivity dominated expansion of output, so that the share of employment in manufacturing fell from 27.2 percent to 18.5 percent over the same period. The light industries' share of the workforce dropped by 5.6 points, while the heavy and chemical industries' share fell by 2.5 points. In addition, the share of workers doing "production" work fell within manufacturing.

Women's labor participation has risen in Korea, but Korean women continue to have lower rates than the OECD average among 25–64 year old persons (59 percent vs. 65 percent). The gap between female participation in Korea and the OECD average is especially large among graduates (57 percent vs. 79 percent). The upward trend in female participation is driven largely by increased work activity among 25–29 year olds, and is thus associated with the decline in marriage rate and falling fertility. Marriage reduces the proportion of women working in offices. While the female to male earnings gap has fallen, particularly among the highly educated, Korean women continue to be paid less than men with equivalent skills (Chapter 4).

Currently Korea is going through a very rapid aging process. Reduced mortality and increased longevity and a precipitous drop in fertility to the lowest level in the world will create the most rapid aging of a population and workforce in history. Life expectancy at birth has increased by more than 25 years during the last 50 years. The total fertility rate decreased from about 4.5 in 1970 to below 1.2 in 2009. This rapid demographic transition, will increase the proportion of the Korean population aged 65 and over from 9.5 percent to 37.3 percent between 2006 and 2050. The under-utilized female labor force could be a valuable human resource substituting for the aging workers who will retire if the incentives for women to work improve.

The 1997 financial crisis increased the level of inequality in the distribution of earnings and family income in Korea. Until the crisis Korea had a relatively low level of income inequality. The financial crisis produced a large jump in inequality that persisted during the recovery. There was another significant jump in inequality in the middle of the 2000s. The rise of inequality took the form of "polarization" of the income distribution, with greater divergence between top and bottom and a hollowing out of the middle of the distribution (Chapter 5).

Compared with other OECD countries, Korea has an exceptionally large proportion of workers in non-regular jobs. In 2009, 42.9 percent of employees were either temporary or daily workers. While regular workers in large firms generally enjoy relative high security and good fringe benefits, the non-regular workers are concentrated in small firms where they have little job security and low wages and benefits. Contributing to the dualistic nature of the Korean job market, non standard employment – which includes workers in contingent and atypical jobs as well as non-regular workers – pays 20 percent or so less than standard employment, after adjusting for labor skills. These pay differences are greater in unionized sectors, where the company-level unions organize regular workers but usually do not organize non-regular workers.

Korea also has a higher proportion of workers in self-employment than most other advanced countries. In part this is because its level of GDP per capita is below that of the main OECD countries, and self-employment is historically higher among countries with low levels of income per capita. But it is also because the share of workers who are self-employed in Korea exceeds the share expected at its level of income. Most of the self-employed are sole entrepreneurs, selling in their own small retail stores. Analysis of the dynamics of transition between work states shows that many of the self-employed come from the ranks of unemployed and laid-off workers. From the 1990s through 2009 the share of workers who were self-employed or unpaid family workers fell, with about half of the drop due to changes in the industrial composition of employment.

Chapter 6 argues that government policies adopted in the post-1997 recovery deepened the duality of the Korean labor market. In order to increase the flexibility of the labor market during the economic crisis, the government relaxed the dismissal law, liberalized the legal restraints for hiring irregular workers and expanded the social safety net. Employers responded to the weaker dismissal law and greater ease of hiring non-regular workers by hiring more non-regular workers. They responded to the expanded social safety net by outsourcing more workers to small companies who generally do not pay social insurance obligations due to the inability of the government to enforce regulations and the exclusion of many non-regular workers. The result was that the reforms increased the divide between the large and small firms instead of creating a more seamless labor market.

II Markets for young workers

The rate of high school graduates enrolling in some form of post-secondary education increased in Korea from 33 percent in 1990 to 82 percent in 2005. The huge growth in the supply of college-educated workers reduced the wage premium between college graduates and high school graduates. The pay difference between junior college graduates and high school graduates virtually disappeared, but the premium for top university graduates remained sizable. Over the same period the increased concentration of employment by industry in general service sectors (wholesale and retail stores, hotels and restaurants), created the potential for mismatch between university-trained new entrants and jobs in traditionally non-university graduate areas. While the job aspirations of young workers rises with education, the sudden swell of the supply of college-educated young workers diminished their prospects of obtaining traditional college-level jobs. By contrast, in the market for low-skilled workers the reduced supply of less educated workers created a relative shortage that induced higher pay and an increased reliance on immigrant labor from lower wage Asian countries.

Chapter 7 documents that the economic crisis was particularly painful to young workers. The unemployment rate for workers aged between 15 and 29 doubled from 6 percent in 1997 to 12 percent in 1998. It had decreased gradually to 8 percent by 2003 and but has remained around 7 percent since 2006. While the unemployment rate is relatively low among OECD countries, many young people in Korea pursue advanced degrees while seeking work or become discouraged and drop out of the workforce. The proportion of employment to population for the age group 15–29 decreased from 45.1 percent in 2003 to 40.5 percent in 2009. For the age group 20–29 it decreased from 61.3 percent in 2002 to 58.2 percent in 2009. Youth unemployment is likely to create long-term loss of income, as it deters the accumulation of human capital in the early stage of one's work life.

Using a micro data set that follows graduates to work, Chapter 8 estimates the extent to which young persons with different levels of education end up in the residual NEET (not in education, employment or training) category. About 23 percent of high school graduates, 12.5 percent of junior college graduates, and 13.9 percent of four-year university graduates are NEETs. In humanities, social sciences and education, the proportion is as high as 15–18 percent. About 4.5 percent of university graduates are unemployed, and substantial additional numbers are enrolled in graduate schools in order to become more competitive in the job market.

In contrast to higher education in most countries, which is dominated by public colleges and universities and is thus highly dependent on governmental policies, the Korean higher education system depends heavily on private universities and the free choice of students and institutions. As the rating of colleges is mainly determined by faculty research performances, many higher education institutions put great emphasis in improving faculty research output in order to improve their rankings. At the same time, Korean universities have been criticized for not adequately training students for jobs, with the implication that research and teaching are substitute activities. Chapter 9 studies the relationship between the labor market performance of students and faculty research output. Graduates tend to have better labor market outcomes from university departments which perform more research, but this relation seems largely due to student admission scores, unmeasured characteristics associated with universities captured by fixed effects, and departmental characteristics. Taking account of these factors, faculty research output and graduates' labor market outcome are essentially unrelated. This rejects the criticism of the effort to improve research based on the view that faculty research substitutes for activities that help graduates succeed in jobs.

III Institutions and policies

The remaining two chapters deal with policy questions. Chapter 10 examines the way in which Korea has responded to the decline in its unskilled workforce via the immigration of foreign workers; Chapter 11 examines its programs to provide vocational training, particularly for young jobless persons.

Table 1.1 shows labor policies and practices in Korea in three periods of time: before the 1987 move to democracy; from 1987 through the financial crisis of 1997; and after the crisis. In the period before the country became democratic labor policies were limited. The main goal of the government was to suppress independent unions and keep wages and benefits low. There was little safety net protection for workers. Democratization brought with it a shift in policy toward workers. The government increased worker protection legislation, introduced a minimum wage law, shortened the statutory workweek, enacted an anti-discrimination law to protect female workers and extended social safety work. In 1988 it introduced a national pension system for workers in workplaces with ten and more employees. In 1989 it began to extend the coverage of the national health insurance from establishments with 500 or more workers to coverage based on location of residence regardless of employment status. In 1995 it introduced unemployment insurance for larger workplaces. Workers, particularly unionized workers in large firms, gain substantial wage hikes.

The financial crisis and subsequent economic difficulty put enormous pressure on the labor market and produced a shift in policy direction toward trying to create greater economic flexibility to recover from the crisis and avoid a future one. In practice this meant adopting policies favorable to firms. To increase market flexibility in reacting to the crisis, the government made it easier for firms to dismiss workers. At the same time, in 1998 it extended unemployment insurance to all employees. In an effort to create a more cooperative labor relations system, the government formed a tripartite commission between the government, labor and management. The crisis exacerbated the dualistic structure of the labor market. Unionized workers in large global companies maintained their high wages and relative job security, while the self-employed, small-scale service and manufacturing industry was forced to absorb increasing numbers of workers.

Table 1.1 Korean labor policies and practices in three periods of time

Policy or practice	Before democracy (1987)	Between democracy and financial crisis	After financial crisis (1997)
Minimum wage		Introduced in 1988	Has been increased continuously
Gender equality/female worker protection		Anti-gender discrimination in employment legislated in 1987.	90 days leave entitlement; paid by employment insurance since 2001; sexual harassment legislation in 2005; affirmative action plan required in public sector and private sector employers with 1,000+ workers in 2006
Industrial accident insurance	Introduced in 1964 for 300+ workplaces		Expanded to all employees in 2000
Employment protection			More liberal dismissal law passed in 1998; increased use of contracts that end in 364 days
National pension system		Started in 1988 for workplaces 10+	Universal coverage with the area plan in 1999; mandatory for all employees in 2003
Labor standards		44-hour week for five days, but with 12 hours overtime at 50 percent	Shortened to 40 hours (2003); applicable to employers with 20+ workers
National health insurance	Introduced in 1977 for 500+ workplaces	Area plan introduced (1989)	Expanded to workplace 5+ (2000); mandatory for all employees in 2003; workplace plan and area plan merged (2003); almost universal coverage in 2006
(Un)employment insurance		Introduced in 1995	Expanded to all employees in 1998
Trade union	Suppressed	Burst of unionism followed by stagnation/decline; lower inequality	Unions weakened; placed in defensive role
Tripartite agreements			Commission established in 1998
Anti-discrimination of irregular workers			Unreasonable discrimination between regular and irregular jobs barred; Maximum two years of temporary employment (2007)

Once the economy recovered from the shock of the financial crisis, the government began expanding social insurance schemes. In 2000 it extended industrial accident insurance to all employees. Previously the insurance was required only for employers with 300 and more employees. The government increased the minimum wage so that it reached 4,320 Korean won per hour (about $4.32 at the going exchange rate) in 2011. It also reduced the legal weekly work-hours to 40 hours per week in 2003 and expanded its coverage to smaller employers. In 1999 it extended the national pension system to all citizens through the area plan based on the location of the applicant, and in 2003 to all employees, essentially making the coverage universal. Similarly, the national health insurance, which had introduced an area-based plan in 1989, expanded mandatory coverage to all employees in 2003. Overall, labor policies have been quite responsive to economic conditions, almost procyclical in their orientation, favoring workers when economic conditions are good but squeezing workers when the labor market faces problems.

The decline in the number of Koreans with limited education willing to work in low-skilled jobs with hazardous working conditions has induced another type of labor policy. These are policies to fill unskilled jobs in "shortage" areas with migrant workers from neighboring Asian countries. The number of foreign workers experienced sustained growth to about 700,000 in 2010, almost 2.5 percent of total employment. More than 90 percent of foreign workers are in low-skill occupations. The influx of migrant workers has been maintained by a guest worker program. The dismissal of foreign workers during the economic downturn created substantial number of illegal migrants, as the job-losers did not want to return to their native countries. The migrant workers and accompanying family members generate social issues of multiculturalism. Given the global competition for highly skilled professionals, it is likely that the next frontier for immigration policy will be to develop policies to attract foreign professional workers (Chapter 10).

The comprehensive employment insurance system introduced in 1998 contained provisions for funding for vocational training programs to help workers be reemployed quickly. Expansion of the insurance program increased the number of subscribers from 4.3 million workers in 1997 to 9.4 million in 2008. In 2009, the vocational training program trained 150,000 of the unemployed. At the same time, the growing demand for life-long vocational and educational training and a more extensive social safety net increased government subsidies for vocation programs outside of the unemployment rolls, so that an additional 90,000 participated in the program. Employers and various designated training facilities and life-long learning facilities also provide worker training programs (Chapter 11). The benefits and costs of these various programs have been only rarely assessed to determine those that work and those that do not.

IV Lessons of the Korean experience

Korea's transformation from an impoverished agrarian economy to a high income industrialized modern economy is the premier example of successful economic development. From the studies in this volume and related work, we draw several lessons about "how Korea did it."

Korea's high growth during the early part of its industrialization involved huge more or less simultaneous investments in both physical and human capital. Korea had a very high domestic savings rate but also borrowed from abroad to finance the capital accumulation. The government policies, however, favored domestic firms over foreign direct investments. At the same time, Korea invested heavily in education through the expansion of the formal school system. Both the government and private citizens spent large sums for primary, secondary, and eventually university education of young people. Households paid a large portion of the costs of primary and secondary education. The private share of expenditure on higher education was one of the highest in the world, with private universities and colleges enrolling more students than public institutions.

By investing heavily in education on the post-Korean war baby boom generation, and then university training, Korea channeled a rapidly growing population from the agricultural sector to the industrial sector. The accumulation of human capital, particularly of young graduates with engineering and management skills, allowed Korean companies to succeed making "exports the engine of growth." Absent the concordant accumulation of human and physical capital, Korea might have failed to sustain its rapid growth. Investment in physical capital would have run into a shortage of skilled labor that might have frustrated further investments in physical capital. The concordance of human capital development with industrialization also played a role in creating a middle class of educated industrial workers and a relatively egalitarian distribution of income, which later helped make the successful political transition from a dictatorial development state to democracy. The dictatorial military governments between 1961 and 1987 were responsible in creating a big-push of industrialization and economic development, while the new middle class in the late 1980s was responsible for establishing the stable democratic regimes that followed.

Korea's legacy from Japanese colonialism of a more equal distribution of income than in many African and Latin American developing countries also is a likely contributing factor in the country's economic success. The rapid social and political reshuffle from monarchy to colonialism to US military rule to dictatorial regime, all in about 50 years, minimized social class distinctions. Social mobility through education and hard work was within the reach of most of the population in the early part of the modernization process.

One of the weaknesses in Korean development was in creating cooperative labor management relations. During the period of dictatorial government and rapid economic development, workers received a relatively small portion of the economic gains. The coalition of the government and large chaebols kept a lid on wage increases and suppressed unions. This left a legacy of radical thinking among many workers and unionists and distrust between labor and management and labor and government that persisted for years. Democratization created a window for the unions to expand their influence, resulting in faster wage increase and better working conditions for union workers, and for other workers as well. But post the 1997 financial crisis, the government's Tripartite Commission that included representatives from employers, workers and the state, was largely ineffective in achieving compromise among the parties. More radical trade unions refused to cooperate within the framework of the commission and dropped out. Workers in small firms and self-employed workers who make up much of Korea's workforce were not properly represented as part of the effort. International comparisons show that better labor–management cooperation is associated with better economic outcomes. In Korea labor strife caused economic and social pain, but failure to attain a more cooperative labor system did not prove to be a barrier to successful development or recovery from the crisis.

V Challenges for the future

To attain the top rung of OECD countries, Korea will have to improve its labor market related policies and institutions in several ways. We list below the major challenges and offer ideas about how to approach them:

A Creating a unified labor market

The Korean labor market has one distinctive feature that differentiates it from those in most highly advanced countries. It is fragmented into segments: the traditional industrial sector, the new knowledge sector, and the informal sector of self-employed persons, unpaid family workers, and small firms.

The traditional industrial sector, dominated by large global firms, most of which are affiliated with chaebols, has high productivity comparable to productivity in the top-rung OECD countries. Wages are high in this sector. During Korea's period of rapid growth, traditional industry was the main locomotive of economic development and growth of employment. But while the traditional sector continues to expand, its share of the workforce has been falling as productivity increases have outpaced the rising demand for output. The traditional sector has a long history of labor and capital conflicts. The increasing supply of university-educated workers, particularly with degrees in science and engineering fields, has boosted the new knowledge sector. This sector is just developing and has yet to expand enough to absorb the new supply of college graduates. The large informal service sector of the self-employed and workers in small family businesses with low productivity, limited safety nets and poor working conditions, remains the employer of a high proportion of Korea's workforce. Approximately one-third of workers in Korea are self-employed or unpaid family workers; 30 percent are non-regular workers (with considerable overlap so the total for the two groups falls short of the sum of the two percentages).

Korean labor market policy should try to reduce the differentials among these sectors to create something closer to a seamless fluid labor market. This would give the country greater flexibility in absorbing external shocks and would reduce earnings inequality and political tension and hostility among different social groups. To do this would require improving productivity in the service sector, increasing employment in knowledge-intensive sectors and reducing confrontation in the traditional industrial sectors.

B *Improving the service sector*

Productivity in the service sector in Korea is just 56 percent that in manufacturing, whereas productivity in service sector is 93 percent of productivity in manufacturing in advanced OECD countries. This means that the rising share of services in employment is a potential barrier to Korea reaching the top rungs of OECD economies unless the country can increase productivity in services massively. Because Korean firms dismiss workers at age 50 or so, 57 percent of workers 50 and over are self-employed, many of whom come from regular jobs in the formal sector. By contrast, 27 percent of younger workers are self-employed. Japan's large firms also dismiss workers at a given age, but many of those workers end up in smaller firms, where they may be more likely to use their skills, rather than self-employed. One possible policy to improve the transition to self-employment would be to develop training programs for workers for self-employment as they approach the dismissal age. In addition, faced with an aging population, Japan has been raising the age at which major firms readjust their workforces, which might also be fruitful in Korea. Finally, Korea's high Internet access and broadband connection should make it a leading center for e-commerce, but at this writing Korea has fewer secure servers than almost any other OECD country.

Greater information about the self-employed would help Korea devise evidence-based policies to improve their situation. Relatively little is known about the flow of self-employed back and forth from the formal sector; income differentials between self-employed and non-regular workers and comparable workers in the formal sector, particularly of the workers who shift between the two sectors; of the use of capital in the informal sector; and of the returns to skill and career paths of those who spend most of their work lives in the informal sector compared to those who enter in their mid-fifties. Without information on the determinants of productivity in the informal sector it is difficult for the government or other interested organizations to devise innovative ways to help businesses and workers raise productivity. Without greater information on injuries in the informal sector, it also difficult to develop programs to improve occupational health and safety and working conditions.

C Absorbing the influx of college graduates

Given that about 80 percent of young Koreans obtain some post-secondary education, Korea needs to find ways to assure that the new college graduates, many with science and engineering degrees, and junior college graduates obtain jobs that use their skills. As one of the lead countries in adapting to the Internet, Korea should be able to improve the process of matching employees and firms through creative use of Internet job boards. Traditionally, firms have relied on the hierarchy of universities to signal graduate skills, but there may be more effective ways for firms to find the type of workers they want by reducing the role of signaling and increasing the importance of actual skills in hiring practices.

In most advanced countries, the proportion of new university graduates who are women exceeds 50 percent. While female college-going has increased in Korea, it lags behind that in other countries, and the Korean job market has not adjusted fully to this growing source of skilled labor. To encourage women graduates to stay in the job market, the country must reduce barriers to their promotion and develop substitutes for household production. Educated women face a dilemma during the childbearing and rearing years as having children harms their career prospects. With its low fertility rate, Korea has a dual policy dilemma: to encourage child-bearing while at the same time encouraging highly educated women to stay in the job market. This could require programs to enable women to take maternity leave and extended leave from work without losing their job skills and employment prospects.

On the demand side, Korea is a world leader in spending on education and R&D. The OECD rated it fourth in the world in investment in knowledge relative to GDP. But Korea ranks low in PhD graduates per person of the relevant age, has few foreign PhD students and virtually no highly skilled immigrants. Moreover, despite its R&D spending Korea's record in papers and citations is mediocre, perhaps because business conducts most R&D, where papers and citations are not that important. Korea is the leading country in the percentage of collaborations with the United States, the leading country in science, which should help it improve its research performance. An increasing proportion of collaborative research papers is also done with China, which is rapidly becoming a giant in the science world. This also should help Korea raise its performance in basic R&D. The increased importance of academic research of international quality in promotion and tenure in university positions should give academics greater incentive for such collaborations and improving the quality of research. In the industrial sector, while Korean firms have an admirable record of R&D and innovation in manufacturing, they lag in R&D on improving service sector productivity. The country rates second among OECD countries in the share of value added in knowledge intensive manufacturing but only fourteenth in the share of value added in knowledge-intensive market services. To raise output in the knowledge-intensive markets, Korea needs to improve the linkage between the corporate R&D sector and the university R&D sector.

D Moving traditional labor sector relations from conflict to cooperation

Labor–management conflict has been falling in advanced countries, with potentially positive impacts on economic performance. Korean labor relations remain marked by labor–management conflict. Strikes are often bitter. Government efforts to establish social dialog between firms and workers from the top down failed in the late 1990s, so something new is needed to improve labor relations. International experience suggests that it is easier to establish cooperation between labor and management at workplaces than at higher levels. Workers generally want to work cooperatively with management while maintaining some independent voice at their workplace to represent their interests to management. In the European Union works councils are a valuable building block for developing national social dialogue. British experience suggests that democratic selection of union leaders is critical for cooperation; it is important that leaders represent members and not some ideological view. American unions have tried to use their pension-fund wealth and aggressive corporate campaigns to pressure particular firms to be more cooperative but have succeeded only intermittently.

Moreover, as the skill of employees and technical requirements of jobs rise, many firms find that some form of profit-sharing and devolution of decisions to workers has productive value. Many US firms pay some part of wages in the form of profits and devolve some authority to workers because this raises firm performance. "Shared capitalism," which ranges from profit-sharing to employee ownership to granting stock options to all employees increases the likelihood of cooperative labor–management relations. It is possible that Korea would do better in achieving a more harmonious labor situation by building cooperative labor–management relations from the enterprise up, through some form of financial and authority sharing, rather than through national dialogue.

E Reducing working hours

Korean workers have the longest work hours among OECD countries. The average number of hours actually worked in 2005 was 2,354 hours, whereas in the United States the average number of hours worked was 1,804 hours and in Japan 1,775 hours. Such long working hours played an important role in the rapid economic development, but are no longer a natural source for either economic growth or improving living standards. Since the early 1980s the number of working hours has been declining gradually but it is still very high from an international perspective. Some decline in hours worked is necessary for Koreans to attain comparable living standards to those in the highest income countries, and possibly to raise productivity as well.

Why do hours worked remain so high? Before Korea reduced legal working hours per week to 40, a natural explanation was that the country was slow to reduce the statutory workweek. But it is the concentration of Korean workers in smaller workplaces and the high proportion that are self-employed to whom the law does not apply that explains much of the long hours in the early 2000s. In addition, the financial crisis may have slowed the reduction in hours worked, as the danger of unemployment created a workplace environment in which workers voluntarily work longer hours in order to increase their job performance and thus their job security.

Reduction of working hours is intrinsically related to the preceding four challenges. Movement toward a single labor market would presumably lead to greater spillover of the practices of large firms and the government sector to smaller employers so that shorter working hours become more popular. Increased efficiency in the service sector is likely to decrease the working hours. Reductions in hours might help keep more educated women in the workforce. And lower hours should contribute to better labor relations in large and unionized workplaces.

F Delivering social safety services to older persons and informal sector workers

Aging of the population is occurring more rapidly in Korea than in virtually any other country. The high and rising proportion of the population in their sixties and seventies and older will increase the demand for social services for the elderly such as health care and pensions. This will strain the resources devoted to investment, which could reduce the rate of economic growth and make it more difficult to pay for social services. In the labor market, the prolonged low fertility rates of the past 20–30 years and increased longevity will reduce labor supply sharply starting in the mid-2020s, reducing the labor resources for growth. The country could find itself with greater demands for social services and less ability to provide them – a recipe for social division and generational conflict.

Aging aside, even after increased coverage of the four major social insurance programs, a substantial portion of non-standard workers are not covered by one or more of the programs. They do not receive many employment-related benefits such as retirement packages, maternity leave, and paid vacations. The delivery of these benefits is one of the key challenges that the Korean labor market faces, because these workers need the expanded social safety net more than anyone else, particularly when they retire from work.

The Korean government required social insurance participation starting from the large employers, because they have stronger financial resources and face pressure from employees. Expanding the scheme to small employers and self-employed workers and their unpaid family workers is difficult. Mandatory imposition of social insurance to the employer adds to the cost of business, which small firms might find hard to meet, given their financial situation. Enforcement is difficult since many workers with limited incomes, as well as employers, prefer to avoid paying costs for future benefits. The challenge is to find a way to encourage the informal sector workers and small firms to participate, for instance through some form of subsidy, without unduly burdening the formal sector to raise money for such subsidies.

VI Conclusion

To move to the next level of economic development, Korea will have to improve the way in which its labor market operates. Expert knowledge from the experiences of other countries, and the studies of Korean practices and policies in this volume, can help the country choose among the options for modernizing its labor system. Since labor practices work best when workers and firms choose them, rather than when they are imposed from the state, it is important to determine what workers want and what management wants. Since so many workers are non-regular or non-standard workers it is particularly important to ascertain the ways to help persons in the informal sector improve their productivity and participation in social programs.

In the Appendix that appears at the end of the book, we briefly describe major data sets available to study the Korean labor market. Most of the data sets are used in the studies reported in this volume. The *Economically Active Population Survey* (EAPS) is a monthly household survey with a size of 30,000. The *Korean Labor and Income Panel Study* (KLIPS) is a longitudinal data set of about 5,000 households and their members, whose ages are 15 and older since 1998. The *Monthly Labor Statistics Survey* (MLSS) surveys workplaces to collect information on wages, working hours and employment. The *Basic Statistical Survey of Wage Structure* (BSSWS) is conducted to identify the wages and working hours of workers by types of occupation and industry who are employed by businesses with five or more regular workers (about 6,500 businesses yearly). The *Household (Income and Expenditure) Survey* has been conducted monthly in order to study the revenue and expenditure pattern of about 27,000 urban households. The *Youth Panel Survey* (YPS) is a longitudinal survey to study the transition from school to work of young people since 2001: the number of observations in the first year was about 8,000. The *Basic Statistical Survey of Business Establishment* (BSSBE) is a census of business establishment conducted annually since 1994. It collects basic information such as location, nature of the business, employment, changes in business for all private businesses, except individual farmers and fishermen. The *Survey on Trends of Labor Demand* (STLD) is a survey of the 15,000 business establishments with five and more employees on current employment and help wanted. The *Graduates Occupational Mobility Survey* (GOMS) is a longitudinal survey that follows about 25,000 of graduates of junior colleges and four-year universities that started in 2004. The quality of these data sets is generally quite high, and can be used not only by Korean scholars but scholars from other countries. The contact information for the data sets can be found in the Appendix as well.

Notes

1 World Bank Group's website, online, available at: http://siteresources.worldbank.org/datastatistics/Resources/GNIPC.pdf.
2 Human Development Reports' website, online, available at: http://hdr.undp.org/en/statistics/.

2 Historical background before and after the financial crisis

Jae-Ho Keum

I Labor market conditions and trends

A Overview of employment and unemployment

Due to the rapid economic growth and a demand for labor that had been increasing for more than three decades, Korea experienced a serious labor shortage as it approached the financial crisis in November 1997. The unemployment rate remained at less than 3 percent for more than ten consecutive years. Analysts argued that the unemployment rate was too far below the non-accelerating wage rate of unemployment (NAWRU). Over the 1990–1997 period, the growth rate of nominal wages averaged around 13 percent (see Figure 2.1). From 1987 to 1997, real wages almost doubled. Wage growth far outstripped productivity growth, undermining the competitiveness of Korean goods at the global marketplace. In addition, rapid increases in wages discouraged a large number of companies from investing.

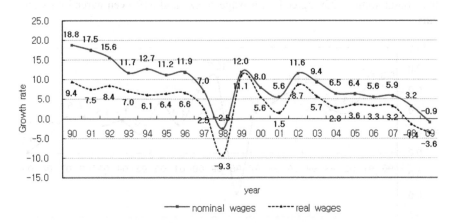

Figure 2.1 Growth rates of non-farming industries nominal and real wages (source: Ministry of Employment and Labor, *Monthly Labor Survey Report*, each year).

Note
Real wage = 100 × nominal wage/consumer price index.

The financial crisis of 1997, which was followed by structural reforms and macro-economic stabilization programs, had a significant impact on the labor market. In 1998, the growth rate of real GDP was −5.7 percent (see Figure 2.2), and the inflation rate rose to 7.5 percent. At the same time, the crisis accelerated the restructuring of the labor market. In order to minimize job losses, the Korean government encouraged the private sector to introduce more flexible manage-ment practices, such as part-time employment, work-sharing, and flexible working hours. Wage flexibility also played an important role in responding to the crisis. As a response to the criticism that labor hoarding within firms was one of the causes of the financial crisis, the Labor Standards Act was amended by the Tripartite Commission. The amendment enabled employers to dismiss redundant workers, opening up ways for enterprises to lower labor costs and improve their competitiveness. Despite the relatively strict conditions for dismissal and, in par-ticular, the requirement that firms should make every effort to rehire the dis-missed workers when intending to hire workers within two years of the dismissal date, many workers lost their jobs through dismissal.

The number of employed persons fell by 1.3 million and the unemployment rate reached 7.0 percent, with the number of unemployed exceeding 1.4 million (see Table 2.1). Most job losses occurred in construction, trade and manufactur-ing sectors. By occupation, non-professional jobs such as machine operators, assemblers and manual laborers were affected the most. After the financial crisis, the proportion of regular workers in total employment decreased, while that of temporary and daily workers increased (see Table 2.5).

In terms of wage adjustments, the growth of nominal wages decreased from 7.0 percent in 1997 to −2.5 percent in 1998, while real wages fell by 9.3 percent in 1998. The results of wage bargaining in 1998 show that agreed wage increases averaged −2.4 percent. Out of 3,337 workplaces which had concluded their bargaining, 2,259 agreed on a wage freeze and 559 even agreed on wage cuts.

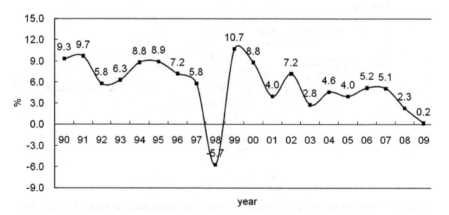

Figure 2.2 Growth rate of real GDP (source: Bank of Korea, *National Account,* each year).

Table 2.1 Trends in labor force participation (thousands, %)

Year	Population aged 15 and over				Labor force participation rate (%)	Unemployment rate (%)
		Labor force				
			Employed	Unemployed		
1980	24,463	14,431	13,683	748	59.0	5.2
1985	27,553	15,592	14,970	622	56.6	4.0
1990	30,887	18,539	18,085	454	60.0	2.4
1995	33,659	20,845	20,414	430	61.9	2.1
1996	34,274	21,288	20,853	435	62.1	2.0
1997	34,851	21,782	21,214	568	62.5	2.6
1998	35,347	21,428	19,938	1,490	60.6	7.0
1999	35,757	21,666	20,291	1,374	60.6	6.3
2000	36,186	22,069	21,156	913	61.0	4.1
2001	36,579	22,417	21,572	845	61.3	3.8
2002	36,963	22,877	22,169	708	61.9	3.1
2003	37,339	22,916	22,139	777	61.4	3.4
2004	37,717	23,370	22,557	813	62.0	3.5
2005	38,300	23,689	22,856	833	61.9	3.5
2006	38,762	23,934	23,151	783	61.7	3.3
2007	39,170	24,166	23,433	733	61.7	3.0
2008	39,598	24,303	23,577	725	61.4	3.0
2009	40,092	24,334	23,506	829	60.7	3.4

Source: National Statistical Office, *Economically Active Population Survey*, each year.

The Korean economy rapidly recovered from its deep recession, mainly owing to the painful efforts of economic restructuring after the financial crisis. Growth resumed with improved export performance and increase in investment. Real GDP grew by 10.7 percent in 1999. Although the unemployment rate remained as high as 6.3 percent in 1999, largely due to the lagging effects of business cycles on the labor market, it started to decrease significantly in 2000. The unemployment rate in 2005 was 3.5 percent, with 833,000 people unemployed.

However, we can hardly say that the financial crisis is over in the labor market. The unemployment rate is still high given that the social safety net is not yet well established. Although the unemployment rate is falling, it is unlikely that it will return to the 2 percent level observed before the financial crisis. Furthermore, the labor force participation rate in 2000 was only 61.0 percent, far below that for 1997. And the number of employed in 2000 was still lower than that for 1997 (see Table 2.1). Even in 2009, the labor force participation rate still failed to reach the level of 1997. The relatively low employment/population ratio and the number of the employed suggest that there are still a large number of discouraged workers who were (in 2009) not looking for jobs because of the economic downturn (see Figure 2.3).

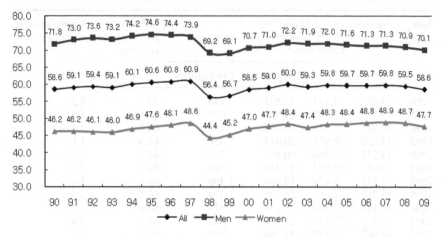

Figure 2.3 Trend of employment/population ratio (source: National Statistical Office, *Economically Active Population Survey*, each year).

B Recent changes in employment structure

1 Female workers play a leading role in employment increase

Largely due to high economic performance, Korea has been able to create jobs for new entrants to the labor market. Since the first Economic Development Plan in the early 1960s, employment has increased rapidly. The number of employed persons increased from 13.68 million in 1980 to 21.21 million in 1997 and 23.51 million in 2009. Over that period, female workers played a crucial role in increasing the employment rate as well as the participation rate. The female participation rate went up from 41.9 percent in 1985 to 49.8 percent in 1997. Finally, in 2006 it recorded 50.2 percent. Various factors such as decreasing fertility, expansion of child-care services, growth of the information technology (IT) industry, and flexible working hours have contributed to this increase. One fact worthy of mentioning is that, after the financial crisis, the labor force participation rate of women, as well as the ratio of women in total employment, continuous to increase while that of men is relatively stable.

Although the labor force participation rate has increased steadily since the 1990s, mainly due to the increased participation of women, the labor force participation rate is still low in Korea when compared to other OECD countries. In 2008, the participation rate of persons aged 15–64 years was 66.0 percent, 4.8 percentage points below the OECD average. As seen in Figure 2.4, the participation rate for women is particularly low. This is widely attributable to the lack of institutional arrangements such as child-care services, maternity leave, and also to sexual discrimination. The strong tendency of women to withdraw from the labor market when they lose their jobs is one of the reasons for this low level of participation.

Table 2.2 Labor force participation by sex: aged 15 and over (thousands, %)

	Number of labor force participants	Labor force participation rate (%)	Number of employed	Male/female proportion of workers (%)
Male				
1990	11,030	74.0	10,709	59.2
1995	12,435	76.4	12,147	59.5
1996	12,650	76.2	12,351	59.2
1997	12,844	76.1	12,483	58.8
1998	12,852	75.1	11,848	59.4
1999	12,881	74.4	11,954	58.9
2000	13,000	74.2	12,387	58.6
2001	13,142	74.2	12,581	58.3
2002	13,411	74.8	12,944	58.4
2003	13,519	74.6	13,031	58.9
2004	13,702	74.8	13,193	58.5
2005	13,854	74.4	13,330	58.3
2006	13,953	74.0	13,445	58.1
2007	14,096	73.9	13,607	58.1
2008	14,182	73.4	13,703	58.1
2009	14,287	72.9	13,734	58.4
Female				
1990	7,509	47.0	7,376	40.8
1995	8,410	48.4	8,267	40.5
1996	8,638	48.9	8,502	40.8
1997	8,938	49.8	8,731	41.2
1998	8,576	47.1	8,090	40.6
1999	8,785	47.6	8,337	41.1
2000	9,069	48.6	8,769	41.4
2001	9,275	49.2	8,991	41.7
2002	9,466	49.7	9,225	41.6
2003	9,397	48.9	9,108	41.1
2004	9,668	49.8	9,364	41.5
2005	9,835	50.0	9,526	41.7
2006	9,981	50.2	9,706	41.9
2007	10,070	50.1	9,826	41.9
2008	10,121	49.9	9,874	41.9
2009	10,047	49.0	9,772	41.6

Source: National Statistical Office, *Economically Active Population Survey*, each year.

2 Employment expansion in the service sector

Due to the successful industrialization, the share of agriculture, fishing and forestry in employment decreased dramatically from the early 1960s. In 2008, only
7.2 percent of total employment is engaged in the primary industries. The
employment share of the manufacturing sector also decreased after reaching 27.2
percent (4,911,000) in 1990. Not only did the employment share go down, but
the number of workers employed in manufacturing also decreased. For example,
the manufacturing sector hired 4,294,000 workers in 2000. Since then, despite

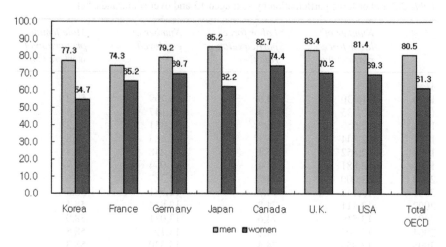

Figure 2.4 Labor force participation rate by sex in 2008, 15–64 year olds (source: OECD, *Employment Outlook*, 2009).

an average annual real growth of 6.4 percent, the number of workers in 2008 had been dropped to 4,079,000. As a result, a new concern, named "Growth without Employment," has been raised among policymakers.

Employment in the services industries continued to increase. The employment share of other services industries such as public service, education, health and welfare (O in Table 2.3) especially has increased dramatically, from 10.9 percent (1,489,000) in 1980 to 23.3 percent (5,493,000) in 2008. The employment share of financial service and real estate (F in Table 2.3) also has increased from 2.4 percent to 13.7 percent during the same period. However, the share and number of workers in sector W (wholesale, retail, hotels and restaurant) has recently decreased, mainly because of industrial restructuring.

3 Increasing share of professional and clerical occupations

By occupational group, the share of employment in craftsman, machine operator, assembler and manual laborer, began trending downward rapidly after the financial crisis after having increased from 1985 to 1995. The widespread enterprise restructuring followed by the financial crisis and efforts for office automation may have contributed to the reduction in the proportion of clerical workers in the late 1990s, but this tendency was reversed as the new millennium began, so that the main losers from the crisis appear to the blue collar workers. The proportion of (associate) professionals increased from 5.8 percent in 1985 to 18.8 percent in 2009, thanks to the growth of knowledge-based industries and enhanced skill requirements for jobs seemingly little impacted by the financial crisis.

Table 2.3 Composition of employment by industry (%)

Year	A	M	E	C	Service				
					Total	W	T	F	O
1980	34.0	21.6	0.3	6.2	37.0	11.9	4.5	2.4	10.9
1985	24.9	23.4	0.3	6.1	44.3	22.6	4.7	3.8	13.3
1990	17.9	27.2	0.4	7.4	46.7	21.8	5.1	5.2	14.6
1995	11.8	23.6	0.3	9.4	54.8	26.5	5.3	8.1	14.9
1996	11.1	22.7	0.4	9.5	56.2	27.3	5.4	8.6	15.0
1997	10.8	21.4	0.4	9.6	57.8	27.7	5.5	9.0	15.5
1998	12.0	19.6	0.3	7.9	60.0	27.9	5.8	9.3	16.9
1999	11.3	20.3	0.3	7.3	61.2	28.3	5.9	9.5	17.4
2000	10.6	19.8	0.3	7.5	61.2	28.2	6.0	10.0	17.1
2001	10.0	19.1	0.3	7.3	62.6	27.2	6.1	10.6	18.6
2002	9.3	19.0	0.2	7.9	63.3	27.1	6.2	10.8	19.3
2003	8.8	19.0	0.3	8.2	63.6	26.4	6.0	11.2	19.9
2004	8.1	19.0	0.3	8.1	64.4	26.0	6.1	11.8	20.6
2005	7.9	18.5	0.3	7.9	65.2	25.4	6.2	12.2	21.4
2006	7.7	18.0	0.3	7.9	66.0	24.9	6.4	12.8	22.0
2007	7.4	17.6	0.4	7.9	66.7	24.4	6.4	13.5	22.4
2008	7.2	17.3	0.4	7.7	67.3	24.1	6.2	13.7	23.3

Source: National Statistical Office, *Economically Active Population Survey*, each year.

Notes
A: Agriculture, fishing and forestry.
M: Manufacturing.
E: Electricity, gas, steam and water supply.
C: Construction.
W: Wholesale and retail trade, accommodation and food service.
T: Transportation, storage, information and communications.
F: Financial and insurance, real estate, renting and leasing.
O: Others including public service, education, health and welfare, etc.

4 High proportion of non-standard workers

Compared to other OECD countries, the Korean labor market has two distinctive characteristics. First, a large number of workers are employed in temporary and daily jobs, which are characterized by short duration and low stability. In 2009, 42.9 percent of employees were either temporary or daily workers (see OECD, 2000 for definitions of "temporary" and "daily"). The incidence of temporary and daily work was particularly high among women, older workers, and the less-educated, while younger and higher-educated male workers performed most regular jobs. In the 1990s, the proportion of temporary and daily workers showed a U pattern (see Table 2.5). It should be noted that the share of temporary and daily workers decreased at the beginning and then increased later. In particular, after the financial crisis, the share of temporary and daily workers increased significantly. For example, the number of daily workers increased from 1,933,000 in the fourth quarter of 1997 to 1,961,000 in the same quarter of 1998. This result reflects the worsening quality of jobs. However, as the economy recovered

Table 2.4 Composition of employment by occupational group (%)

Year	Legislator and senior manager	(Associate) professional	Clerical	Service and sales	Agriculture and fishery	Craftsman, machine operator and assembler	Manual laborer
1985	1.5	5.8	11.5	26.3	24.6	17.4	12.9
1990	1.5	7.2	13.0	25.7	17.8	19.7	15.1
1995	2.5	13.9	12.6	22.1	11.1	26.7	11.2
1996	2.6	14.4	12.6	22.6	10.6	26.2	10.9
1997	2.4	15.1	12.5	23.1	10.3	25.6	11.0
1998	2.5	16.3	12.4	23.6	11.5	23.3	10.4
1999	2.3	16.9	11.3	23.7	10.7	23.2	11.8
2000	2.2	16.6	11.6	23.8	10.0	23.5	12.2
2001	2.4	16.6	12.4	26.2	9.4	23.0	9.9
2002	2.6	16.7	12.7	26.1	8.9	22.9	10.2
2003	2.7	17.4	14.3	25.2	8.3	21.7	10.5
2004	2.7	15.4	14.6	25.7	7.5	21.9	12.2
2005	2.6	15.7	14.8	25.2	7.5	21.9	12.4
2006	2.6	16.6	14.6	24.8	7.2	21.7	12.6
2007	2.6	17.3	14.5	24.3	6.9	21.3	13.1
2008	2.3	18.6	14.8	24.1	6.7	20.9	12.7
2009	2.3	18.8	15.3	23.4	6.5	19.3	13.4

Source: National Statistical Office, *Economically Active Population Survey*, each year.

Table 2.5 Composition of employment by employment status (%)

Year	Wage worker				Non-wage worker		
		Regular[1]	Temporary[2]	Daily[3]		Self-employed	Unpaid family worker
1990	60.6	32.8	17.5	10.2	39.5	28.0	11.4
1992	62.7	36.0	17.4	9.3	37.3	27.2	10.1
1994	62.9	36.4	17.5	9.0	37.1	27.1	10.0
1996	63.3	36.0	18.7	8.6	36.7	27.4	9.3
1997	63.2	34.3	20.0	8.9	36.8	27.8	9.0
1998	61.7	32.8	20.3	8.6	38.3	28.2	10.2
1999	62.4	30.2	21.0	11.2	37.6	28.1	9.5
2000	63.1	30.2	21.8	11.1	36.9	27.7	9.1
2001	63.3	31.1	21.9	10.3	36.7	28.1	8.6
2002	64.0	31.0	22.0	11.0	36.0	27.9	8.1
2003	65.1	32.8	22.6	9.6	34.9	27.3	7.7
2004	66.0	33.8	22.5	9.7	34.0	27.1	6.9
2005	66.4	34.6	22.1	9.7	33.6	27.0	6.6
2006	67.2	35.4	22.2	9.5	32.8	26.5	6.3
2007	68.2	36.8	22.1	9.3	31.8	25.8	6.0
2008	68.7	38.2	21.5	9.0	31.3	25.3	5.9
2009	70.0	39.9	21.7	8.4	30.0	24.3	5.7

Source: National Statistical Office, *Economically Active Population Survey*, each year.

Notes
1 Regular worker – contract term is either at least one year or does not have any specific term.
2 Temporary worker – contract term is shorter than one year but longer than or equal to one month.
3 Daily worker – contract term is less than one month.

from the financial shock, the proportion of temporary and daily workers started to reduce. Currently the share of non-regular workers (temporary plus daily workers) is 42.9 percent, which is 9.2 percent points lower than the record high 52.1 percent in 2000.

While temporary and daily workers are often counted as "non-regular" workers it is important to note that a large number of those workers have worked for more than one year. In the *Labor Force Survey*, any worker who does not receive either severance payment or medical insurance and other benefits is regarded as temporary, even if his or her tenure is more than one year.

To measure the size of "non-regular" workers more accurately, the National Statistical Office adapted a new definition of "non-regular" workers and has estimated its size every year since 2002. From now on we will use a new terminology – "non-standard" – to make a distinction between these different definitions of "non-regular" workers. As shown in Table 2.6, the ratio of non-standard workers in August 2009 was 34.9 percent (5,754,000 workers) of all wage workers, which was much lower than that of temporary and daily workers.

Smaller firms have larger proportions of non-standard workers than do large firms. While, in 2009, the ratio of non-standard workers in large enterprises with 300 and more employees was just 17.1 percent, half of employees were

Table 2.6 Composition of wage workers by employment type (%, thousands)

Year/month	Standard workers	Non-standard workers			
		Sub-total	Contract work[1]	Part-time[2]	Atypical[3]
2001/8	73.2 (9,905)	26.8 (3,635)	13.8	6.5	12.6
2002/8	72.6 (10,190)	27.4 (3,839)	14.7	5.7	12.4
2003/8	67.4 (9,542)	32.6 (4,606)	21.3	6.6	11.9
2004/8	63.0 (9,190)	37.0 (5,394)	24.7	7.3	13.4
2005/8	63.4 (9,486)	36.6 (5,482)	24.1	7.0	12.7
2006/8	64.5 (9,894)	35.5 (5,457)	23.6	7.4	12.6
2007/8	64.1 (10,180)	35.9 (5,703)	22.3	7.6	13.9
2008/8	66.2 (10,658)	33.8 (5,445)	20.4	7.6	13.3
2009/8	65.1 (10,725)	34.9 (5,754)	21.3	8.7	13.9

Source: National Statistical Office, *Economically Active Population Survey: Supplementary Survey*, each year.

Notes
1 Contract work: workers having a fixed contract term.
2 Part-time: workers whose working hour is less than 36 hours per week.
3 Atypical: dispatched workers, in-house working, call workers, etc.

non-standard in small businesses with less than five workers (see Table 2.7). As a result, two-thirds of non-standard workers were employed in small enterprises with less than 30 employees. In August 2009 only 6.0 percent of all non-standard workers were employed in large enterprises with more than 300 employees (see Figure 2.5).

5 High proportion of non-wage workers

The incidence of non-wage workers in Korea is the highest among OECD countries (Figure 2.6). The proportion of self-employed remained relatively unchanged at 27–29 percent during the 1990s while the proportion of unpaid family workers fell to about 10 percent of total employment (see Table 2.5), reducing the proportion of non-wage workers (see Figure 2.7). In 2009, the number of self-employed persons was 5,711,000, which made up for 24.3

Table 2.7 Proportion of "non-standard" workers by size of firm: August 2009 (%, thousands)

Size of firm (number of employees)	1–4	5–9	10–29	30–99	100–299	300 and more
Proportion of non-standard workers	44.5	40.3	40.3	32.0	23.5	17.1
Number of wage workers	3,058	2,740	3,714	3,309	1,656	2,002

Source: National Statistical Office, *Economically Active Population Survey: Supplementary Survey*, August 2009.

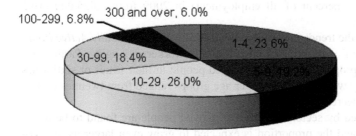

Figure 2.5 Proportion of "non-standard" workers by size of firm (source: National Statistical Office, *Economically Active Population Survey: Supplementary Survey*, August 2009).

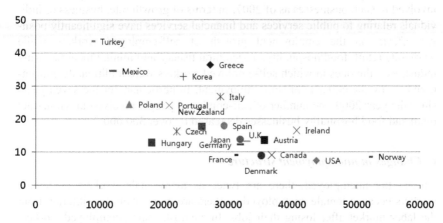

Figure 2.6 Proportion of non-wage workers and per capita GDP (purchasing power parity) in selected countries, 2006 (source: OECD, *OECD Factbook*, 2008).

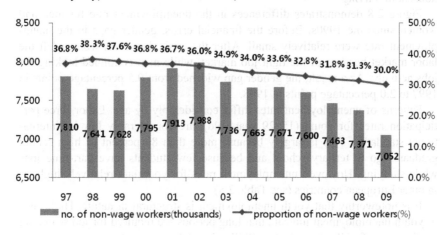

Figure 2.7 Trends in non-wage workers (source: National Statistical Office, *Economically Active Population Survey*, each year).

percent of all employment; while the number of unpaid family workers dropped to 1,341,000 (5.7 percent of all employment) in 2009 from 2,025,000 (10.2 percent) in 1998.

According to the trends in self-employment of the *Economically Active Population Survey*, self-employed and unpaid family workers are aging. Particularly since 2002, the proportion of self-employed people in their fifties or sixties has increased sharply while that of younger age groups ranged from twenties to thirties rapidly has decreased.

When analyzed by sector, most self-employed people are found to be in the services sector, and the proportion is expected to grow even larger as the economic landscape is increasingly dominated by services. Within the services sector, the self-employed population is concentrated on wholesale, retail, food and hospitality businesses, with 33.4 percent of total self employed workers involved in such businesses as of 2007. In terms of growth rate, business or individuals relating to public services and financial services have significantly positive effects on the employment growth of self-employed workers while wholesale/retail, food/hospitality, agricultural/fishery and mining/manufacturing industries – the ones in which self-employed workers were traditionally concentrated – saw the collapse of self-employment. In particular, for the seven years since the year 2000, the number of self-employed people involved in wholesale/retail and food/hospitality businesses decreased by over 300,000.

C Changes in unemployment structure

Among the unemployed, there are twice as many male workers as female workers because female unemployed workers are more likely to withdraw from the labor market after losing their jobs. In contrast, male unemployed workers tend to continue seeking jobs since they hold the main responsibility for the household's living.

Figure 2.8 demonstrates differences in the unemployment rate for men and women since the 1990s. Before the financial crisis, gender gaps in the unemployment rate were relatively small. After the crisis, however, women left the labor market because of the tight job market, while men continued looking for jobs actively. As a result, the gender gap widened from 0.5 percentage points in 1997 to 2.0 percentage points in 1998.

Patterns of unemployment rates differ considerably by age. Labor force participation rates for youth (15–29 years old), are considerably low by international standards. This is largely because more than 80 percent of high school graduates go to tertiary school and because few students have part-time jobs while studying. However, unemployment rates for youth are relatively high, as in other European countries (see Table 2.8).

It is noteworthy that youth unemployment is structural in nature. High rates of youth unemployment indicate that long periods are required for job searching on the part of college graduates. Skill mismatches may also generate serious school-to-work transition problems for many young entrants, particularly for

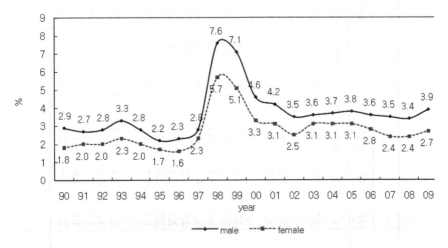

Figure 2.8 Unemployment rates by gender (source: National Statistical Office, *Economically Active Population Survey*, each year).

female entrants who studied liberal arts in college. In 2009, the official number of unemployed youth was 324,000, which made up 39.1 percent of total unemployment. However, if we include youth who do not participate in the labor market because of reasons such as "preparing for examination" and "taking rest without any specific activities," the youth having difficulties finding jobs is 1,082,000 and the quasi-unemployment rate is as high as 21.5 percent. Thus, the real situation is much more difficult for youth, and the official statistics may underestimate the seriousness of youth unemployment.

Compared to other age groups, the unemployment rates for those aged 60 and over were always low. The main reason for this is that older workers also tend to withdraw from the labor market when they lose their jobs. But the rapid aging of the population raises a serious concern, which is that the unemployment rate of the aged will dramatically increase in the near future.

Figure 2.9 illustrates trends in unemployment rates by the educational attainment. Traditionally, the unemployment rate was higher for "tertiary education" than for "high school graduates." However, the gap in unemployment between the two groups has narrowed over time and finally reversed after the financial crisis. In 2000, unemployment rates for "high school graduates" and "junior college graduates or more education" were 4.3 and 3.3 percent, respectively.

According to an empirical analysis (see Chapter 7 of this volume), there was a replacement of less-educated workers with highly educated workers after the financial crisis, as less-educated workers were forced to leave their jobs in favor of highly educated workers. Another explanation is that the shrinking employment in the manufacturing and construction industries, where a large number of less-educated workers are employed, might have contributed to increasing the

Table 2.8 Unemployment rates by gender, age, and educational attainment (thousands, %)

	Year												
	1997	1998	1999	2000	2001	2002	2003	2004	2005	2006	2007	2008	2009
Total number of unemployed	568	1,490	1,374	913	845	708	777	813	833	783	733	725	829
Total	2.6	7.0	6.3	4.1	3.8	3.1	3.4	3.5	3.5	3.3	3.0	3.0	3.4
Sex													
Male	2.8	7.8	7.2	4.7	4.3	3.5	3.6	3.7	3.8	3.6	3.5	3.4	3.9
Female	2.3	5.7	5.1	3.3	3.1	2.5	3.1	3.1	3.1	2.8	2.4	2.4	2.7
Age													
15–29	5.7	12.2	10.9	7.6	7.5	6.6	7.7	7.9	7.6	7.4	6.7	6.8	7.6
15–19	9.8	20.8	19.5	13.8	13.3	1.1	12.1	13.4	11.6	9.8	8.1	9.3	11.0
20–24	7.1	14.8	12.8	9.3	8.9	7.5	9.2	9.4	9.4	9.4	8.2	8.8	8.9
25–29	4.1	9.3	8.5	5.7	5.8	5.5	6.1	6.2	6.1	6.2	5.9	5.6	5.7
30–39	1.9	5.7	5.3	3.4	3.0	2.8	2.9	2.9	3.2	2.9	3.0	3.0	3.4
40–49	1.5	5.6	5.2	3.3	2.8	1.9	2.1	2.2	2.4	2.2	1.9	2.0	2.3
50–59	1.2	5.3	5.1	2.9	2.6	1.8	2.0	2.2	2.3	2.1	1.9	1.9	2.3
60 and over	0.8	2.4	2.3	1.3	1.1	1.0	0.9	1.1	1.2	1.3	1.2	1.1	1.4
Education													
Middle school or less	1.5	5.9	5.2	3.3	2.9	2.1	2.0	2.3	2.4	2.2	2.0	2.1	2.3
High school	3.3	8.3	7.6	4.8	4.3	4.1	4.1	4.3	4.3	3.9	3.6	3.6	4.1
Tertiary Education	3.0	5.9	5.4	4.0	3.8	3.5	3.5	3.3	3.2	3.2	3.1	2.8	3.2
Junior college	3.5	8.5	7.6	5.9	5.4	4.7	4.9	4.5	4.6	4.1	4.3	3.6	4.0
Four year college/university	2.7	4.9	4.5	3.1	3.1	2.9	2.9	2.8	2.6	2.8	2.5	2.5	2.9

Source: National Statistical Office, *Economically Active Population Survey*, each year.

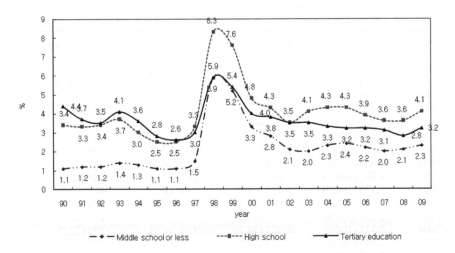

Figure 2.9 Unemployment rates by education (source: National Statistical Office, *Economically Active Population Survey*, each year).

unemployment rate for less-educated workers. However, the gap in unemployment between "high school graduates" and "junior college graduates or more education" has narrowed in recent years.

II Wages and working hours

A Wages

The wage level increased sharply in the late 1980s due to the labor shortage and trade union activities. For example, the nominal wage increased by 21.2 percent in 1989. During the period from 1991 to 1993, the Korean economy was confronted with a downturn, but the tendency toward higher wages continued. Even if the government adopted a policy suppressing rapid wage hikes, wages have still increased indirectly through the expansion of fringe benefits. Nominal wages increased at the robust rate of 127.9 percent between 1990 and 1997.

With the financial crisis that hit Korea in late 1997, however, nominal wages decreased by 2.5 percent, down 9.5 percentage points from the previous year, while real wages shrunk by 9.3 percent, down 11.8 percentage points from the previous year. Also, in 2009, due to the global financial crisis nominal and real wages decreased by 0.9 percent and 3.6 percent, respectively.

As of the end of 2009, the total monthly average wage per full-time worker in all industries except for agriculture was 2,875,000 Korean won (see Table 2.9). The total wage consists of three parts: regular wages (normal wages and other consecutive allowances); extended wages (overtime payment, night work allowance and holiday allowances); and special wages (including bonuses and performance-based pay). For a typical full-time worker, the regular wage,

Table 2.9 Total average monthly wage by category, all industries except agriculture (KRW 1,000, %)

Year	Total wage	Regular wage	Extended wage	Special wage
1980	176 (100.0)	129 (73.3)	26 (14.8)	21 (11.9)
1985	324 (100.0)	239 (73.8)	39 (12.0)	46 (14.2)
1990	642 (100.0)	444 (69.2)	70 (10.9)	128 (19.9)
1995	1,222 (100.0)	828 (67.8)	111 (9.1)	283 (23.2)
1996	1,368 (100.0)	925 (67.6)	117 (8.6)	326 (23.8)
1997	1,463 (100.0)	1,012 (69.2)	118 (8.1)	333 (22.8)
1998	1,427 (100.0)	1,050 (73.6)	100 (7.0)	276 (19.3)
1999	1,599 (100.0)	1,114 (69.7)	131 (8.2)	354 (22.1)
2000	1,727 (100.0)	1,196 (69.3)	149 (8.6)	383 (22.2)
2001	1,825 (100.0)	1,274 (69.8)	149 (8.2)	402 (22.0)
2002	2,036 (100.0)	1,436 (70.5)	144 (7.1)	456 (22.4)
2003	2,228 (100.0)	1,567 (70.3)	150 (6.7)	511 (22.9)
2004	2,373 (100.0)	1,677 (70.7)	157 (6.6)	539 (22.7)
2005	2,525 (100.0)	1,795 (71.1)	173 (6.9)	557 (22.1)
2006	2,667 (100.0)	1,918 (71.9)	181 (6.8)	567 (21.3)
2007	2,823 (100.0)	2,047 (72.5)	191 (6.8)	586 (20.8)
2008	2,891 (100.0)	2,207 (76.3)	187 (6.5)	497 (17.2)
2009	2,875 (100.0)	2,220 (77.2)	179 (6.2)	477 (16.6)

Source: Ministry of Employment and Labor, *Monthly Labor Survey Report*, each year.

Note
( ) indicates the ratio of each category.

extended wage and special wage, in Korean won, were 2,220,000; 179,000; and 477,000, respectively, in 2009.

The larger the firm size, the higher wages are. Assuming that the wage in a workplace with 10–29 employees is 100, the wage in large enterprises with 500 and more employees was 167.4 in 2006. As shown in Figure 2.15, the wage gap by company size has widened significantly since 2002. Globally competitive large companies have grown rapidly as they have kept pace with the trends of globalization and use of IT while SMEs relying solely on domestic demand or subcontractors doing work for larger firms have been sidelined from the overall growth trend. Such a widening gap between large companies and SMEs causes the gap between the rich and poor and other social conflicts.

Moreover, by education level, high school graduates received the monthly wage of 2,327,000 won in 2008, only 63.9 percent of university graduates' 3,642,000 won. The wage level for those with just a middle school education or lower is even smaller at 1,919,000 won, just about 52.7 percent of that of university graduates. Meanwhile, the average monthly wage of two-year college graduates is 2,452,000 won, about 67.3 percent of that of university graduates, which is not much higher compared with high school graduates. When analyzed by age, the wage level goes up sharply with age, peaking at age 40 and declining afterward, resulting in an inverted U shape. The wage level is the highest for those in their forties because most wage workers quit jobs in their late forties or early fifties.

Table 2.10 Monthly wages by size of firm (KRW 1,000)

Year	10–29	30–99	100–299	300–499	500 and more
1980	166	177	173	182	178
1985	308	314	308	340	344
1990	549	572	603	698	741
1995	1,082	1,108	1,175	1,334	1,511
1996	1,188	1,233	1,323	1,517	1,693
1997	1,283	1,342	1,418	1,619	1,774
1998	1,255	1,307	1,382	1,570	1,765
1999	1,376	1,439	1,561	1,794	2,019
2000	1,497	1,567	1,713	1,973	2,195
2001	1,606	1,680	1,785	2,135	2,313
2002	1,705	1,856	2,067	2,357	2,718
2003	1,808	2,005	2,230	2,474	3,043
2004	1,945	2,124	2,387	2,683	3,327
2005	2,081	2,259	2,517	2,822	3,541
2006	2,187	2,413	2,646	2,943	3,660
2007	2,331	2,574	2,836	3,064	3,939
2008	2,195	2,442	2,529	3,124	
2009	2,187	2,492	2,519	3,050	

Source: Ministry of Employment and Labor, *Monthly Labor Survey Report*, each year.

B Working Hours

With the legislation of the Labor Standards Act in 1953, Korea adopted a working hour system of eight hours a day and 48 hours a week. After the revision of the Labor Standards Act in 1989, the statutory working hours are eight hours a day and 44 hours a week, excluding rest periods, regardless of the type of business.

With the revision of the Labor Standards Act, however, beginning in July 2004, the working hour system of eight hours a day and 40 hours a week (five-day workweek) has been introduced by stages according to the size of enterprise. From July 2005, the five-day workweek is legally mandated for companies with 50 or more employees. Overtime work is possible for up to 12 hours a week, provided that it is agreed upon by both labor and management. And in the case of overtime work, the employer should pay 50 percent or more of normal wages.

Based on all industries except agriculture, the average working hours of Korean workers reached 52.5 hours per week in 1986. After that, the average working hours started to decline. In 2009, the average weekly working hours was 41.2. The normal working hours decreased to 37.3 hours per week, and overtime working hours decreased to four hours per week as shown in Figure 2.10. Regarding firm size, the larger the firm, the shorter the average working hours.

Even though the average working hours of Korean workers has been declining during last two decades, Koreans still work longer than comparable workers of other OECD countries. As seen in Figure 2.11, in 2006 a typical Korean worker worked for 2,305 hours, which is the highest among OECD countries.

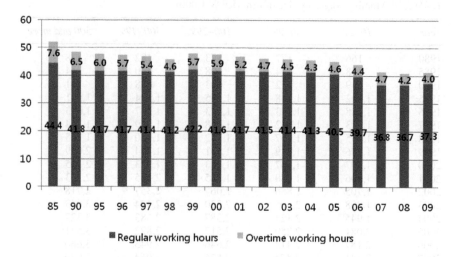

■ Regular working hours   ▪ Overtime working hours

Figure 2.10 Changes in the working hours per week (source: Ministry of Employment and Labor, *Monthly Labor Survey Report*, each year).

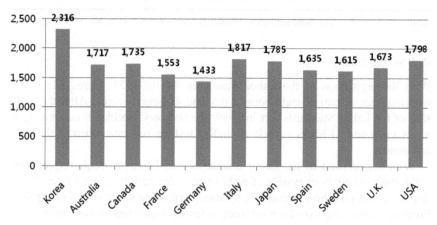

Figure 2.11 Average annual hours actually worked per person in employment, 2007 (source: OECD, *Employment Outlook*, 2009).

In addition, the share of part-time workers, who work less than 36 hours per week, is the lowest among OECD countries. The proportion of part-time workers was only 6.2 percent in 1996, and has increased continuously over the years to reach 13.2 percent in 2009. This shows that recently the labor market situation has deteriorated and that many jobseekers have difficulties finding regular jobs.

III Challenges in the labor market

There are two major challenges facing the Korean labor market: the problem of mismatches and the widening gap among workers. The problem of mismatch includes youth unemployment, increasing activities of women, employment of older workers and skill mismatch, while widening gap among laborers includes growth of non-standard workers, long-term unemployment and decreasing job stability. However, in this chapter only five issues will be discussed.

First, one of the key issues to be addressed is the youth unemployment problem. As of 2009, 39.1 percent of the unemployed are in the 15–29 age group. The unemployment rate of those in the 15–29 age group was the highest among all age groups. However, the actual number of individuals looking for jobs is estimated to be much higher than the official figure. This is because many discouraged youth are not counted. One of the main causes for high youth unemployment is the high entrance rate to tertiary education. Currently more than 80 percent of high school graduates advance to college. Combined with the recent economic depression, this increases the number of unemployed graduates.

The job crunch among the youth is also visible in the employment/population ratio. Due to the high university advancement rate, Korea's youth employment rate is relatively low compared with other countries, and it has been declining quite sharply since 2004. Specifically, the youth employment rate was 45.1 percent in 2004 and it dropped as low as 40.5 percent in 2009, a level similar to that of the 1998 financial crisis. Such a serious youth employment challenge deters the development of human resources in the early stage of one's career, triggering long-term loss of income throughout one's life.

Second, gender equality is another issue to be addressed. In the past, female labor force participation followed a U pattern, as shown in Figure 2.12. However, due to various factors such as increased education opportunities for women, development of a child-care system, and changed social attitudes for female workers, more and more women are willing to participate in the labor market.

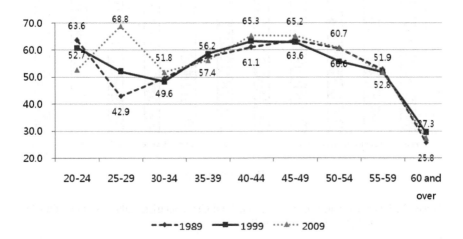

Figure 2.12 Female labor force participation rates by age group (source: National Statistical Office, *Economically Active Population Survey*, 1989, 1999, 2009).

However, most female workers belong to the secondary labor market, and the gender gaps in wages are larger than in other countries as shown in Figure 2.13. Furthermore, Korea has not fully addressed gender-based discrimination. Although discrimination against women has decreased in Korea in recent years and women have been increasingly active in many areas of society, the wage gap between men and women remains unchanged since the Asian financial crisis (see Figure 2.14). Also, according to the KLIPS (*Korean Labor and Income Panel Study*) data, the gender–wage gap remains unaltered within the range of 0.581(1999) and 0.607(2003) for the last ten years. When calculated based on the hourly wage, the relative wage for women even decreased rather than increased.

The analysis rejects the general perception that discrimination against women has been reduced in the job market, at least as reflected in relative wages. An increasing number of women have become working members of society, but as non-standard workers or employees working for SMEs. And women workers are concentrated in SMEs and non-standard jobs. These factors help explain why the gender–wage gap has not narrowed despite the obvious improved position of women in society.

Third, the worsening of the income distribution structure should also be addressed, which we call "polarization." As the proportion of "non-standard" jobs has increased significantly, the income gap among workers has also increased in recent years. Given that the increase in non-standard workers has

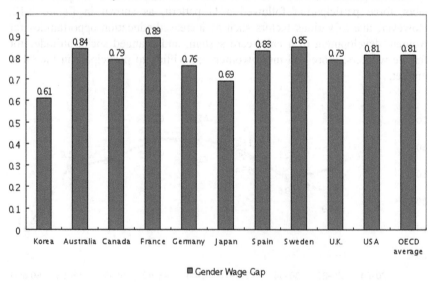

Figure 2.13 Gender wage gap in selected OECD countries, 2005 (source: OECD, *Employment Outlook*, 2007).

Note
The gender wage gap is calculated as the ratio of median earnings of female workers relative to male workers.

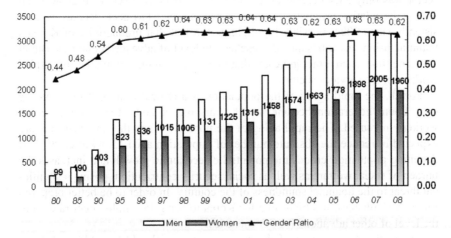

Figure 2.14 Men and women's average monthly wage and gender ratio (women/men) (source: Ministry of Employment and Labor, *Monthly Labor Survey Report*, each year).

been a common trend in most advanced countries, a key question might be how and to what extent these non-standard workers should be protected in terms of basic labor standards and active labor market policies. Especially after the financial crisis that hit Korea in late 1997, the wage gap between large-sized firms and SMEs has widened, as shown in Figure 2.15.

The imbalance in industrial productivity is another challenge that needs to be addressed. In the case of Korea, productivity of the services sector is significantly lower than that of the manufacturing sector, while other countries witness similar output per worker in both the manufacturing and the services sectors. For example, based on the added value obtained, output per worker in the services

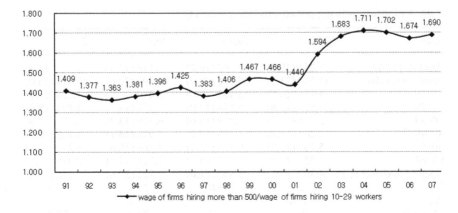

Figure 2.15 Firm size and wages (source: Ministry of Employment and Labor, *Monthly Labor Survey Report*, each year).

sector was only 54.4 percent of that of the manufacturing sector in 2008. Even worse, the relative productivity of the services sector has been decreasing consistently since 2004, possibly highlighting the fact that productivity of Korea's manufacturing sector has already reached the level of advanced countries. But at the same time, such a fact indicates that there are a significant number of surplus workers in the services sector.

Fourth, the rapid aging of the population is a critical issue in Korea. As the baby boom generation became 43–51 years old in 2005, the average age of workers increased. The rapid aging of the population and the low birth rate are expected to reduce the absolute number of population aged 15–64 after 2017. A declining population erodes the potential of economic growth and increases the burden of social welfare as well as social security contribution, posing a significant threat to the financial soundness of the country. In order to be better prepared for such challenges, it's high time for Korea to bring its employment rate up to the level of other advanced OECD countries.

Lastly, the deterioration of the non-wage sector should be addressed. Self-employed workers felt a sense of loss compared with wage workers because of stagnant sales and income since 2002/2003. During the period from 2002 to 2007, the nominal wage of wage workers grew 46.2 percent, while that of the self-employed went up just by 11.6 percent. Meanwhile, as large size businesses have a much better chance of becoming successful, self-employed individuals in small size businesses are held back, or more likely to be in danger of being pushed out of business. Of all self-employed individuals, women, elderly people, low educated workers, and small business owners stand higher chances of falling below the poverty line. In addition, the income gap is widening even within the self-employed population

The problem is that such grave situations facing self-employed individuals are not temporary. Of course, the latest global financial crisis has worsened the difficulties facing self-employed people, increasing the number of businesses

Table 2.11 Changes in population structure (thousands, %)

Year	2005	2010	2020	2050
Aged 0–14 (A)	9,241 (19.2)	7,907 (16.2)	6,118 (12.4)	3,763 (8.9)
Aged 15–64 (B)	34,530 (71.7)	35,611 (72.9)	35,506 (72.0)	22,424 (53.0)
15–19	3,136 (6.5)	3,402 (7.0)	2,440 (4.9)	1,558 (3.7)
20–29	7,587 (15.8)	6,834 (14.0)	6,471 (13.1)	3,494 (8.3)
30–39	8,534 (17.7)	8,099 (16.6)	6,770 (13.7)	3,773 (8.9)
40–49	8,209 (17.1)	8,376 (17.1)	7,948 (16.1)	4,423 (10.4)
50–59	5,137 (10.7)	6,713 (13.7)	8,166 (16.6)	6,260 (14.8)
60–64	1,927 (4.0)	2,187 (4.5)	3,711 (7.5)	2,916 (6.9)
Aged 65 and over (C)	4,367 (9.1)	5,357 (11.0)	7,701 (15.6)	16,156 (38.2)
C/B	12.6	15.0	21.7	72.0
A/B	26.8	22.2	17.2	16.8
(A+C)/B	39.4	37.2	38.9	88.8

Source: National Statistical Office, *Forecast of Future Population*, November 2006.

shutdown and bankruptcy filings since late 2008. However, the problems associated with self-employment have existed ever since the 2003 credit crunch and, even without the latest crisis, restructuring measures such as pushing noncompetitive small businesses out of the market were already inevitable. The recent global financial crisis created the triggers to accelerate the restructuring of the self-employed.

Under such circumstances, a considerable number of self-employed individuals being pushed out of the market are expected to fall below the poverty line. The current lack of attention and policies on self-employed workers on the part of government is likely to worsen the situation for the self-employed who are placed in the blind spot of government assistance measures.

References

Korea Labor Institute, "Abroad Labor Statistics," 2006.
Ministry of Employment and Labor, *Monthly Labor Survey Report*, each year.
National Statistical Office, *Economically Active Population Survey*, each year.
National Statistical Office, *Economically Active Population Survey: Supplementary Survey*, each year.
National Statistical Office "Forecast of Future Population," November 2006.
OECD, *OECD Employment Outlook*, 2007, 2009.
OECD, *OECD Factbook*, 2008.

3 Tertiarization of employment

Jai-Joon Hur

I Introduction

Employment in the Korean manufacturing industry has been declining since 1990, not only in the share of total employment but also in absolute numbers. The value-added share of manufacturing in the total GDP has been stable at around 24 percent since 1990; however, in this period, due to the decline of the construction industry, which explained 9.5 percent of the GDP on average in the pre-crisis period but currently explains 6.3 percent of the GDP, the combined share of manufacturing and construction value-added has shown a tendency to decline.

If the reduction of manufacturing and construction is represented by the head of a coin, expansion of the service industry constitutes the tail, comprising one of the key features in the structural changes of the Korean economy since 1990. Besides, the manufacturing industry has tertiarized itself. As R&D, design, maintenance and consumer finance become more important in the value chain than the manufacturing process itself, firms such as Samsung Electronics and LG Electronics have increased their workforces in R&D and design. Currently more and more traditional manufacturing or equipment firms are selling solutions rather than intermediate goods or equipment alone. A growing proportion of service work within those manufacturing companies is causing them to resemble service firms.

The growth of the service industry and the acceleration of tertiarization in the Korean economy since 1990 have been influenced by three factors. To begin with, the income increase has pushed up the demand for service goods (Oh 2005). At the same time, changes in the environment of international trades, particularly the so-called China Shock (Choi *et al.* 2005; Kim 2006), have reduced employment in the manufacturing sector. Also, as information and communication technology (ICT) diffused in the 1990s, production processes became more high-skilled and capital-intensive, and new knowledge-intensive jobs have come into existence, tertiarizing the composition of employment (Hur *et al.* 2002).

This study analyzes features of tertiarization of the Korean economy, comparing them with the experiences of other OECD countries. Here tertiarization includes the rise of the service share in production, intermediate input, and trade, as well as the increase in employment in the service industry and in service jobs in the overall economy. Though the service industry is growing in employment and production, its productivity growth is decelerating.

According to Baumol (1967), the economic development and the consequent income growth will raise the demand for service goods. As the productivity grows slower in the service industry than in manufacturing, prices of service goods increase at a higher rate. The results are a shift of labor to the service industry. Thus, tertiarization will bring in both a productivity and growth slow-down in the overall economy.

However, productivity growth of all the service industries is not necessarily slower than that of manufacturing. Therefore, the result of tertiarization is not as gloomy as Baumol (1967) predicts. For instance, if tertiarization is accompanied by a growing proportion of communication and other business services whose productivity growth is comparable to that of manufacturing, the tertiarization may not necessarily lead to productivity slow-down.

Besides, all the service goods are not final goods as is assumed by Baumol (1967). When service goods are used as intermediary input, the productivity growth of the overall economy can grow providing the total factor productivity growth of the intermediary good-producing service industry is positive (Oulton 1999).

This study will first investigate the overall and sector-specific aspects of terti-arization. Drawing on the features of tertiarization in progress on the one hand, and the implications of Baumol (1967) on the other hand, this study will discuss policy implications.

This chapter is composed of five sections. Section II examines the various aspects of tertiarization of employment and reasons for the fast expansion of service employment. Section III investigates tertiarization in production, focus-ing on the growing share of production as well as the intermediate input of serv-ices. Section IV summarizes the main characteristics of tertiarization in Korea. Lastly, in Section V we discuss policy implications for ensuring more and better jobs in the tertiarizing Korean economy.

II Tertiarization of employment

The tertiarization of employment can be captured via two aspects: one is the rise in employment of the service industry, and the other is the rise in non-production and high-skilled jobs. Service industry employment is increasing with the expan-sion of the service industry and, simultaneously, the number of non-production and high-skilled jobs are also growing in the overall economy.

A The rise of employment in the service industry

Figures 3.1a, 3.1b and 3.1c show the change in employment by sector over the period 1993–2008. Agriculture, mining and manufacturing recorded a net

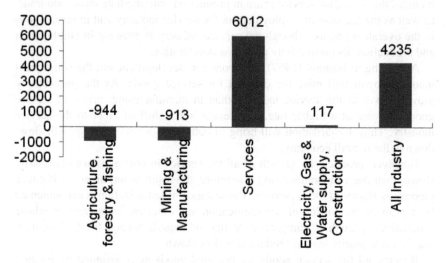

Figure 3.1a Changes in employment by industry, 1993–2008 (thousands) (source: Statistics Korea, *Economically Active Population Survey*).

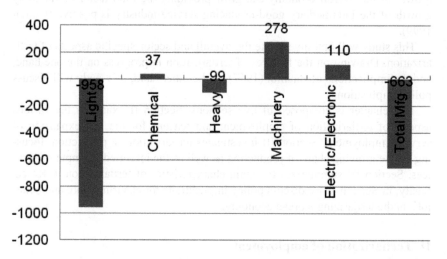

Figure 3.1b Changes in manufacturing employment by sub-sectors, 1993–2008 (thousands) (source: Statistics Korea, *Economically Active Population Survey*).

decrease of 0.9 million jobs, while service industry jobs increased by six million. Employment in the sub-sectors of manufacturing showed a different evolution from one sub-sector to another. The employment cut in manufacturing mostly resulted from the light industry sector. Specifically, during 1993–2008, the light and the heavy industries lost, respectively, 958,000 and 99,000 jobs, whereas the number of workers in the chemical, machinery and electric/electronic industries all rose.[1]

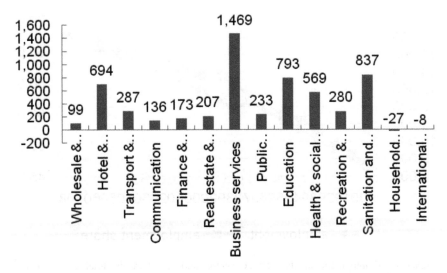

Figure 3.1c Changes in service employment by sub-sector, 1993–2008 (thousands) (source: Statistics Korea, *Economically Active Population Survey*).

Among the 14 different sub-sectors in the service industry, business service, hotel and restaurant, sanitation and others, and education service represented more than 62 percent of the increase in service employment. More precisely, over the 1993–2008 period, the service industry as a whole experienced an increase of 5.7 million workers, including 1.5 million in business services, about 694,000 in hotel and restaurant, 837,000 in sanitation, 793,000 in education services and 1.9 million in the other service industries.

The share of the service industry in total employment continued to increase from 46.7 percent in 1990 to 67.3 percent in 2008 (Figure 3.2). The employment share of the service industry in Korea as of 2008 was comparable to that of Germany, Japan, Spain, Ireland, Australia and Italy (Figure 3.3). However, it has grown at a faster rate in Korea than in any other OECD countries during the previous two decades. When compared with Japan, Ireland and Germany, Korea's service employment share rose by 20.7 percent over the period 1990–2008, higher than 12.8 percent, 11.8 percent and 11.0 percent in Germany, Ireland and Japan, respectively, over the same span.

Within the service industry, however, the employment trends differ among sub-sectors (Figures 3.4a and 3.4b). Among the employment shares of the four sub-sectors (producer services, distributive services, personal services and social services), the largest increase in employment share is found in producer services, with a 6.6 percent rise during the period 1993–2008.[2] This increase was largely attributable to an employment increase in business services. During the same time, personal services registered a 5.4 percent rise, which is mainly attributable to a rise in sanitation and other services, and hotel and restaurant business.

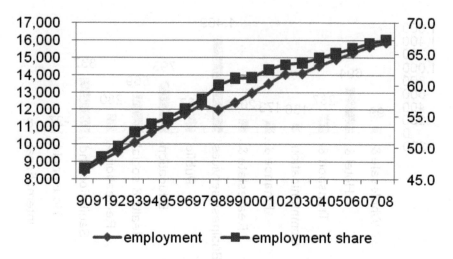

Figure 3.2 Employment in the service sector and its share in total employment, 1990–2009 (thousands, %) (source: Statistics Korea, *Economically Active Population Survey*).

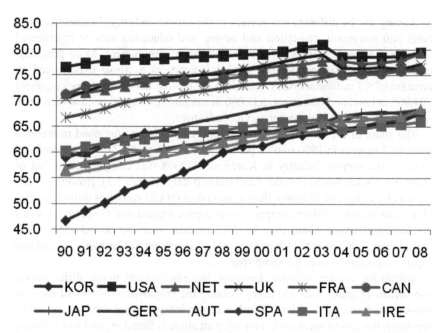

Figure 3.3 Shares of the service sector employment in selected OECD countries (source: OECD *STAN database* 2005).

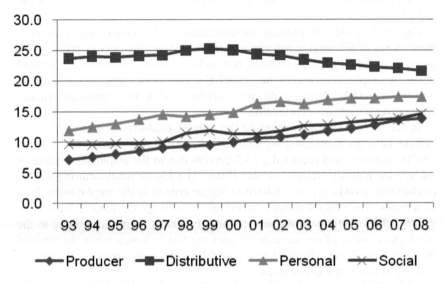

Figure 3.4a Evolution of employment shares by service sub-sector: employment shares of four service sectors.

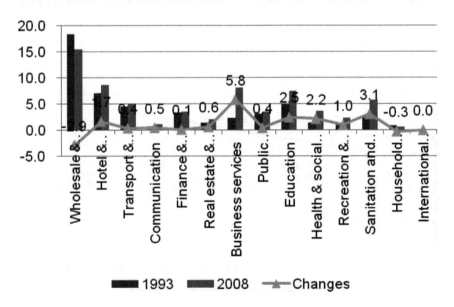

Figure 3.4b Evolution employment shares by service sub-sector: changes in employment shares by sub-sectors, 1993–2008.

The 4.9 percent increase in social services mostly came from health, social work, and education services.

Figures 3.5a and 3.5b illustrate the correlation between the changing employment shares of the service industry and the manufacturing–service productivity growth gap for 17 OECD countries, one including Korea and the other without Korea. A simple regression of the 17 OECD countries including Korea reveals a positive correlation between the two variables, while the regression without Korea reveals a negative correlation.

In the 1990s, Korea experienced the biggest productivity growth gap, 7.3 percent between manufacturing and the service industry among the selected OECD countries, and recorded a 13.3 percent rise in the employment share of the service industry, relative to the 1980s. The higher manufacturing-service productivity growth gap was related to higher growth in the employment share of services. The general increase in income pushed up the demand for service goods, but productivity in the service industry almost stagnated, leading to the employment share of service industry growing fast in Korea, while the demand for service goods was absorbed by reasonable productivity growth in the service industry in other OECD countries.

In the 2000s, the similar trend continued as in the 1990s. The productivity growth gap between manufacturing and service industry amounted to 5.3 percentage points with productivity growth of manufacturing and service industry being

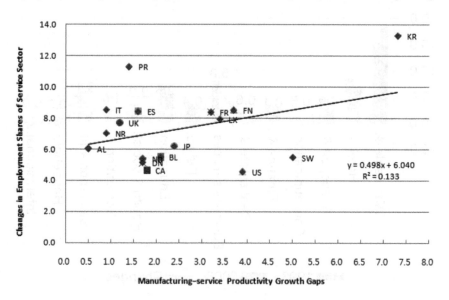

Figure 3.5a Changes in productivity growth gap and the percent shares of service employment: including Korea (source: OECD, *STAN database 2005*).

Note
The productivity growth gap refers to the difference of labor productivity growth rates between manufacturing and service in the 1990s, while the change in employment shares refers to the difference of the average employment shares of service between the 1980s and the 1990s.

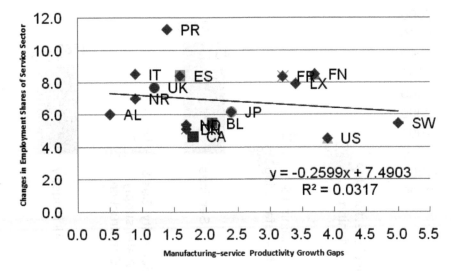

Figure 3.5b Changes in productivity growth gap and the percent shares of service employment: without Korea (source: OECD, *STAN database 2005*).

Note
The productivity growth gap refers to the difference of labor productivity growth rates between manufacturing and service in the 1990s, while the change in employment shares refers to the difference of the average employment shares of service between the 1980s and the 1990s.

6.4 percent and 1.1 percent per annum, respectively, and the rise in employment share of the service industry demonstrated 7.0 percentage points. The Korean economy seems to have remained in "Baumol's World" since the 1990s in the sense that the income increase combined with slower productivity growth of the service industry contributed to the expansion of service employment.

Meanwhile, the structural changes of the Korean economy in the 1990s were characterized by not only tertiarization but also informatization. The slower growth in productivity of the service industry also implies that informatization did not lead to greater productivity in the sector.

B The increase of non-production and high-skilled workers

Figures 3.6a and 3.6b describe the changes in the number of non-production and high-skilled jobs between 1993 and 2009.[3] Over this period, total employment increased by 4.2 million, while the number of non-production jobs grew by 4.6 million. That is, the new jobs created by business start-up or business expansion were mostly in non-production, and most of the jobs lost due to business closure or curtailment were imputed to production workers.

The net loss of jobs during the observed period numbered about 913,000 in agriculture, but a mere 2,000 were non-production jobs and 5,000 were high-skilled jobs. In mining and manufacturing, non-production jobs increased

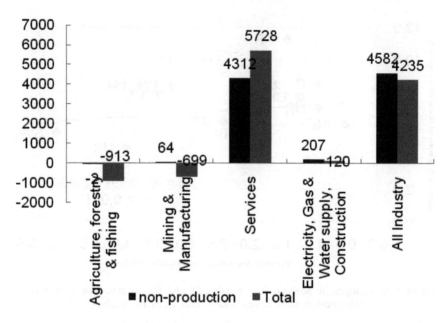

Figure 3.6a Changes in non-production employment, 1993–2009 (thousand persons) (source: Statistics Korea, *Economically Active Population Survey*).

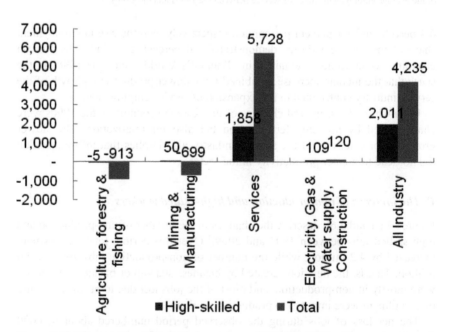

Figure 3.6b Changes in high-skilled employment, 1993–2009 (thousand persons) (source: Statistics Korea, *Economically Active Population Survey*).

by 64,000 and the number of high-skilled non-production jobs increased by 50,000, while 699,000 total jobs were lost. This implies that 763,000 production workers' jobs were lost and low-skilled non-production workers' jobs increased only by 14,000 during the observation period. In the electricity, gas, water, and construction sector, a total of 120,000 jobs were increased, while net job creation of non-production workers was 207,000, 109,000 of which were high-skilled non-production jobs. In the service industry, 5.7 million jobs were newly increased, with 4.3 million and 1.9 million of them being, respectively, non-production jobs and high-skilled jobs. These facts clearly indicate that tertiarization of jobs is under way in all industries.

Table 3.1 summarizes the changes in shares of high-skilled jobs and non-production jobs during the 1993–2009 periods. In the whole economy, the share of high-skilled jobs rose by 5.8 percentage points over the period, while the share of non-production jobs rose 10.5 percentage points. The share of high-skilled and non-production jobs in the overall economy grew more than the share of those jobs in the service or manufacturing industry, because the service industry, which has higher proportion of high-skilled and non-production jobs than the other industries, grew rapidly.

In summary, tertiarization of employment has progressed at a rapid pace, not only driven by the growth of the service industry but also in the form of the rising share of service jobs in non-service industries.

III Tertiarization in production

Tertiarization also progressed in production. This phenomenon also has two dimensions: the rise in the value-added of the service industry, and the rise in the share of the service products used as intermediate input.

A The rise in the value-added of services

The share of service industry in total value-added grew consistently from 51.5 percent in 1990 to 60.3 percent in 2008 (Figure 3.7). This level of value-added

Table 3.1 Changes in high-skilled and non-production jobs (%, %point)

	1993	1995	2000	2005	2007	2009	1993–2009
High-skilled jobs							
All	15.3	16.4	18.9	20.9	22.0	21.1	5.8
Manufacturing	9.7	11.3	14.3	16.6	18.2	13.2	3.5
Service	22.5	22.7	24.1	25.3	26.1	25.6	3.1
Non-production jobs							
All	49.2	49.9	54.3	59.8	59.7	59.8	10.5
Manufacturing	26.0	26.3	27.0	34.1	35.6	33.8	7.8
Service	77.3	76.5	76.2	78.4	76.5	75.2	−2.1

Source: Statistics Korea, *Economically Active Population Survey.*

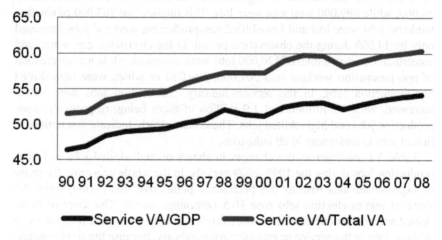

Figure 3.7 Share of the service industry value-added, 1990–2008 (%) (source: Bank of Korea, *National Accounts*).

share is one of the lowest among OECD countries. In most of the OECD countries, the service industry represented about 70 percent of the total value-added.

Meanwhile, the composition of the sub-sectors went through changes (Tables 3.2a, 3.2b). Largely due to the substantial growth of real estate, rental and business services, the share of producer services in the service industry rose by 5.1 percentage points, from 14.9 percent in 1990 to 20.0 percent in 2008. By contrast, distributive services remained almost the same in its share over the same period, despite the considerable growth of communications services because the share of wholesale and retail, and transport and storage activities dropped. The share of personal services in the service industry went down in its share, from 5.5 percent to 4.4 percent. Social services showed a 5.3 percentage point increase, with public administration, educational service, and health and social work activities each rising by 1.3–2.3 percentage points.

Table 3.2a Changes in shares of value-added production by four aggregate service industries (%, % point)

	1990	1995	2000	2005	2008	1990–2008
Producer	14.9	18.3	20.1	19.9	20.0	5.1
Distributive	17.3	15.0	15.0	17.5	17.3	0.0
Personal	5.5	6.2	6.2	4.4	4.4	−1.0
Social	11.9	12.3	13.1	15.9	17.2	5.3
Total	49.5	51.8	54.4	57.7	58.9	9.4

Table 3.2b Changes in shares of value-added production by industry of national account classification (%, % point)

Services	1990	1995	2000	2005	2008	1990–2008
Producer						
Finance/insurance	5.8	6.9	6.9	6.9	6.6	0.8
Real estate/lease	9.1	11.5	13.2	8.1	7.9	2.7
Business service	3.8	4.8	5.1	4.9	5.4	1.6
Distributive						
Wholesale/retail	10.5	8.4	7.9	8.3	8.6	−1.9
Transport/storage	6.8	6.6	7.1	9.2	8.7	1.9
Communications	2.0	1.9	2.4	4.7	4.3	2.4
Personal						
Hotel/restaurant	2.5	2.7	2.9	2.4	2.4	−0.1
Other personal services	2.9	3.4	3.3	2.0	2.0	−0.9
Social						
Public administration	5.2	5.3	5.7	6.2	6.5	1.3
Education	4.7	5.0	5.0	6.0	6.5	1.8
Health/social work	1.9	1.9	2.4	3.7	4.2	2.3
Total	49.5	51.8	54.4	57.7	58.9	9.4

Source: The Bank of Korea, *National Accounts*.

B The rising proportion of intermediately used service output

Not only does the service industry account for a growing share in total value-added, but also the proportion of service output in total output and that of intermediately used service output is increasing. The share of service input in total intermediate input increased from 25.4 percent in 1990 to 31.6 percent in 2007 (Table 3.3).

The import of service goods has also grown. Over the period 1990–2007, the share of service import in total imports rose from 5.9 percent to 14.6 percent, whereas the share of manufactured imports declined from 74.8 percent to 62.7 percent over the same period. This growth of service imports is largely attributable to business services.

Although the share of intermediately used service output has continued to grow, it is much lower than in other OECD countries. For example, the proportion of service output used as intermediate input was 50.3 percent in Japan in 2000, while it was limited to 31.6 percent in Korea in 2007. This implies that the extent of tertiarization in the Korean economy is relatively weak in the sense that the service industry is providing only a limited proportion of intermediate goods.

Furthermore, the share of service input in total intermediate input decreased between 2000 and 2005 while it remained invariant between 2005 and 2007. Some service sectors are less specialized so that they do not provide quality services. Productivity is low in some service sectors and they provide services only at high price. Therefore, Korean firms are purchasing a limited proportion

Table 3.3 Outputs, intermediate inputs and imports (%)

	1990	1995	2000	2005	2007	Japan (2005)
Manufacturing						
Manufacturing output in total output	49.6	47.1	46.0	46.3	46.5	31.9
Intermediately used manufacturing output out of total manufacturing output	72.8	69.1	72.6	74.6	75.7	70.9
Tangible input* in total intermediate input	74.6	69.5	68.1	68.4	68.4	49.7**
Manufactured imports in total imports	74.8	75.1	66.9	63.8	62.7	61.4
Service						
Service output in total output	30.3	34.6	39.4	40.0	40.4	57.2
Intermediately used service out of total service output	34.3	35.2	38.4	40.1	41.1	36.3
Service input in total intermediate input	25.4	30.5	31.9	31.6	31.6	50.3**
Service imports in total imports	5.9	9.8	13.4	14.1	14.6	13.5

Source: Bank of Korea, *Input–Output Tables.*

Note
* Includes agriculture, mining, electricity, gas, water, and construction as well as manufacturing.
** As of 2000.

of domestic services. Instead, they either purchase from abroad or produce in-house. This is likely to limit expansion of the service market and obstruct in turn a further increase in productivity of the service industry.

Baumol (1967) predicts that, as the service industry is slower in productivity growth than manufacturing, the economic growth rate will slow down as the share of services goes up. According to Oulton (1999), however, when services are used as intermediate goods, the productivity growth of the whole economy may increase so long as the intermediate service input sector achieves positive growth of the total factor productivity.

According to the total factor productivity estimates made by Lee and Song (2005), over the period of 1970–2001, the productivity growth in manufacturing remained high over the period from 1970 to 2001, while the growth of total factor productivity in services was very slow or even negative. Though ICT was diffused in Korea in the 1990s, this was hardware-oriented, and the productivity of the service industry has not grown as fast. Lee and Song (2005) estimate that in finance, insurance, real estate and business services, which are a major sup-plier of services for intermediate input, both per capita labor productivity and total factor productivity recorded negative growth over the 1970–2001 period. Even in the light of Oulton's prediction, Lee and Song's findings suggest that the productivity of the Korean economy was most likely to have been slowing down with tertiarization in progress over the period of 1970–2001.

IV Characteristics of tertiarization

A The fastest structural change among OECD countries

Figure 3.8 illustrates the speed of structural change, measured by the modified Lilien Indicator, in selected OECD countries over the period 1980–2002. OECD countries differ substantially with respect to the speed of structural change. Korea, Germany, Australia, Spain and Portugal belong to the rapidly changed group throughout the 1980s and the 1990s. Above all, the speed of structural change was the fastest in Korea among the OECD countries throughout the entire observation period.

The same countries show different speeds of structural change depending on the period. In the dominant parts of OECD countries, the speed of change was more rapid in the 1980s than in the 1990s. However, Korea, Germany and Finland went through more rapid changes in the 1990s than in the 1980s.

The share of service employment increased at a speed of 4.5 percent per annum in the 1990s, but slowed down to 2.5 percent in the 2000s (Table 3.4). In the 1990s, the demand for service goods increased. However, the annual productivity growth of the service industry was no more than 1.6 percent, 6.9 percentage points lower than the productivity growth in manufacturing. Consequently,

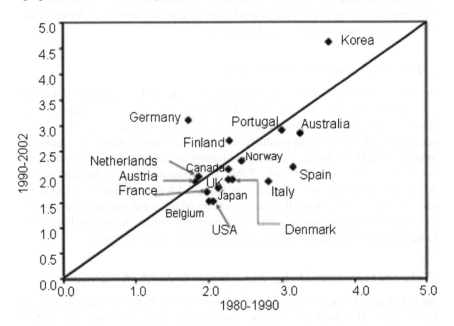

Figure 3.8 Speed of structural change in selected OECD countries (source: Wölfl 2005).

Note
Modified Lilien Indicator, based on employment per industry. Data for 1980–1990 for Germany refer to West-Germany. The results are computed on the basis of the shares of disaggregated services industries in total employment, using STAN-employment data at the lowest level of aggregation possible.

Table 3.4 Growth rates of GDP, employment and productivity (%)

	1980–1990	*1990–1998*	*1998–2009*
GDP			
Total economy	9.7	5.8	4.2
Manufacturing	12.3	5.8	6.8
Service	8.4	6.1	3.7
Employment			
Total economy	2.8	1.3	1.0
Manufacturing	5.3	−2.6	−1.3
Service	5.3	4.5	2.5
Productivity			
Total economy	6.9	4.6	3.3
Manufacturing	7.0	8.5	8.1
Service	3.1	1.6	1.2

Source: Bank of Korea, *National Accounts.*

Note

Statistics Korea, *Economically Active Population Survey.*

increasing demand for services led to the rapid growth of service employment. The productivity gap between manufacturing and the service industry in the 2000s is still comparable to that of the 1990s.

B Low productivity of the service industry

In terms of the employment share, the Korean service industry is about 7 percentage points lower than the average OECD. Meanwhile, the value-added share is about 15 percent lower compared to other OECD countries. This discrepancy results from the fact that the productivity of Korean manufacturing is comparable to other OECD countries, but the productivity of the service industry falls far below the OECD average level. Table 3.5 compares the productivity of the service and manufacturing industries of Korea with those of other OECD countries. The table shows that all countries except Mexico and Slovakia have higher productivity in the service industry than Korea. In contrast, the productivity of the Korean manufacturing industry is comparable to the OECD average.

C The rise in producer services and reduction in distributive services

Some changes in the composition of sub-sectors within the service industry are noteworthy. The producer service employment share recorded the highest increase among four categories of service sectors, with its value-added share increase comparable to social services. Business services had sharply grown in employment explaining 39.2 percent of the total employment increase in the service industry between 1993 and 2008, but the production of value-added had increased much less (Tables 3.6a, 3.6b and Table 3.7), implying that its

Table 3.5 Productivity of services and manufacturing (US$1,000/person)

Productivity of service industry			Productivity of manufacturing and energy industry		
Country	2006	2007	Country	2006	2007
1 Luxembourg	91.8	92.6	Norway	171.3	162.4
2 United States	71.3	–	Ireland	151.4	167.3
3 Belgium	61.5	61.7	United States	99.6	–
4 France	58.9	–	Canada	98.9	–
5 Italy	58.1	58.4	Finland	95.3	103.0
6 Ireland	56.5	57.8	Belgium	92.7	95.8
7 Japan	56.3	–	Netherland	89.8	91.6
8 Greece	53.4	55.4	Sweden	89.7	91.5
9 Switzerland	53.3	–	United Kingdom	83.6	85.2
10 Sweden	52.1	52.5	Japan	79.4	–
11 Netherlands	51.2	51.6	Korea	77.5	83.1
12 Norway	50.9	52.0	France	76.1	–
13 Germany	49.8	49.9	Switzerland	73.8	–
14 New Zealand	49.6	–	Luxembourg	71.6	72.8
15 Canada	49.2	–	Germany	70.1	72.8
16 Finland	48.6	48.9	Denmark	68.2	66.7
17 United Kingdom	48.3	50.2	New Zealand	66.8	–
18 Spain	48.2	48.6	Italy	57.6	57.7
19 Denmark	47.8	47.8	Greece	56.1	56.9
20 Portugal	38.0	38.8	Spain	54.5	56.2
21 Poland	37.9	–	Slovak	48.8	–
22 Hungary	34.9	35.5	Czech	41.8	44.3
23 Czech	34.8	35.6	Mexico	40.5	–
24 Korea	30.9	31.6	Poland	39.0	–
25 Mexico	28.1	–	Hungary	38.0	40.3
26 Slovak	26.8	–	Portugal	33.0	34.5

Source: OECD 2008, *National Accounts.*

productivity performance was not relatively high. Therefore, the increase in employment and value-added share of producer services was due to productivity increase in real estate and lease on the one hand, and employment expansion of business services on the other hand.

Wholesale and retail dropped in both its share of employment and value-added, leading consequently to the decline of the share of distributive services. The most influential factor which brought about this dramatic change was most likely to have been the opening of the retail and wholesale market to foreign investment in the mid-1990s and the consequent restructuring in the sector.

The opening of the wholesale and retail market, diffusion of ICT, and expansion of the communication industry have contributed to a productivity increase, which is salient from the fact that the changes in the value-added share of distributive services, measured in volume, recorded the highest increase (Table 3.7). Notwithstanding the 5.4 percentage point increase in employment during the 1993–2008 period, the value-added share of personal services in volume

Table 3.6a Changes in employment shares by four aggregate service industries (% point)

	1993	2005	2008	1993–2008
Producer	7.2	12.2	13.8	6.6
Distributive	23.7	22.6	21.6	−2.0
Personal	11.9	17.1	17.4	5.4
Social	9.7	13.3	14.6	4.9
All services	52.5	65.2	67.4	14.9

Source: Statistics Korea, *Economically Active Population Survey.*

Table 3.6b Changes in employment shares by industry of KSIC (% point)

Service	1993	2005	2008	1993–2008
Producer				
Finance and insurance	3.4	3.3	3.5	0.1
Real estate and lease	1.5	2.2	2.1	0.6
Business services	2.3	6.7	8.2	5.8
Distributor				
Wholesale and retail	18.4	16.4	15.5	−2.9
Transport and storage	4.6	5.0	5.0	0.4
Communication	0.7	1.2	1.1	0.5
Personal				
Hotel and restaurant	7.0	9.0	8.7	1.7
Cultural activities	1.3	2.2	2.3	1.0
Sanitation and others	2.7	5.4	5.8	3.1
Domestic services	0.9	0.6	0.6	−0.3
Social				
Public administration	3.2	3.5	3.6	0.4
Education	5.0	6.9	7.4	2.5
Health and social work	1.5	2.8	3.6	2.2
Total	52.5	65.2	67.4	14.9

Source: Statistics Korea, *Economically Active Population Survey.*

Table 3.7 Changes in shares of value added by service industry, in volume: 1990–2008 (%, % point)

	1990	1995	2000	2005	2008	1990–2008
Producer	18.1	20.8	20.1	19.9	19.7	1.6
Distributive	13.8	13.5	15.0	17.5	17.4	3.6
Personal	5.8	6.3	6.2	4.4	4.2	−1.5
Social	16.9	14.7	13.1	15.9	15.8	−1.1
Total	54.5	55.4	54.4	57.7	57.1	2.5

Source: Bank of Korea, *National Accounts.*

decreased because of low productivity growth. Meanwhile, the increase of the valued-added share of social services, confirmed in Table 3.2, is due to a large increase in relative prices (Table 3.8) with negative productivity growth. Consequently, the value-added share of social services in volume declined by 1.1 percent over the period 1990–2008 (Table 3.7).

D Reverse trends in nominal and real GDP shares

Figure 3.9 shows the changing share of the service industry in value-added, both in volume and current prices. This figure reveals that on the whole, except for the 1988–1998 period, the value-added share of service industry does not run parallel, but rather in opposing directions. In nominal terms, the value-added share of services rose from 51.5 percent in 1990 to 60.3 percent in 2008. The share of services in real terms has been showing a trend decrease since 1998.

In Canada, France, Germany, Italy, Japan, the United Kingdom, the United States and Australia, both the real and the nominal share of services increased in the 1990s, as the real value-added share of services and the relative prices increased simultaneously (Wölfl 2005). In Korea, however, the productivity growth in the service industry has been very slow and, as a consequence, its share has been falling sharply since the 1998 financial crisis (and continues to do

Table 3.8 Growth rate of value-added prices by industry of national account classification (% per annum)

Service	1990–1995	1995–2000	2000–2005	2005–2008	1990–2008	2000–2008
Producer						
Total value-added	8.2	2.6	2.9	1.5	4.1	2.4
Manufacturing	7.8	0.6	0.5	0.5	2.6	0.5
Services	9.3	4.3	4.2	2.5	5.4	3.6
Finance/insurance	5.2	5.8	4.1	−1.8	3.9	1.9
Real estate/lease	13.1	5.4	2.8	3.2	6.5	2.9
Business service	12.0	4.6	5.6	5.2	7.0	5.5
Distributive						
Wholesale/retail	5.5	2.6	2.9	3.3	3.6	3.1
Transport/storage	8.7	0.8	4.0	−0.1	3.7	2.5
Communications	1.5	−2.2	−1.1	−0.7	−0.6	−0.9
Personal						
Hotel/restaurant	9.1	3.9	2.0	3.7	4.8	2.6
Recreation/cultural activities	4.6	−0.4	4.6	2.2	2.8	3.7
Other personal services	10.4	2.7	3.4	2.5	5.0	3.1
Social						
Public administration	12.2	5.8	7.3	3.9	7.7	6.0
Education	13.3	6.0	6.7	5.5	8.1	6.2
Health/social work	9.5	10.3	10.6	3.7	9.1	8.0

Source: Bank of Korea, *National Accounts.*

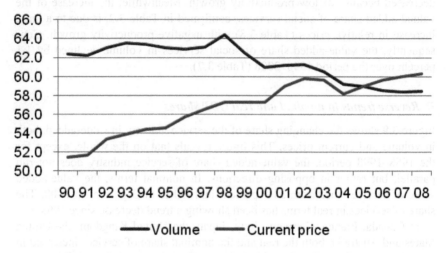

Figure 3.9 Value-added share of service industry (source: Bank of Korea, *National Accounts*).

so). The difference in trends between the nominal and real shares of the service industry is due to the fact that the service industry has been slower than other industries in productivity growth but faster in the rise of relative prices.

Table 3.8 shows the value-added price inflation rates for the manufacturing and service industries. The table shows that prices grew much faster in the service industry than in manufacturing even though the negative growth has been found in communication services since the second half of the 1990s. In all the industries, the inflation rate was higher in the 1990s than in the 2000s. Over the entire period, social services showed the highest price increase and the price increase in distributive services was the lowest.

V Summary and conclusion

Over the last two decades, the Korean service industry grew rapidly in its share in both employment and production, to the extent that the pace was the fastest among OECD countries. In addition to this, the proportion of non-production and high-skilled workers has increased over the entire economy.

The share of service production both in value-added and output has also been growing. In addition, the proportion of intermediately used service output has been on the rise. The productivity gap between manufacturing and services is bigger in Korea than in any other OECD country. The rise in income has increased the demand for service goods, but productivity in the service industry has failed to meet the growing demand, resulting in an expansion of the service employment at the fastest rate.

Given the wide productivity gap between manufacturing and services and low productivity in the service industry, the Korean economy seems to remain in

"Baumol's World," where tertiarization brings in both productivity and growth slowdown in the overall economy.

Meanwhile, not all the service industry shared the common trend. Employment growth was the highest in the producer services sector, it was negative in the distributive services sector. Productivity growth was the highest in the distributive services but slow in personal and social services. Two contrasting sectors were business services and distributive services. Business services employment grew sharply, but productivity growth was not remarkable. Productivity increase was remarkable in wholesale and retail services due to intensified competition and diffusion of information technology. However, its employment share dropped sharply.

Although the share of intermediately used service output has continued to grow, the Korean service industry, compared to other OECD countries, provides only a limited proportion of intermediate goods. This is because service firms have failed to provide manufacturing and other service firms with relevantly specialized services on the one hand, and because professional services are frequently expensive on the other hand. Consequently, Korean firms purchase a limited proportion of domestic services, and, in turn, this tends to limit expansion of the service market and a further increase in productivity of the service industry.

That less than 10 percent of SMEs have ever purchased consulting services, along with a too high price for lawyer services, is only a small tip of an iceberg. Meanwhile, though the service industry is growing in both employment and production, productivity growth is slowing down consistently and those jobs created are low-wage ones, raising challenges to policy decision makers.

To enhance the productivity and the probability of good job creation through business openings, improving the competition environment, enhancing competition, and streamlining regulations on business opening will be necessary. In any case, what seems important is that more strategic consideration should be given to an increased role of the service output as an intermediary input. When the Korean service industry expands its market by providing more inputs to manufacturing and other industries with increased productivity, not only can tertiarization progress without confining the Korean economy from in Baumol's World, but it will also contribute to ensuring more and better jobs.

Notes

1 Notwithstanding the revisions of the industry classification, coherence of the industrial classification is maintained for the period 1993–2008. Light industry is defined as sectors 15–22 and 36–37, chemical industry as sectors 23–25, heavy industry as sectors 26–28, electric/electronic industry as sectors 30–32, and machinery industry as sectors 29 and 33–35 in the eighth amended industrial classification code.

2 In terms of 1-digit level of Korean Standard Industry Classification (KSIC), producer services include finance and insurance (K), real estate and rental (L), business services (M); distributive services include wholesale and retail (G), transport (I) and communications (J); personal services include hotel and restaurant (H), recreational, cultural, and sporting services (Q), other public repairs and personal services (R) and domestic

services (S); and social services include public administration, national defense, and social security administration (N), educational services (O), health and social work services (P) and foreign and international organizations (T).

3   High-skilled or high-skilled non-production workers refer to legislators, senior officials and managers (0), professionals (1), and technicians and associate professionals (2) of 1-digit level classification in the fifth revised Korean Standard Classification of Occupations (KSCO). Non-production workers designate high-skilled workers plus clerks (3), service workers (4) and sales workers (5). The fourth and fifth amendment of KSCO has enabled a coherent grouping of workers by skill level since 1993.

References

Baumol, William, "Macroeconomics of Unbalanced Growth: The Anatomy of Urban Crisis," *American Economic Review*, 57(2) 1967, pp. 415–426.

Choi, Yong-Seok, Moon-Joong Tcha and Jong-Il Kim, *Impact of Chinese Economic and Trade Growth on Korean Economy*, KDI, 2005.

Hur, Jai-Joon, Hwan-Joo Seo and Young Soo Lee, "ICT Investment and the Demand for Skilled Workers," *Kyong Je Hak Yon Gu*, 50(4) 2002, pp. 267–292.

Kim, Jong-il, "Structural Changes and Employment Issues in Korean Economy," mimeo, 2006.

Lee, Jong-Hwa and Cheol-Jong Song, "The Sector-specific Analysis of the Key Factors in Korean Economy, for 1970–2001," *Kyong Je Hak Yon Gu*, 53(2) 2005, pp. 99–144.

Oh, Joon-Byeong, "The Analysis on the Determinants of Changes in the Industrial Structure of Korea: focusing on the discussions of deindustrialization," *Kyong Je Hak Yon Gu*, 53(1) 2005, pp. 155–174.

Oulton, Nicholas, "Must the Growth Rate Decline?: Baumol's Unbalanced Growth Revisited," *Working Paper 107*, Bank of England, London, 1988.

Wölfl, Anita, "Productivity Growth in Service Industries An Assessment of Recent Patterns and the Role of Measurement," *STI Working Paper 2003–07*, OECD, Paris, 2003.

Wölfl, Anita, "The Service Economy in OECD Countries," *STI Working Paper 2005–03*, OECD, Paris, 2005.

4 Female employment structure and policy agenda in Korea

Hyewon Kim

I Introduction

Korea does not fully utilize its female workforce. With an aging society and demographically driven future labor shortage, Korea will face great pressure to remedy this situation and increase the opportunities for women, especially highly educated women, or suffer substantial slowdown of growth and difficulty in funding its commitment to retirees. The female employment rate of those aged 15–64 in Korea stands at 52.2 percent as of 2009. This does not differ much from the OECD average of 56.5 percent (OECD 2010). However, if we compare the 25–54 age bracket, which excludes senior age groups and young student groups, Korea stands at 59.8 percent and shows a somewhat big discrepancy with the OECD average of 65.3 percent. Moreover, if we compare the employment rate of females with a college-level education between the ages of 25 and 64, the difference is even greater, with Korea at 61.1 percent as of 2008 and the OECD average of 79.4 percent.

These figures indicate that the female workforce in Korea is underutilized. In other words, we already have sufficient potential to address the aforementioned threats posed by aging society and labor shortage. This chapter aims to examine female employment in Korea, which will serve as an alternative to resolve the quantity imbalance which may face the Korean labor market in the future. Section II will focus on the employment structure and the occupational segregation between genders, while Section III will examine the wage difference between genders and gender inequality. Section IV will look at the poor level of female economic participation in Korea and analyze core factors behind this problem, i.e., childbirth and marriage. Section V will present some policy issues.

II Female employment structure

A Employment structure by industries and occupations

The rapid growth experienced by Korea can be characterized as a continuous reduction of primary industries coupled with brisk growth in the manufacturing and service industries. In the 1970s and 1980s, the employment share of the manufacturing industry showed fast growth, only to peak in 1990 and plummet from 1992, falling to 16.3 percent as of 2009. In contrast, the service sector has continued to record steady growth. The employment share of the service sector, which stood at 44.5 percent in 1985, rose to 55.1 percent in 1995 and 68.5 percent as of 2009. In order to examine this growth in detail, let us divide the service industry into the subcategories of personal services, distributive services, social services, and producer services (see Singlemann 1978, Elfring 1988).

If we look at the employment share for each subcategory as a percentage of total employment, the employment share of distributive services reached its peak in 2000 and is now on the decline. In comparison, employment in producer services is increasing at a rapid pace.[1]

Traditionally, the proportion of females in the manufacturing, construction and utilities industries has been low, while the proportion in the service sector has been relatively high. Personal and social services are mostly comprised of interpersonal services, and therefore considered to be female-friendly business. Table 4.1 shows the ratio of female employment share in industry j over male employment share in industry j. If the value for industry j is higher than 1, then that industry has relatively high female employment. We find that the proportion of women in the manufacturing industry is continuing to decline. The personal and social service industries were traditionally female-dominated but have recently taken different directions. There has been a great inflow of men into the

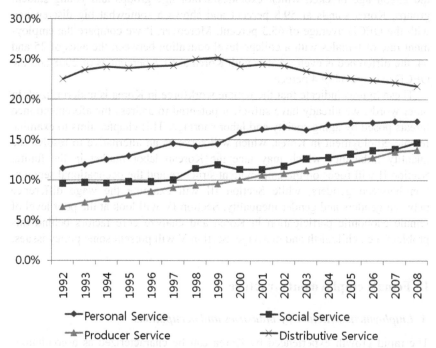

Figure 4.1 Changes in employment share of each of four service industries (source: *Economically Active Population Survey*).

Table 4.1 Relative ratio of female employment to male by industry

	1992	1995	2000	2005	2009
Forestry and fishery	1.37	1.37	1.29	1.23	1.19
Mine and manufacturing	0.95	0.84	0.78	0.70	0.65
Construction and utilities	0.17	0.16	0.14	0.14	0.16
Personal service	2.55	2.68	2.11	2.03	1.95
Social service	1.20	1.30	1.56	1.96	2.11
Producer service	0.99	1.15	0.90	0.85	0.91
Distributive service	0.83	0.84	0.86	0.85	0.78

Source: *Economically Active Population Survey.*

personal service sector after the financial crisis in 1998, taking the female–male ratio down from 1:2.55 to 1:1.94. In contrast, the social service sector has continued to see an increase of women, pushing up the ratio from 1:1.2 in 1992 to 1:2.25 as of 2009. In the case of producer services, which have shown the fastest growth in terms of employment, the rate of growth in female employment is slightly behind that of male employment in the 2000s.

Next, let us move on to the features of the distribution of female and male workers by occupation. The most noticeable feature of the occupational distribution for women is that about half of women are in elementary occupations or sales and service jobs. While only 26 percent of men hold such jobs, the rate of women is twice that at 47.9 percent in 2008. Such a concentration of women in elementary occupations and sales and service jobs has remained nearly unchanged for a long time.

The biggest change during the past decade is the huge decline in the ratio of females working in plant, machine operator and assembly jobs. This is correlated with the large drop in the number of female employees working in the manufacturing industry. The ratio of female employment in manufacturing fell by more than 50 percent, from 16.5 percent in 1993 to a mere 6.9 percent in 2008. In comparison, the ratio for males showed only a slight decline in the same period, from 35.3 percent to 30.9 percent.

With regard to clerical jobs, the percentage of males has stood at 12 percent with hardly any change, while the percentage of women has risen slightly. The rate of both male and female employment increased greatly in the case of professional jobs with hardly any difference in the rate of growth. A breakdown of age groups shows that single women from ages 20 to 29 mostly hold clerk jobs and professional/semi-professional jobs, while married women from ages 40 to 49 are concentrated in sales and service jobs and elementary occupations (more than 50 percent), as well as plant, machine operator and assembly jobs (more than 20 percent).

The analysis of this data poses difficulty as they are influenced by both age and cohort factors. In other words, it is difficult to determine whether single women in their 20s with clerk jobs and professional/semiprofessional jobs will continue to hold such jobs 20 years down the road or switch to elementary occupations or sales and service jobs, which are currently held by married women in their forties. It is also difficult to say whether married women in their forties work mostly in elementary occupations and sales and service jobs because of the cohort factor, in that they were born between 1955 and 1964, or because of the age factor, in that they are now in their forties.

B Employment structure by employment form

The status of women in the labor market can be evaluated by their employment status. Recently, non-regular employment has become an issue in the Korean labor market, and the fact that there is a high rate of women among non-regular workers has made the issue a gender-related one. If we are to define non-regular employment as a job status, 32.8 percent of male wage-earners are employed on a non-regular basis on August, 2009 while the rate for women is a whopping 55.8 percent, showing that non-regularly employed women far outweigh men.[2]

However, this high rate of non-regular employment among women is not a phenomenon that suddenly appeared after the Asian financial crisis. The rate of female non-regular employment was already 62 percent in 1990 and has not changed a great deal for the past 20 years or so. But it is also true that the shock of the financial crisis affected the increase of non-regular employment around 2000.

The high share of non-regular employment among women is not a phenomenon specific to Korea alone. There tends to be a high ratio of women working in part-time or fixed-term jobs all around the world. This high rate of female

Table 4.2 Composition share by employment type: female

Year	Non-wage worker[a]	Unpaid family worker[a]	Wage worker[a]	Permanent worker[b]	Temporary worker[b]	Daily worker[b]	Non-regular worker[b]
1963	0.78	0.56	0.22			0.48	
1965	0.79	0.58	0.21			0.35	
1970	0.71	0.50	0.29			0.32	
1975	0.71	0.48	0.29			0.23	
1980	0.61	0.37	0.39			0.21	
1985	0.52	0.31	0.48			0.23	
1990	0.43	0.24	0.57	0.38	0.40	0.23	0.62
1995	0.40	0.21	0.60	0.43	0.41	0.17	0.57
2000	0.38	0.19	0.62	0.31	0.46	0.23	0.69
2005	0.33	0.14	0.67	0.38	0.45	0.17	0.62
2009	0.29	0.12	0.71	0.44	0.43	0.13	0.56

Source: *Economically Active Population Survey.*

Notes
a Comparison with total employment.
b Comparison with wage workers.

Table 4.3 Relative female to male ratio

Year	Nonwage worker	Unpaid family worker	Wage worker	Permanent worker	Temporary worker	Daily worker	Non-regular worker
1963	1.24	3.11	0.59			1.25	
1965	1.28	3.50	0.55			1.10	
1970	1.29	3.76	0.64			1.23	
1975	1.33	4.00	0.62			0.96	
1980	1.27	5.16	0.75			1.08	
1985	1.23	6.95	0.83			1.60	
1990	1.17	9.96	0.90	0.58	1.77	1.74	1.76
1995	1.18	12.62	0.91	0.63	2.03	1.34	1.77
2000	1.08	9.81	0.96	0.53	1.74	1.59	1.69
2005	0.97	10.94	1.02	0.61	1.81	1.31	1.64
2009	0.93	9.89	1.03	0.66	1.93	1.19	1.69

Source: *Economically Active Population Survey.*

non-regular employment is in part related to the needs of women as labor suppliers. Women who wish to continue economic activities after marriage and childbirth tend to search for jobs where they can manage their time flexibly in order to accommodate child rearing and housekeeping.

In addition, a change in the occupation and industry composition affects the increase in non-regular jobs among women. In the case of elementary occupations and sales and service jobs where female employment is concentrated, more than 80 percent of the jobs are temporary or daily jobs. As for clerk jobs that have a high female preference, the proportion of temporary or daily jobs has grown threefold since the 1990s, from 12 percent to 36 percent. In terms of employment status, the service sector is an industry high in temporary or daily employment. As we have seen, the service sector has continued to expand its employment proportion. A shrinking manufacturing sector with a relatively low share of non-regular employment has also played a part in the high level of non-regular employment for women. It should be noted that such a trend did not appear suddenly after the Asian financial crisis, however.

III Wage gap between genders

A Change in wage gap

The wage gap between genders is considered to have continued to decline in the Korean economy. However, the evaluation of measurement and comparison of a gender–wage gap depends on which data are used and whether other factors are controlled or not. The Ministry of Labor's *Monthly Labor Statistical Survey* is frequently referred to in cases of gender–wage gap. The relative wage for women in 1980 was only 45 percent that of men but continued to grow, reaching 62.3 percent as of 2004.

The *Monthly Labor Statistical Survey*'s relative wage index between genders is incomplete in that it does not reflect the difference in human capital between men and women or the difference in job or industry composition. A lower wage difference is natural if the educational level of women is low. Jeong (2005) has calculated the relative wage level between men and women after controlling for such differences using wage equation estimation. The wage function graph shown in Figure 4.2 depicts the estimated wage difference after factoring in educational level, tenure, and age using the data from the *Survey Report on Wage Structure*.

We can see that the relative wage gaps have continued to reduce whether we make a simple comparison or use a wage function. Many past studies used the methodology of Oaxaca (1973) to approach the reasons behind such relative wage gaps and wage gap trends. Park (1984) shows that the gender–wage gap from 1971 to 1980 was less influenced by differences in productivity from personal characteristics. Uh (1991) shows that 45 to 50 percent of the gender–wage gap could be explained by a difference in human capital by means of the 1989 *Survey Report on Wage Structure*. Similarly Keum (2000) shows that about 40 percent of the gender–wage gap could be explained by the difference in human capital between genders using 1998 data from the *Korean Labor and Income Panel Study* (KLIPS).

Yoo (2001) applies the Oaxaca method to analyze the trend and the driving force which reduced wage disparity from 1984 to 1999. His study confirms that the wage gap caused by a difference in human capital has decreased in size. This trend is also confirmed in Jung (2007). In Jung (2007), the decline of the productivity-related gap exceeded that of the non-productivity-related gap from 1985 to 2005.

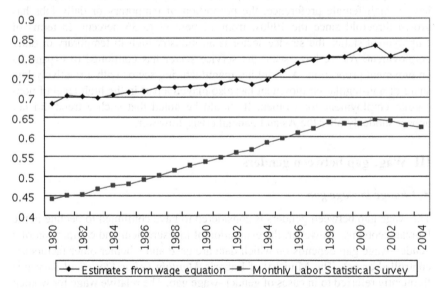

Figure 4.2 The trend of the relative wage of female worker compared to male (source: Jeong 2005).

There remain questions which should be addressed. One of the most important problems is the reason why the gender–wage gap has not declined in the 2000s. The differences in human capital between men and women almost disappeared. But the next driving force which will reduce the wage gap is yet to come.

B Wage differences by gender, Korea vs. Sweden vs. United States

Sweden has a high female participation rate in economic activities but suffers from both a severe occupational segregation as well as a glass ceiling that makes it very difficult for women to advance upwards into well-paying jobs. Since the 1990s, the wage disparity between genders in Sweden can mostly be explained by a wage gap not in the lower wage groups but the higher wage groups. Figure 4.3, which is from Albrecht *et al.* (2003) shows the observed gender gap at each percentile in the wage distribution in Sweden. As the figure shows, there is virtually no wage disparity in the low wage groups, but the wage of women is only 85 percent of men in the middle group. This level drops to 82 percent in the seventy-fifth percentile and even further to about 70 percent in the upper tenth percentile range.

As for the United States, there is a minor wage disparity in the lower tenth percentile, but the gender–wage gap grows wider as the wage level increases (see Figure 4.4). In the middle wage groups, the relative level of female wage to male wage is as low as 75 percent that of men. The gender–wage gap declines in the higher wage group. This implies that the promotion and advancement of women into well-paying jobs is relatively easy in the United States.

In terms of wage disparity, Korea appears to have moved from a Swedish model to a US model during the past two decades. As displayed in Figure 4.5, the

Table 4.4 Decomposition of gender–wage gap (won, %)

	1984	1988	1994	1997	1999
Total wage disparity between gender	159,800	216,941	459,073	565,387	530,253
(amount/ratio)	(100.0)	(100.0)	(100.0)	(100.0)	(100.0)
Wage disparity from human capital	50.8	50.8	38.2	38.3	43.0
Difference in education level	15.3	14.7	10.0	10.2	11.5
Difference in tenure	17.1	22.0	20.3	20.7	23.0
Difference in career	18.4	14.2	7.8	7.4	8.5
Wage disparity from discrimination	49.2	49.2	61.8	61.7	57.0
Wage discrimination	50.2	47.5	63.7	62.4	71.0
Discrimination in job allocation and promotion	−1.0	1.7	−1.8	−0.7	−14.0

Sources: Yoo 2001, table 10, p. 227; data: tape of the *Survey Report on Wage Structure*, Ministry of Labor.

Notes
1 The wage difference between men and women has been divided.
2 Career refers to a career outside of the current job and is calculated as: age − years of education − years of tenure − 6.

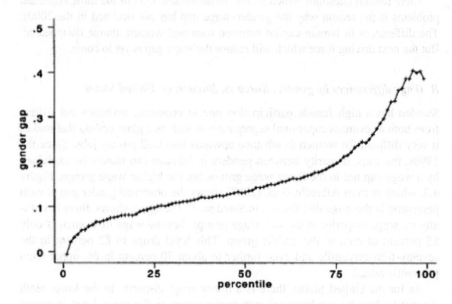

Figure 4.3 Gender log wage gap, Sweden, 1998 (source: Albrecht *et al.* 2003).

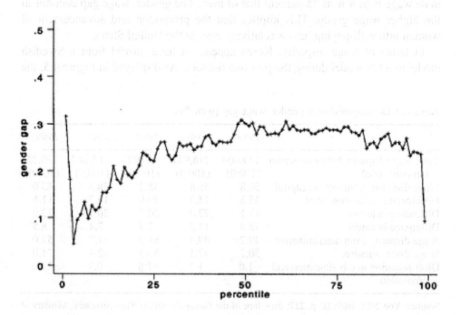

Figure 4.4 Gender log wage gap, United States, 1999 (source: Albrecht *et al.* 2003).

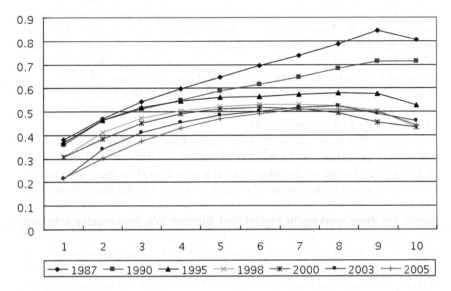

Figure 4.5 Gender log wage gap, Korea, 1987–2005 (source: *Basic Survey of Wage Structure*).

wage disparity was smaller in the low wage groups and higher in the high wage groups in 1984. In 1999, however, an increase in wage levels led to a greater wage gap that showed a slight decline in the middle-range wage groups and above.

Hwang (2003) explains this change to be a testimony of polarization within women. There has been a rise in both unskilled low-wage labor and high-skilled high-wage labor. Hwang (2003) points out that the income disparity within women has a positive aspect in that it reflects a greater number of well-educated women entering high-skilled careers. Keum (2002) not only examines the issue of occupational segregation but also promotion, which is a major reason behind the glass ceiling. According to that analysis, men have twice the possibility of promotion than women, confirming that there is indeed a glass ceiling. As tenure had a positively significant influence on the possibility of promotion, reducing the career interruption of women would play a significant role in enhancing their chances for promotion. However, the higher possibility of promotion for men than for women has an adverse effect on female tenure because it discourages women from keeping attachment with labor market.

We can see that the glass ceiling is being broken partially in certain areas of the labor market. We can see some evidence in the changes in the distribution of age, education level and tenure of working women based on the *Survey Report on Wage Structure*. This survey only includes data of regular jobs and therefore does not include information on temporary or daily labor.

The age distribution of employees in the *Survey Report on Wage Structure* does not show the typical double peaks that are found in the *Economically Active*

Population Survey. This may be because married women who reenter the labor market after their mid-thirties usually find non-permanent jobs and are therefore not captured in the *Survey Report on Wage Structure.* We can see that the proportion of married women has increased over the past 20 years, especially elderly women, and this is also confirmed in the tenure data. In 1981, only 8 percent of women had tenure of five years and over but this surged to 32 percent in 2001. The career length of women has also risen continuously. The percentage of women with careers of five years and over expanded to 41.7 percent in 2001 from only 12.8 percent in 1981.

Many scholars who have studied the female labor market in Korea conclude that there is an increase in the number of women in relatively well-paying jobs on the one hand while on the other there is a growth in elementary occupations. This dual structure in the female labor market is linked to the discontinuation of careers. Women who maintain employment without exiting from the labor market are those working in high-skilled superior jobs who receive relatively high wages. In contrast, the women who discontinue their careers and later reenter the labor market become concentrated in low-skilled low-wage jobs. Women with a higher education who have chosen to build their careers are continuously pressured and tempted to leave the labor market due to a male-oriented working culture, marginalization from social networks, low possibility of promotion, and a workplace culture that does not accommodate family life. In the next section, we will examine the changes in female labor supply which have direct ties to career discontinuation.

IV Changes in the female labor supply

A Changes in female economic participation and international comparison

Female participation in the labor market has continued to grow in Korea. The economic participation rate of females aged 15 and over reached 52.2 percent as of 2009 – a big leap from 37 percent recorded in 1963. While the overall trend has been positive, the shock of the Asian financial crisis caused a temporary snag in female economic participation. The female economic participation rate which was close to 50 percent right before the Asian financial crisis fell back to early 1990s levels after the crisis. However, this figure increased with the economic recovery and surpassed pre-crisis levels in 2005.

It may seem that the female economic participation rate has grown considerably, but international comparisons prove that the growth is not so remarkable. During the 30 years leading up to the Asian financial crisis, the economic participation rate of women in Korea rose from 40 percent to 50 percent, whereas the United States made the same increase of 10 percent during the 13 years between 1960 and 1973, jumping from 42 percent to 53 percent. In the case of Sweden, the participation rate grew by 30 percent within two decades, from 39 percent in 1960 to 69 percent in 1980.

An analysis of the different age groups can provide a detailed picture of the changes in female economic participation and help our understanding on the structure of female participation in economic activities. Figure 4.6 shows the female economic participation rate for the different age groups. Active participation by women in their twenties has contributed largely to the growth in the economic participation rate of women, while the rate of participation from women in their thirties has been at a standstill since 1995. (Keum 2002, p. 10) There are a few points worth noting. First, economic participation for women in their late twenties was very low in 1985 but has shown an extraordinary increase up until 2010. Second, the stagnant growth of participation from women in their early thirties remains a long-standing issue and is playing a decisive role in the M-shaped curve of female economic participation in Korea.

One of the most important reasons why such an M-shaped curve persists is because marriage and childbirth greatly decrease female economic activities. The participation trough shifted from the late twenties to the early thirties because women postponed marriage and children to a later age than before.

Figure 4.7 shows the economic participation rate of single women by cohorts groups. As can be seen in Figure 4.7, the economic participation rate of single women has remained stable. Although there is a small dip with age, the participation rate maintains above 70 percent and does not show a big difference between cohorts. Figure 4.8 is a measure of the economic participation rate for married women by cohort groups. The participation rate for married women by age groups shows a typical U-shaped curve, and the shape after age 30 of the older cohort group is almost the same as that of the younger cohort groups. However, the economic participation rate for married women in their early and late twenties is increasing at a rapid pace.

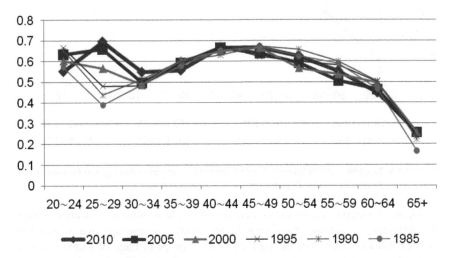

Figure 4.6 Female economic participation rate by age (source: *Economically Active Population Survey*, June, each year).

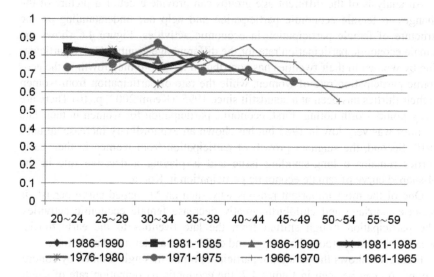

Figure 4.7 Economic participation rate of single women by cohort groups (source: *Economically Active Population Survey*, June, each year).

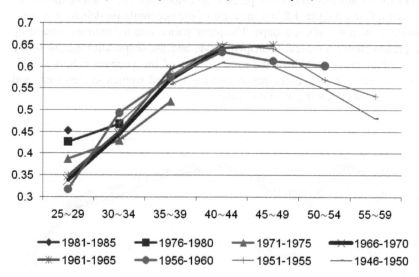

Figure 4.8 Economic participation rate of married women by cohort group (source: *Economically Active Population Survey*, June, each year).

Figure 4.9 displays how the percentage of single women has changed within the different age groups. As shown in the figure, the average age of married women has increased over the past 20 years. The percentage of single females under the age of 35 is growing considerably, particularly for those between the ages of 25 and 29. Single females accounted for 16 percent of those between ages

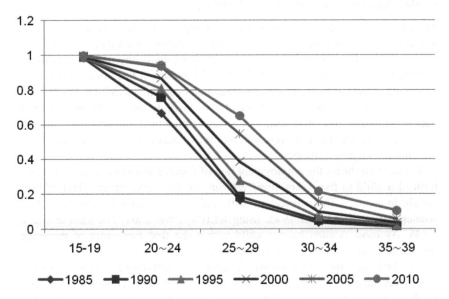

Figure 4.9 Percentage of women who are single (source: *Economically Active Population Survey*, June, each year).

25 and 29 in 1985, but this number rose to 65 percent in 2010. Higher education for women has had a big influence on the sharp increase of single women in this age group, which also affected the growing economic participation of women. There is also a growing body of single females between the ages of 30 and 34, increasing from less than 4 percent 25 years ago to nearly 20 percent recently.

Changes in the time series for the economic participation rate of an age group is influenced by factors such as changes in the singles ratio and changes in the economic participation rate of both married and single females. As singles have a higher economic participation rate than married people, a rise in the singles ratio acts as a force that pushes up the economic participation rate within the age groups.

According to Kim (2006), the continuous rise in the early thirties singles ratio during the past decade increased the economic participation rate of female in their early thirties. That force was offset, however, by a decline in the economic participation of married females in their early thirties, which explains that female participation rates in the early thirties have not changed for 20 years. The reason for the small decrease in the economic participation rate of married women in their early thirties is that women are having their first child at a later age and thus the burden of childcare is now felt in the early thirties rather than the late twenties. In recent years the main period of childcare is diffused and postponed and the late thirties became a trough in female economic participation (Figure 4.6). The next section will examine how female economic participation contracts as a result of marriage and childbirth.

B Marriage, childbirth, and female labor supply

The employment rate for women declines steeply with marriage and childbirth in Korea. While it is still the most representative labor force survey in Korea, the *Economically Active Population Survey* does not contain any data on the time of marriage or the age or number of children. Therefore, it has limitations in analyzing the effects of marriage and childbirth on economic activities. The KLIPS, which has been compiled by the Korea Labor Institute since 1998, includes rich data on marriage and childbirth, as well as employment and economic activity status, making it suitable for research into the effects of marriage and childbirth on female economic activities.

Figure 4.10 shows the employment rate of females from two years before the birth of a child to five years after. We can see the career break effect of birth clearly in Korea.[3] This subsection will analyze the economic activities of all women who married after 1995, using KLIPS, 1998–2004. The sample size is 1,046. As most women have a child within the first five years of marriage, women had one or more children no older than age 5.

The first analysis is to compare the economic activity of women two years before marriage and five years after marriage. As we see in Table 4.5, 48 percent of the women had been employed two years prior to marriage. This figure dropped considerably to 27 percent five years after marriage. The probability of working women becoming unemployed is 0.73. Similarly, the probability of unemployed women staying jobless is 0.74, and just 43 percent of the employed women were likely to have the same job after marriage.

We can find different patterns between different employment types. There is a greater probability of wage workers becoming unemployed compared to

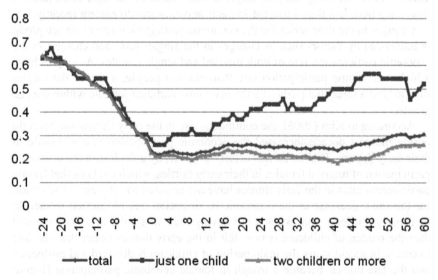

Figure 4.10 Employment rate of female around birth of child (source: *Korean Labor and Income Panel Study*, Kim 2010).

Table 4.5 Changing status of employed two years before marriage

Prob(U|E)	Prob(Ei|Ei)	Percentage of employed two years before marriage	Percentage of employed five years after marriage
0.73	0.43	0.48	0.27

Source: *Korean Labor and Income Panel Study* (KLIPS).

non-wage workers (see Table 4.6): 93 percent of working women were wage workers two years prior to marriage, but this dropped to 65 percent after five years of marriage. As wage workers have limitations in using their time, many women move towards non-wage labor: 26 percent of wage workers convert to non-wage employment, as non-wage work is advantageous in balancing family and work. While 93 percent of the women had regular jobs before marriage, this figure declined to 78 percent after marriage. The increase in non-regular employment is due to the single unemployed women who enter non-regular employment, as well as the 10 percent or so who move from regular employment to non-regular employment after marriage. Table 4.6 also shows that there was a higher probability of non-regular workers becoming unemployed than regular workers becoming unemployed. Females in regular jobs before marriage find it difficult to give up their jobs because of the high expected wage of regular employment. The probability of people keeping their jobs after marriage was about 40 percent for regular workers. Conversely, there was a zero probability of non-regular workers keeping the same job.

The proportion of part-time workers is very small, at only 6 percent before marriage. However, this rises to 14 percent for women five years after marriage. This increase is influenced more by unemployed people choosing part-time jobs as their first job after marriage rather than full-timers switching to part-time employment. Part-time jobs can be better for balancing work and family. However, the probability of unemployment is almost the same for both part-timers and full-timers. Of those who stayed employed after marriage, full-time workers had a greater chance of keeping the same job.

Table 4.6 Comparison between employment types

	Prob(U|E)	Prob(E|U)	Prob(Ei|Ei)	Percentage of employed two years prior to marriage	Percentage of employed five years after marriage
Wage worker	0.75	0.65	0.39	0.93	0.65
Non-wage worker	0.47	0.35	0.68	0.07	0.35
Regular worker	0.73	0.69	0.40	0.93	0.78
Non-regular worker	0.90	0.31	0.00	0.07	0.22
Part-timer	0.79	0.20	0.40	0.06	0.14
Full-timer	0.79	0.80	0.58	0.94	0.86

Source: *Korean Labor and Income Panel Study* (KLIPS).

There was a big disparity across occupations. Those with elementary occupations had the highest probability of becoming unemployed after marriage, followed by female clerks and semi-professionals. It may come as a surprise that semi-professionals are highly likely to become unemployed. Given the inadequate remuneration for semi-professionals, however, it is not so surprising. Although semi-professionals have a high probability of unemployment, the likelihood of such workers keeping their jobs is quite high as long as they continue to work after marriage. Semi-professionals are divided clearly into those who continue to work and those who do not. The percentage of semi-professionals is increasing, although few unemployed people find jobs in this sector and many semi-professionals become unemployed. This is because many people who worked as female clerks as singles switch to semiprofessional jobs after marriage. Single women account for a large percentage of office work: 43 percent of women work in clerk jobs. However, female clerks leave the labor market in masses five years after marriage, and there are few new entries. Female clerks also show a tendency to move to other jobs. Many female clerks advance upwards to become semi-professionals and even step down to lower levels. We cannot see such an active movement in other jobs.

When the unemployed enter the market anew, many women enter service jobs followed by sales and then professional jobs. Therefore, the proportion of service and sales jobs increases notably compared to that before marriage.

The analysis thus far shows that marriage and childbirth are causing a severe discontinuation of careers for Korean women, and that single women are overly concentrated in office work only to exit the labor market after marriage. Cost (2000) conducted a historic analysis on the process of growing female employment in the United States and found that, when female employment in the United States was centered on office work, there was a pattern where women left the labor market with marriage and childbirth and returned to the labor market after their children had grown up. Cost (2000) also noted that the exponential growth in female employment in the United States appeared with a pattern of women moving from office work to career jobs. Based on this analysis, it seems difficult

Table 4.7 Comparison between employment statuses

	$Prob(U|E)$	$Prob(E|U)$	$Prob(Ei|Ei)$	Percentage of employed two years prior to marriage	Percentage of employed five years after marriage
Permanent workers	0.54	0.45	0.85	0.86	0.54
Temporary workers	1.00	0.16	–	0.02	0.09
Daily workers	1.00	0.05	–	0.02	0.03
Self-employed	0.09	0.15	0.80	0.08	0.16
Unpaid family worker	0.00	0.19	1.00	0.03	0.18

Source: *Korean Labor and Income Panel Study* (KLIPS).

Table 4.8 Comparison between occupations

	Prob(U|E)	Prob(E|U)	Prob(Ei|Ei)	Percentage of employed two years prior to marriage	Percentage of employed five years after marriage
Upper management	0.00	0.00	1.00	0.00	0.01
Professionals	0.54	0.15	0.69	0.13	0.18
Semi-professionals	0.73	0.08	0.64	0.10	0.12
Office workers	0.77	0.12	0.39	0.43	0.19
Services	0.68	0.22	0.40	0.06	0.15
Sales	0.67	0.18	0.15	0.08	0.16
Agriculture and fishery	0.50	0.01	1.00	0.00	0.03
Craft workers	0.84	0.08	0.00	0.04	0.07
Assembly	0.71	0.06	0.14	0.05	0.04
Elementary labor	0.86	0.09	0.00	0.10	0.05

Source: *Korean Labor and Income Panel Study* (KLIPS).

to discard the M-shaped curve from the female employment rate in Korea in the near future. From a different perspective, there is the possibility of expansion in female career jobs, as the United States experienced, because Korea has a steadily increasing share of female professionals and highly educated women.

V Conclusion: prospects of female employment policy in Korea

Labor policy about female employment can be divided into policies for gender equality in employment and policies for work–family balance. Gender-equal employment policies are mostly comprised of anti-discrimination policies that focus on equal opportunities for women in employment, as well as some policies that encourage female employment and expand employment opportunities. Work–family policies are made up of maternity protection, childcare support policies and flexible work policy.

In the case of gender-equal employment policies, it is most notable that affirmative action programs in employment have been introduced recently. In Korea, affirmative action has been implemented since March 2006 and requires all public companies and some private businesses with 500 plus employees to annually submit their status of male and female employment. If the female employment rate does not meet the target rate, the employer is required to prepare and submit an "Action Plan for Proactive Employment Improvement" and then file a follow-up report one year after the action plan has been implemented. Employers who fail to submit such reports are punished with fines of up to three million won. However, some have criticized that there are no sanctions against companies whose plans are unsatisfactory or who do not execute their plans.

Maternity leave is stipulated under the Korean Labor Standards Act. Duration of maternity leave in Korea was extended from its original 60 days up to 90 days in 2001, and the employer's burden was reduced. Parental leave of 12 month is available until the child is six years old, and starting in 2007, a monthly parental leave benefit of 500,000 won is provided. According to the Ministry of Labor, many eligible women do not use parental leave after maternity leave, although this usage rate grew considerably recently (21 percent in 2003 and about 40 percent at the end of 2008, see Ministry of Labor 2005, Kim 2010). According to Lee *et al.* (2004), lower-wage workers tend not to take advantage of parental leave, which indicates that the current parental leave benefit is insufficient enough to induce workers to take leave.

Looking back on the female employment policies of advanced countries, countries that successfully reached a high female employment rate can be divided into two types. The first are North European countries that enhance female employment with the state taking responsibility of childcare, providing maternity and parental leave, and guaranteeing, through policy, employment after the leave period. In this case, the factors that hinder female employment are removed using government expenditure. The second are countries following the US model where government investment into childcare is minimal and maternity and parental leave is virtually nonexistent compared to that of Northern Europe. Despite such restrictions, female employment in these countries can be high because inequality in employment, promotion and wages can be reduced, and women return to the labor market voluntarily in pursuit of high wages. As a result, the employment rate of women was greatly enhanced as well-educated career women succeeded in moving up the corporate ladder through promotion.

The rich pool of well-educated women in Korea can potentially be used as key human resources. We need to devise female employment policies which fit the environment of the Korean labor market by reviewing the pros and cons of both the US and the North European models. Whether we look at the unionization rate or job safety level, we should consider the fact that the Korean labor market is closer to the US model, which stresses more flexibility, than the North European model, which underlines safety. In addition, the institutional environment of Korea is not same as the United States. Social policy systems in Korea have many common elements with the European system. We present some basic policy directions that should be included in a Korean female employment policy, which reflect the complex environment of the Korean labor market and social system.

First, the government needs to make greater investment into childcare and the system should be more employment-friendly and quality-focused. There is a lot of public and academic criticism towards low-cost and low-quality childcare services in the liberal model. There is a great demand for high-quality childcare services in Korea. High-road strategy, i.e., high spending and high-quality childcare service, is promising in achieving a high female participation rate in Korea. Second, many studies have proven that excessively long parental leave undermines the competitiveness of women in the labor market. In particular, the discontinuation of careers deters women from entering jobs that require high skills from the start and produce high value-added. Given that fiscal and economic resources are limited, it would be more effective for the government to invest in childcare rather than provide lengthier parental leave from work. Flexible use of part-time work in the childcare period should be promoted. In addition the incentive for the returner from parental leave should be designed and provided. Third, it is important to reduce discrimination towards women in terms of wages and especially promotion in decent jobs, such as professional and managerial jobs. If high profits were given to successful career women, the opportunity costs for well-educated women leaving the labor market would be great and would serve as an impetus in nurturing a mass of highly productive female labor. Fourth, there is a need to create jobs in the social service sector for married women who have discontinued their careers. As the external labor market is underdeveloped in Korea, it is difficult for married women to reenter the labor market with sufficient remuneration and fair treatment according to their skill and experiences. We need interventionist policies to promote female-friendly jobs for middle-aged women – for example, social service jobs. What should be noted is that there is a need to plan long-term career paths for any job that is created. In particular, jobs must be diversified and developed so that married women with secondary educations will perceive those jobs as promising rather than as dead-end jobs.

Notes

1 The employment data of 2009 is available. But the time series show overshooting phenomena due to the change of the industry classification code. So we present 1992–2008 data in Figure 4.1.
2 A hot debate about the definition and measurement issues of non-regular employment exists in Korea. According to another definition, 28.2 percent of men are non-regular workers on August, 2009 while the rate for women is 44.1 percent (National Statistics Office 2009).
3 Some numbers between Figure 4.10 and Table 4.5 are inconsistent due to the difference of data. We use the data of women who gave birth in 2001 and 2002 in order to produce Figure 4.10.

References

Ahn, Joo-yeop, "Forecast of Labor Supply and Demand 2005–2020," Korea Labor Institute, 2005.

Albrecht, James, Anders Bjorklund and Susan Vroman, "Is There a Glass Ceiling in Sweden," *Journal of Labor Economics*, 21(1) 2003, pp. 145–177.

Cost, Dora L., "From Mill Town to Board Room: The Rise of Women's Paid Labor," *Journal of Economic Perspectives*, 14(4) 2000, pp. 101–122.

Elfring, Tom, "Service Sector Employment in Advanced Economies," *A Comparative Analysis of its Implications for Economic Growth*, Aldershot, UK: Gower Publishing Company Limited, 1988.

Hwang, Su-gyeong, "Occupational Choice and Employment Structure of Women," Korea Labor Institute, 2003.

Jeong, Jin-ho, "Wage Gap and its Change," *Wage and Labor Market in Korea*, Korea Labor Institute, 2005.

Jung, Jin Hwa, "Korea Wage Gap: Do the Marital Status of Workers and Female Dominance of and Occupation Matter?," *Korean Journal of Labor Economics*, 30(2) 2007, pp. 33–60.

Keum, Jae-ho, "Changes in Female Labor Market and Policy Directions," *Korean Journal Regulation*, 9(2) 2000, pp. 157–185.

Keum, Jae-ho, "Current State of Female Labor Market and Policy Issues," Korea Labor Institute, 2002.

Kim, Hyewon, "Analysis of Changes in Female Participation Rate in Korea," *Monthly Labor Review*, Korea Labor Institute, 2006.

Kim, Hyewon, "Career Break of Women and Policy Agenda," 2010 Equal Employment Policy Seminar, unpublished paper, 2010a.

Kim, Hyewon, "Work–Family Balance Policy in Low Fertility and High Ageing Era," *Monthly Labor Review*, 64, Korea Labor Institute, 2010b.

National Statistics Office, "Report of Special Economically Active Population Survey in August, 2009," 2009.

Oaxaca, Ronald, "Male–Female Wage Differentials in Urban Labor Markets," *International Economic Review*, 14(3) 1973, pp. 693–709.

OECD, "Employment Outlook," OECD, 2010.

Park, Se-il, "Problems of Female Labor Market and Gender Wage Gap," *Wage Structure in Korea*, KDI, 1984.

Singlemann, Joachim, *From Agriculture to Services: The Transformation of Industrial Employment*, Beverly Hills: Sage Publications, 1978.

Uh, Soo-bong, "Female Labor Market in Korea," Korea Labor Institute, 1991.

Yoo, Gyeong-Jun, "Gender Wage Gap and Discrimination," KDI Policy Review, KDI, 2001.

5 Income polarization and rising social unrest*

*Ki Seong Park and Donggyun Shin***

I Background

There is great concern about how income distribution has evolved in Korea. Special attention has been given to bipolarization of income distribution. Bipolarization, a shorthand expression for the phenomenon of the disappearing middle class and formation of two segregated income classes, has emerged in some developed countries, the United States and the United Kingdom in particular. The fear is that, when a country is divided into two societies, every democratic decision is very costly, and more importantly, conflicts are likely between the two groups. This is the point emphasized by Esteban and Ray (1999) among others.

There are conceptual differences between polarization and inequality (Wolfson 1994; Esteban and Ray 1994). While inequality represents dispersion around the global mean, polarization emphasizes clustering around local means. While rising inequality between groups increases both the overall inequality and the polarization measure, rising within-group inequality is expected to increase only the inequality measure. On the contrary, a distribution becomes more polarized when within-group dispersion becomes smaller. As such, the phenomenon of the disappearing middle class is better captured by polarization, specifically bipolarization, than by rising inequality. In addition, if one is concerned about their negative social consequences, it is not inequality per se but polarization that matters. Indeed, unlike the conventional inequality measures such as the Gini index, polarization measures are designed to reflect changes in income distribution that are likely to indicate social tensions or unrest.

The question of why a society is bipolarized in terms of the income distribution is not easily answered. One possible explanation may be jobless growth, which is commonly observed in many advanced economies. As technological changes work favorably to only a fraction of a society, presumably the top portion of the entire distribution of workers, income distribution becomes clustered around two poles, leaving the middle class less weight. In Korea, the employment to real GDP ratio has decreased from 98.5 in 1981 to 28.8 in 2008. The reduction of the employment–real GDP ratio has been most pronounced in the manufacturing sector, where the figure went down dramatically from 131 in 1981 to 16.4 in 2008 (*KLI Labor Statistics*).

In fact, accumulated evidence suggests that Korea is not completely free from the possibility of developing a centrifuging society, which is characterized by the disappearance of the middle class and formation of two societies. In addition to the jobless growth hypothesis, industrial shifts from the manufacturing to the non-manufacturing sector are expected to raise the level of bipolarization, as income dispersion is typically greater in the non-manufacturing than in the manufacturing sector. Industries are often dichotomized into the growing sector and the declining sector, e.g., the fast-growing information technology (IT) sector and the declining non-IT sector.

It is commonly believed that the 1997 exchange rate crisis played a significant role in making the earnings distribution more bipolarized. In an effort to overcome the recent financial crisis, the Korean economy introduced various measures to enhance labor market flexibility, such as dismissal for managerial reasons, a flexible work hour system, and the dispatched worker system. Extending labor market flexibility, however, which aims at firms enhancing competitiveness, came at the cost of increased job instability. According to Keum and Cho (2000), the average job tenure among wage and salary workers decreased from 6.62 years in 1996 to 6.19 years in 1998. The reduction of the average tenure was mainly attributed to the sharp decrease in the average tenure among non-standard workers. For example, the average tenure among non-standard workers was 4.53 years in 1996, compared to 3.06 years in 1998. On the contrary, the figure among standard workers went up slightly from 6.48 years in 1996 to 6.63 years in 1998 (ibid.). Evidence shows that both the reduced tenure among non-standard workers and the increased share of them among total workers are responsible for the overall reduction in the average tenure level. Indeed, strengthened employer–employee relationships in the standard sector, accompanied by the growing portion of the flexible marginal sector, characterizes the process of making the labor market flexible in Korea as well as many developed countries.[1] This process hypothesizes the formation of segmented labor markets as a consequence of achieving labor market flexibility.

While these arguments may explain rising inequality and/or bipolarization in the distribution of labor income, it truly neglects the role of non-labor income in the evolution of the distribution of total income. This point will be addressed in a subsequent section, where the distribution of labor earnings is found to exhibit a weak tendency of bipolarization relative to the distribution of total income. More importantly, income may not be an accurate measure of the standard of living. It has often been argued that, due to rising asset inequality, the standard of living has become unequal to the historically unprecedented level since 2002.

The very fact that a society splits into two mutually exclusive groups implies that every democratic decision is highly costly, and conflicts between the two groups are likely to arise, which works as an impediment to further economic development. As will be discussed in Section V, bipolarization of income distribution also reduces the expected lifetime income of individuals in the low-income class, which in turn reduces both the marginal cost of crime and the incentive to supply labor in the legal labor market. As a result, crime rates are expected to be higher and labor supply to be lower in a more bipolarized society, other things being constant. With all these social and economic consequences considered, it is extremely important to understand the phase and characteristics of the evolution of the distribution of income.[2]

This chapter investigates how income distribution has evolved in Korea since the 1997 exchange rate crisis, and discusses causes and consequences of bipolarization of income distribution. In Section II, we highlight the conceptual differences between polarization and inequality. We also briefly discuss measurement issues related with income bipolarization. Section III investigates how income distribution has changed since the 1997 exchange rate crisis. It concludes that the distribution of total family income has become much more bipolarized than unequal since the crisis. To put it differently, the nature of the problem associated with income distribution is characterized by bipolarization rather than rising inequality.

Section IV discusses the characteristics of the bipolarization process. Of particular interest is the analysis of what happened to the middle class, to confirm whether there was a tendency for it to shrink, as was claimed by the United Kingdom and the United States among others. The size of the middle class is found to be negatively correlated with the level of bipolarization, mobility from the low to the upper income class decreases as income distribution is bipolarized, and non-labor income, especially income from real estates, plays a major role in the dramatic bipolarization of income distribution in Korea.

Section V is devoted to the economic and social consequences of income bipolarization. While existing studies focus on collective actions between polar groups as a result of polarization, following Lee and Shin (2007) and Lee and Shin (2011), we study how individual behaviors are affected by bipolarization of income distribution. We find that the amount of labor supplied to the legal paid market is lower when income distribution becomes more bipolarized, other things being constant. This result is interpreted as the consequence of an increased marginal opportunity cost of labor supply (or reduced marginal cost of crime), as the expected lifetime income of individuals in the lower-income class is reduced by the lowered upward income mobility. More importantly, it is found that the bipolarization measure is a better predictor of labor supply (or crime) than the conventional inequality measure. Extensions of Becker (1968) would suggest that, as income distribution becomes more bipolarized, the expected lifetime income of individuals in the lower income class is reduced, which works in the direction of lowering the marginal cost of crime. Evidence from the United States and Korea generally concludes that, with all the other variables controlled for including the degree of income inequality, crime rates become higher as income distribution becomes more bipolarized. Section VI concludes.

II Conceptual and measurement issues

A Inequality and polarization

While the concept of polarization has been widely used in political science and sociology, it is relatively new in economics. This concept is often erroneously equated with the concept of rising inequality. However, as noted repeatedly by Foster and Wolfson (1994), Wolfson (1994, 1997), Esteban and Ray (1994), and Duclos *et al.* (2004), the two terms have fundamentally different concepts. In fact, the notion of polarization has been developed as a result of some dissatisfaction in the use of conventional inequality measurements to deal with the level of social unrest. The axioms of inequality measurement fail to adequately distinguish between convergence to the global mean and clustering around local means (Esteban and Ray 1994, p. 821), and the concept of polarization can run counter to the Pigou–Dalton axiom underlying the conventional inequality measures.

To illustrate, suppose there are six income levels, (1, 2, 3, 4, 5, 6), with equal population shares. Consider now income redistribution between 1 and 3 and between 4 and 6, which leads to only two income levels, 2 and 5 with 50 percent of population shares. That is, the distribution after the transfers becomes (2, 2, 2, 5, 5, 5). Clearly overall inequality has decreased by this mean- as well as median-preserving transfers. However, it can be seen that the society is now more "clustered," and the middle class has disappeared. In this sense, the society is more bipolarized, and the tensions between the below-average class and the above-average class have intensified. As in this example, while the Pigou–Dalton Principle of Transfers can be applied to between groups, it no longer applies to within groups. And, it is possible that a given distribution displaying little inequality is concentrated around a few mutually separating poles in the income space. In sum, while the two concepts are closely related, polarization places more emphasis on clustering or formation of sub-groups, and the conventional concept of inequality fails to explain a certain type of distribution change, such as the declining middle class.

Why should we pay particular attention to polarization? Justifying the measurement of polarization, Esteban and Ray (1994, p. 820) stress that "the phenomenon of polarization is closely linked to possibility of articulated rebellion and revolt and to generation of social tension and unrest in general." In a follow-up study, Esteban and Ray (1999) try to identify the type of distributions under which social conflict is most likely. A question arises then of the relative importance of polarization over rising inequality in predicting social unrest. This is so because economists as well as sociologists have long believed that inequality causes disadvantaged groups engage in criminal activities: when wealth is inequitably distributed, those at the bottom of the distribution feel they have little to lose by engaging in unlawful behaviors. Lee and Shin (2007) and Lee and Shin (2011), however, find that crime is more likely to occur when the income distribution becomes more polarized than unequal. They go on to explain that, individuals at the bottom of the distribution have greater incentive to commit crimes when, for a given degree of income inequality, income distribution is more bipolarized so that upward income mobility is less likely. To put it differently, from the viewpoint of individuals in the low class, it is not inequality per se but the chance of upward mobility that determines their expected lifetime incomes. In Section V this point will be discussed in more detail.

B Measurement issues

Esteban and Ray (1994) postulate that an individual in a society is subject to two forces: he feels identification with those he considers to be members of his "own group," and alienation from those he considers to be members of "other groups." Effective antagonism an individual has in a society increases with alienation, which is fueled by some sense of identification as well. Polarization is defined as the sum of all effective antagonism in a society. A practical question is how to define the identification and the alienation function in an income space and how to construct the overall measure of bipolarization based on these functions. We first introduce the simple ER (Esteban and Ray) index (Esteban and Ray 1994) and then the extended ER index by Esteban, Gradin and Ray (EGR) (Esteban *et al.* 1999), which is followed by a discussion of some recent development made by Lee and Shin (2007, 2011).[3]

Let us assume that the entire distribution is divided into two groups: the rich and the poor. Let y be the cut-off level of income that divides the entire distribution between the two groups. Let π be the population share of the lower-income group. That is,

$$\pi = \int_a^y f(x)dx$$

where $f(x)$ is the density function of the income distribution with the support of the distribution being contained in some bounded interval (a, b). Then, the simple ER bipolarization index is defined as follows.[4]

$$ER(\alpha) = \left\{ \left| \mu_H - \mu_L \right| \cdot \pi^\alpha + \left| \mu_H - \mu_L \right| \cdot (1-\pi)^\alpha \right\} \cdot \pi \cdot (1-\pi) \qquad (1)$$

where α is called a sensitivity parameter and falls – in order to be consistent with a set of axioms – in the interval (0, 1.6). The higher the value of α is, the greater is the difference between the bipolarization index and the Gini index computed based on group means. In fact, the simple ER index is nothing but the group-mean-based Gini index when α equals zero. μ_H and μ_L are the conditional mean of the high and the low-income group, respectively. Equation (1) has the form of the population mean of the interaction of two functions. π^α and $(1-\pi)^\alpha$ are identification functions of the low- and the high-income groups, respectively, while the alienation function is represented by $\left| \mu_H - \mu_L \right|$.

In Equation (1), the ER index increases in $\left| \mu_H - \mu_L \right|$. The more alienated the two groups, the more bipolarized the distribution. However, the ER measure is not monotonic in π. In fact, it can be shown that the right-hand side of Equation (1) is maximized when $\pi = 0.5$, implying that conflict between the two groups is the most likely when the two groups have equal shares of the entire population as 0.5.

Because $\mu_L = L(\pi)/\pi$ and $\mu_H = \{1 - L(\pi)\}/(1 - \pi)$, Equation (1) becomes

$$ER = \{\pi^\alpha + (1-\pi)^\alpha\}\{\pi - L(\pi)\} \tag{2}$$

where $L(\pi)$ denotes the ordinate of the Lorenz curve of the income density function at the point π.

Equation (1) or (2) may represent the total level of antagonism, when all individuals in the low- and high-income groups have the same income level as μ_H and μ_L, respectively. This two-spike representation of the entire distribution is truly subject to some degree of measurement error. Definitely, the ER index overstates the true degree of bipolarization. To minimize the error, Esteban et al. choose the cut-off income level that minimizes the area between the original Lorenz curve and the piece-wise linear Lorenz curve. They show that the cut-off level is the population mean in the case of bipolarization. Put together, the extended EGR bipolarization measure has the following form.

$$EGR(\alpha, \beta) = \{\pi_\mu^\alpha + (1 - \pi_\mu)^\alpha\}\{\pi_\mu - L(\pi_\mu)\} - \beta(G - G_p) \tag{3}$$

where $\pi_\mu = \int_a^\mu f(x)dx$, μ is the population mean, G is the Gini index for the original income distribution, G_p is the group-mean-based Gini index, and β represents the weight we put on the measurement error, $(G - G_p)$, in downscaling the simple ER measure computed from the two-spike representation of the population distribution.[5] Many existing studies compute the level of bipolarization using Equation (3).

The EGR measure, however, implicitly assumes symmetry of the alienation function: focusing on their bipolarization measure, the rich are assumed to feel as much alienated against the poor as the poor feel against the rich. Unlike Esteban et al., Lee and Shin (2007, 2011) allow for the possibility that the poor feel greater antagonism against the rich than the rich do against the poor. This is important for the purpose of measuring the degree of social unrest more effectively, and thereby using it to explain negative social consequences such as the crime or suicide rate. Lee and Shin (2007) suggest the following alternative measure of bipolarization.

$$B(\alpha, \beta, \theta) = \frac{\mu_H - \mu_L}{\mu}\pi_\mu(1 - \pi_\mu)\left\{(1-\theta)(\pi_\mu)^\alpha + \theta(1 - \pi_\mu)^\alpha\right\} - \beta(G - G_p), \tag{4}$$

where the degree of the asymmetry is determined by the value of θ. Specifically, since $0 \leq \theta \leq 0.5$, the low-income group feels more alienation to the high income group than the high income group feels to the lower. The asymmetry gets severer as θ goes to zero. As an extreme case, if $\theta=0$ then the rich do not feel any alienation to the poor; if $\theta=0.5$ then the degree of alienation is symmetric to both groups, which is the case of the EGR index.

Lee and Shin (2011) finally propose a further developed bipolarization measure, which has the following simple form.

$$B(\alpha,\theta) = \frac{\mu_H - \mu_L}{\mu} \pi_\mu (1-\pi_\mu) \left\{ (1-\theta)\left(\frac{\pi_\mu}{G_L/G}\right)^\alpha + \theta\left(\frac{1-\pi_\mu}{G_H/G}\right)^\alpha \right\}, \qquad (5)$$

where G_L and G_H represent the Gini indices of the low and the high income class, respectively. In this specification, the identification function is represented by the term $\left(\pi_k \big/ G_k/G\right)^\alpha$, $k=L, H$, which is a ratio of two terms. A person in group k feels more identified when the group's population share (numerator) is greater. Let us call this term a "scale effect." At the same time, the person feels more identified when, for a given population share, individuals' income levels in the group he/she belongs to are more clustered around the local mean so that the denominator becomes smaller. This term is called a "clustering effect." The denominator measures the *relative* dispersion of the within-group income distribution, which can be more meaningful than the absolute dispersion measure, G_k, since changes in G_k also alter the overall income inequality G. Two factors make $B(\alpha, \theta)$ superior to $B(\alpha, \beta, \theta)$. First, unlike $B(\alpha, \beta, \theta)$, $B(\alpha, \theta)$ does not depend on β. That is, as pointed by Lee and Shin (2011), while statistical significance of estimated $B(\alpha, \beta, \theta)$ depends on β, inference based on $B(\alpha, \theta)$ is robust with respect to β. Second, while $B(\alpha, \beta, \theta)$ considers the difference between the overall Gini index and the group-mean-based Gini index as the clustering effect for both the low- and the high-income groups, $B(\alpha, \theta)$ adopts group-specific clustering effects.[6]

Most of the discussion in Section III and Section IV is based on the revised index in Equation (4), $B(\alpha, \beta, \theta)$, mainly because of its comparability in the form and magnitude of the index with the original EGR index that is commonly used in existing studies. In addition, when we make international comparisons in the speed of bipolarization, we use the original EGR index for Korea just as for the other countries.

III Evolution of income distribution: rising inequality or bipolarization

While many studies have investigated inequality of income distribution in Korea,[7] only a few have been dealing with the bipolarization issue. They are Choi (2002), Shin and Cheon (2005), Shin and Shin (2007), and Shin (2007). While these studies generally lead to the same conclusion regarding the trend in bipolarization of income distribution, they differ in many details, including the following. While Choi analyzes repeated cross-sectional data from the

Household Income and Expenditure Survey (HIES) for the 1982–2001 period using both the simple ER index and the Wolfson index, Shin and Cheon's (2005) and Shin and Shin's (2007) analyses are based on the EGR index and longitudinal data from the *Korean Labor and Income Panel Surveys* (KLIPS) for the 1997–2003 period. Shin (2007) reanalyzes the KLIPS data for the 1997–2004 period, using the reformulated EGR index in Equation (4). Unlike previous studies, he investigates additionally the causes and characteristics of bipolarization.

For the purpose of explaining how income distribution has evolved since the 1997 exchange rate crisis, this section and the next extend Shin's (2007) and some of Shin and Shin's (2007) analyses by including more recent waves of the KLIPS surveys. We heavily depend on Shin (2007) because of his usage of the revised index and analysis on causes of bipolarization. We borrow from Shin and Shin's (2007) discussions regarding the relationship between bipolarization and income mobility and comparisons across countries in the speed of rising inequality and bipolarization. The KLIPS data adopted by these studies are believed to be more reliable for the current purpose than other data sets from repeated cross-sections such as the HIES for the following reasons. First, the KLIPS has been collecting information on total disposable household income which most existing studies in other countries have been based on. This is important especially when we want to compare the results across different countries. Second, the KLIPS represents the entire population better than the HIES as the latter limits the sample to the households in the urban area, whose heads have labor income, and with at least two family members. Third, for the purpose of studying the connection between bipolarization and income mobility, we need longitudinal information on individual household incomes. In 1998, the KLIPS selected a random sample of approximately 5,000 households and has tracked them annually until 2008. With the 2009 survey skipped due to the budget problem, 11 waves of surveys from 1998 through 2008 are available.

The total income in the KLIPS is defined as the sum of labor earnings and non-labor income, with the latter being composed of financial income, real estate income, income from social insurance, transfer income and other sources of income. Because each year's survey collects information on household income by income components for the preceding calendar year, the sample period covers from 1997 through 2007 in terms of the income year. It is worth noting that the Korean government took the International Monetary Fund's bailout package late 1997. Therefore, our sample period enables us to investigate how the income distribution has evolved after the exchange rate crisis from its pre-crisis status.

To check the characteristics and quality of the income data in the KLIPS, Shin and Shin (2007) compute the Gini index from the KLIPS sample and compare it with the official figure reported by the National Statistical Office (NSO). For the 1997–2003 period, the average of Gini indices is 0.419, in comparison with 0.310 of the average Gini index reported by the NSO for the same period. It should be noted at this point that, unlike the KLIPS sample, the HIES sample the NSO uses to compute the Gini index focuses on labor earnings of household heads who are not self-employed. When only labor earnings are used from the KLIPS sample to compute the Gini indices, the average figure is reduced to 0.358. When self-employed workers are excluded additionally from the sample, the average Gini index is further reduced to 0.312, which is virtually identical to the figure presented by the NSO. To put it another way, the Gini indices provided by the NSO tend to understate the true income inequality by excluding non-labor income and the self-employed from its sample.

Figure 5.1 displays bipolarization indices exhibited by the distribution of disposable household income for the 1997–2007 period.[8] For statistical inferences for changes in the bipolarization index, the 95 percent confidence interval is presented for each year's bipolarization index. Initially, α is set to 1.3 and, to put a greater weight to the low-income class, θ is assumed to be 0.25. Changing these parameter values, however, makes little difference in the final result. It is obvious from Figure 5.1 that the income distribution has been bipolarized for the entire sample period. Specifically, the bipolarization index went up by 120 percent during the sample period: it increased from 0.0709 just before the crisis, 1997, to 0.156 in 2007. The estimated change (0.085) in the index is statistically significant.

Most of the increase in the bipolarization index was made right after the crisis, 1997–1998 and 1998–1999, which is consistent with the result by Shin and Cheon (2005). After 1999, the index generally maintained its level until 2007. This pattern is robust with respect to different values of α, changing the weight, θ, and even exclusion of extreme values of household income.

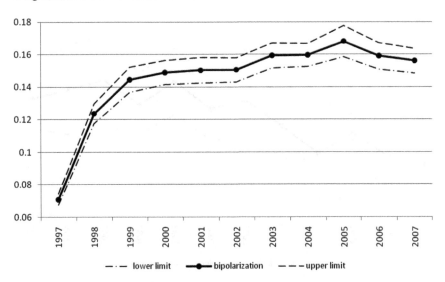

Figure 5.1 Trend in bipolarization of the income distribution (source: *Korea Labor and Income Panel Survey* from 1997 through 2007.

Note
The OECD equivalence scale as well as the family weight is applied to compute per capita family income. The 95 percent confidence interval is constructed using standard error estimates obtained by the jackknife variance estimation method. $B(1.3, 1, 0.25)$ is used to compute bipolarization indices).

Figure 5.2 shows Gini coefficients for our sample period. First, there is no strong upward trend in income inequality. The Gini coefficient increased from 0.404 in 1997 to 0.428 in 2007, and the increase is not statistically significant. This suggests that the nature of the problem associated with the income distribution lies in bipolarization rather than in rising income inequality. This finding replicates those of Shin and Cheon (2005), and Shin and Shin (2007, 2011). It is consistent with what Choi (2002) found based on the *Household Expenditure Survey* data for the 1982–2001 period. Second, the movement of the Gini coefficient does not necessarily coincide with the movement of the bipolarization index. For the 1998–1999 period, the income distribution was more polarized when the inequality measure was decreased. The two measures also moved in opposite directions for the 2001–2002 and 2003–2004 periods. In sum, the two types of measures are different indicators of what is happening to the underlying income distribution, and, from 1997 2007 period, the distribution of household income in Korea has been much more bipolarized rather than unequal.

In Figure 5.3,[9] we attempt to compare trends in bipolarization of household income among several OECD countries including Korea. The sample period covers from the early 1970s to the mid-1990s for most countries. Only Korea has a relatively short sample period, covering the 1997–2004 period. All the estimates in Figure 5.3 are based on the original EGR index in Equation (3) and correspond to the case of $\alpha = 1.3$. To highlight international differences in the speed of bipolarization, for each country, Figure 5.3 displays the level of bipolarization

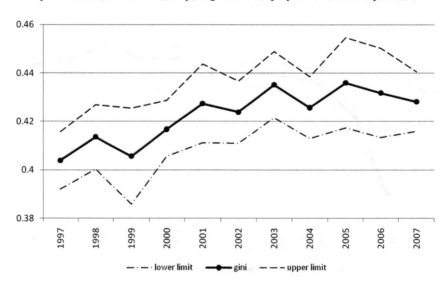

Figure 5.2 Trends in income inequality (source: *Korea Labor and Income Panel Survey* from 1997 through 2007.

Note
The OECD equivalence scale as well as the family weight is applied to compute per capita family income. The 95 percent confidence interval is constructed using standard error estimates obtained by the jackknife variance estimation method.

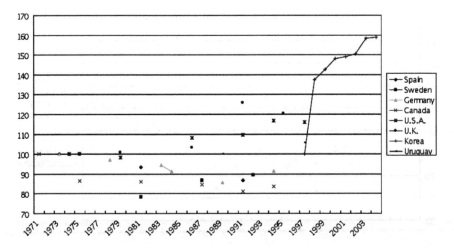

Figure 5.3 Trends in income bipolarization among selected countries (source: Spain: Gradin 2002; Uruguay: Gradin and Rossi 2006; Korea: Shin 2007; Sweden, Germany, Canada, the United States, and the United Kingdom: Esteban *et al.* 1999).

Note
For all countries, $\alpha = 1.3$. For each country, the initial year's index value is set at 100, and those of following years are expressed as percentages of the initial value.

of the first year set at 100, with following years' index values expressed as percentages of the initial one. For example, bipolarization in the United States increased by 16 percent in 1997 relative to 1974. In comparison, Korea recorded a 59 percent increase in the bipolarization measure for the seven years from 1997 to 2004. In fact, among all country-year cases except for Korea, the most dramatic episode of increase in bipolarization comes from the United Kingdom for the 1986–1991 period, where the index increased by 22 percent for five years. Indeed, Korea recorded the most dramatic episode of increase in bipolarization of the income distribution among all the countries included in the sample. Among the countries in Figure 5.3, the United States and the United Kingdom have also increased the level of bipolarization over time. In Sweden, bipolarization experienced a significant decrease in 1975–1981, and increased its level thereafter. The other countries have generally decreased the level of polarization over time.

Figure 5.4 makes cross-country comparisons in the trend of income inequality expressed by the Gini coefficient. As in Figure 5.3, for each country, the Gini coefficient of the first year is set to be 100 and subsequent years' indices are expressed as a percentage of the initial one. Two things are notable at this point. First, unlike the case of bipolarization, Korea does not show the greatest increase in income inequality. For the seven years from 1997 to 2004, the Gini coefficient increased by 5.6 percent. In comparison, the United Kingdom marked a

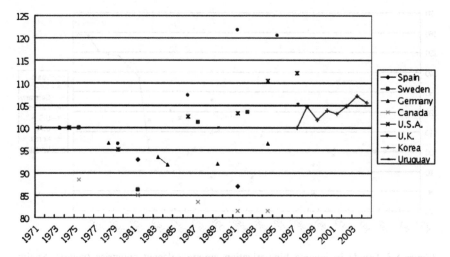

Figure 5.4 Trends in income inequality among selected countries (source: Spain: Gradin 2002; Uruguay: Gradin and Rossi 2006; Korea: Shin 2007; Sweden, Germany, Canada, the United States, and the United Kingdom: Esteban *et al.* 1999).

Note
Indices with initial year=100.

14 percent increase for the five years from 1986 to 1991, the United States a 7 percent increase for the three years from 1991 to 1994, and Sweden showed a 17 percent increase for the six years from 1981 to 1987. This observation reconfirms our previous conclusion that the problem associated with income distribution in Korea lies in polarization rather than in rising inequality. Second, polarization and income inequality are two different indicators of the underlying income distribution. As just mentioned, Korea experienced the most dramatic increase in bipolarization among all countries while showing a moderate increase in income inequality. Since 1981, Sweden observed a mild increase in bipolarization, in comparison with a sharp increase in income inequality for the same period. Canada has a mild but steady decrease in bipolarization except for the last period, but experienced a rapid and steady decrease in income inequality.

IV Characteristics of bipolarization of the income distribution

A Labor earnings vs. non-labor income

We investigate whether the dramatic increase in bipolarization is mainly attributed to bipolarization of labor earnings or that of non-labor income. Given that bipolarization of the total income was mainly driven by bipolarization of earnings, appropriate labor market policies would be desirable. Otherwise, measures to mitigate bipolarization should be sought outside of labor market policies.

To that effect, we re-compute the bipolarization measure using only labor earnings from the same KLIPS data.

In Figure 5.5, the dashed line represents bipolarization indices exhibited by the distribution of household labor earnings, implying that there is no clear upward trend in bipolarization of labor earnings for the 1997–2007 period. The index went up by only 7.68 percent in 2007 relative to 1997, which is far smaller than the 120 percent obtained from total household income (solid line). Non-labor income, therefore, played a major role in the rapid bipolarization of the total household income. Evidence from the *Occupational Wage Survey* (OWS) data is generally consistent with the findings from the KLIPS.[10] According to Shin and Shin's (2007) analysis of the OWS data, in 2003, the bipolarization measure of labor earnings increased only by 13 percent relative to the 1997 level. In sum, the dramatic increase in the level of bipolarization of total household income is mainly attributed to the non-labor income rather than labor earnings. Shin (2007) also reported that, among the entire households, the proportion of those households that had only non-labor income increased from 11 percent in 1997 to 14 percent in 2004. He also reported that, among those households that had labor income, the proportion that had non-labor income additionally increased from 21 percent in 1997 to 49 percent in 2004. Certainly, the rapid bipolarization process since the 1997 crisis is not irrelevant to these households' efforts to diversify income sources. Shin's (2007) more detailed analysis found

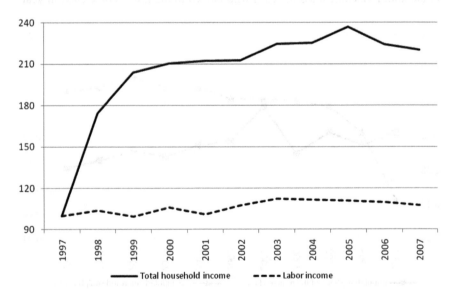

Figure 5.5 Trends in bipolarization of labor earnings (source: *Korea Labor and Income Panel Survey* from 1997 through 2004).

Note
The OECD equivalence scale as well as the family weight is applied to compute per capita family income. $B(1.3, 1, 0.25)$ is used to compute bipolarization indices. The initial year's index value is set at 100, and those of following years are expressed as percentages of the initial value.

that, among five different sources of non-labor income (financial income, income from renting real estates, transfer income from family members or government, income from social insurance, and other sources of income), real estate income together with transfer income from family members or government is mostly responsible for the dramatic increase in the bipolarization of total household income after the crisis.

B Declining the middle class and upward mobility[11]

Figure 5.6 depicts the population share of the middle class (solid line connecting squares) along with the estimated polarization index (dashed line connecting triangles). In computing the former, we follow Wolfson (1994) to define the middle class as between 75 and 150 percent of the median income. To put two series with different scales in one graph, we use different scales of axes with the left one being for the middle class share. It is noticed that the middle class has been generally shrinking, as the income distribution has been bipolarized over time. For a decade after the crisis, the population share of the middle class is reduced by two percentage points: from 40 percent in 1997 to 38 percent in 2007.

Figure 5.7 displays changes in the degree of bipolarization between two adjacent years along with various measures of mobility across different income groups. The "middle-to-low" mobility is defined as the proportion of individuals in the middle-income class in year *t* who moved to the low-income class in year

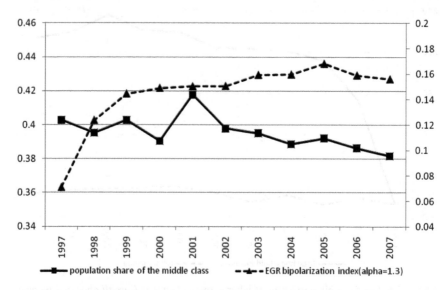

Figure 5.6 Bipolarization and the declining middle class (source: *Korea Labor and Income Panel Survey* from 1997 through 2003.

Note
The middle class is defined by those households whose annual income is between 75 and 150 percent of the median income. *EGR*(1.3, 1) is used to measure the degree of income bipolarization).

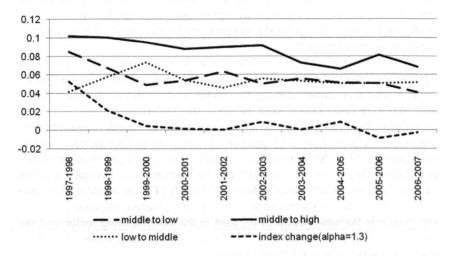

Figure 5.7 Changes in polarization and income mobility (source: *Korea Labor and Income Panel Survey* from 1997 through 2003).

$t+1$. The other two series are defined in a similar fashion. For the 1997–1998 period, when the index increased to the greatest extent, mobility from the middle to the high and from the middle to the low class were high relative to that from the low to the middle class. A similar pattern was observed for the 1998–1999 period when the income distribution was also more polarized. As the level of bipolarization decreased slightly for two consecutive years, from 2005 to 2006 and from 2006 to 2007, the mobility from the low to the middle class came to exceed that from the middle to the low class in 2007.

Cross-correlations in Table 5.1 show that an increase in the level of bipolarization is positively correlated with mobility from the middle to the high as well as to the low class. As emphasized by Levy and Richard (1992), Wolfson (1994), and Esteban and Ray (1994), among others, bipolarization refers to a case in which observations move from the middle of the distribution to both tails. It should be noted that, despite the arbitrariness of the definition of the middle class, bipolarization has been accompanied by a substantial volume of mobility from the middle- to the high-income class. At the same time, bipolarization

Table 5.1 Cross-correlations of mobility and changes in polarization

	Middle → low	*Middle → high*	*Low → high*	*Δ Polarization*
Middle → low	1			
Middle → high	0.6575	1		
Low → middle	−0.4720	0.1490	1	
Δ Polarization	0.8582	0.5895	−0.3153	1

Source: *Korea Labor and Income Panel Survey* from 1997 through 2007.

changes are negatively correlated with the mobility from the low to the middle class. As will be discussed in a subsequent section, weak mobility from the low to the middle class has a strong negative implication about the social consequences of polarization.[12]

Although not reported in a separate table, Shin and Shin (2007) show that bipolarization has more unfavorable effects on the low-education group than on the high-education group. Among household heads with college education or over who were in the middle class in year t, the proportions of those who were upgraded to the high class, maintained their status, and were downgraded to the low class in year $t+1$ are 27.5 percent, 65.5 percent, and 6.9 percent, respectively, for the 1997–2003 period. Comparable figures for high school graduates or under are 20 percent, 65.3 percent, and 14.7 percent. Bipolarization also has more unfavorable effects on older household heads (45 year or older) than relatively younger ones (44 years or younger). Finally, income dispersion is typically greater in the non-manufacturing than in the manufacturing sector, and the rising level of bipolarization is not irrelevant of the great exodus of workers from manufacturing to non-manufacturing.

C Bipolarization and business cycles

Another concern associated with bipolarization of income distribution is whether it can be explained by certain economic variables. If changes of polarization are closely related with general business cycle conditions, expansionary fiscal policy can be sought to mitigate the level of polarization. However, when the causes of polarization are irrelevant of business cycles but rather structural, well-targeted policy measures might be desirable.

To address this issue at the descriptive level, Figure 5.8 contrasts estimated bipolarization indices with unemployment rates and growth rates of real gross domestic product. For the 1997–1998 period, when the income distribution was drastically bipolarized, the unemployment rate went up greatly, and the economy recorded a minus growth rate, suggesting a close link between polarization and economic and/or labor market conditions. Beyond 1998, however, even when the unemployment rate has been decreasing, and went back almost to its pre-crisis level in 2007, bipolarization has been maintaining or increasing its level. This in turn implies that bipolarization of the income distribution in Korea may not be reversible, even in the face of future economic growth. Shin's (2007) formal analysis concludes that there exists a strong upward trend in the bipolarization index even after either the unemployment rate or the growth rate is controlled for.

V Economic and social consequences of bipolarization[13]

Why should we particularly worry about bipolarization? What are economic and social consequences of bipolarization? As noted by Esteban and Ray (1994) and Wolfson (1994), polarization has important implications for political cohesion

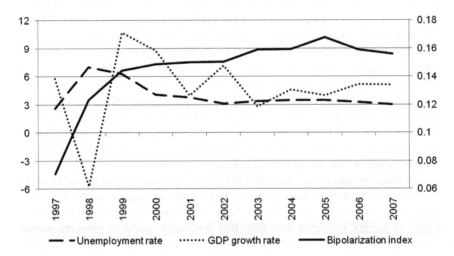

Figure 5.8 Unemployment rates, growth rates and bipolarization (data source: *Korea Labor and Income Panel Survey* data is used to compute the polarization index, measured by *B*(1.3, 1, 0.25). Data for the unemployment rate and the growth rate of real gross domestic product are obtained from the National Statistical Office).

and democratic decision making. The very fact that the distribution of individuals' attributes in a society is bipolarized implies that a social consensus on the same subject is costly. Indeed, the polarization index developed by Esteban and Ray (1994) and Esteban *et al.* (1999) is intended to reflect the level of social conflict or social unrest in general. Esteban and Ray (1999) try to identify the type of distributions under which social conflict is most likely.

Despite the repeated efforts to explain social conflicts theoretically based on the phenomenon of bipolarization, there is little empirical analysis of the bipolarization–conflict relationship, presumably because of the data problem. Not enough observations exist that reflect group conflicts, such as riots or revolts, although history has witnessed them occasionally. Conventional inequality measures may not be appropriate in explaining these collective actions. The differences manifested in great inequalities tend to deprive the lower strata of the strength and resources to organize successful collective action (Blau and Blau 1982 p. 119).

In this section, we take another path to explore the potential negative economic and social consequences of the bipolarization of income distribution. Unlike existing studies that focus on between-group conflicts as a political or social consequence of polarization, we attempt to explain how bipolarization affects "individual crime." In fact, much effort has been made by economists and sociologists to find the relationship between crime and income inequality, as well summarized by Kelly (2000), Fajnzylber *et al.* (2002), and Demombynes and Ozler (2005) among others. Despite the common prediction of positive association between inequality and crime, economic and sociological theories vary depending on which aspect of social phenomena is operative in their theories. Economic models of crime suggest that the more unequal an income distribution is, the greater the gap between benefits and costs of crime, the higher will be the (property) crime rate. In this analysis crime results from differential returns from legal and illegal activities.[14] By contrast, the sociological theory of relative deprivation emphasizes social tensions generated by the poorer who feel disadvantaged and unfair when compared with the richer. As noted by Fajnzylber *et al.* (2002, p. 2), however, it is difficult to determine whether any observed positive crime–inequality relation, results from monetary incentives–disincentives of crime or from social strain or disorganization.

Although the theoretical relationship between income inequality and crime is clear, empirical studies have found mixed results in measuring the link. For example, most cross-sectional comparisons across states and cities in the United States or across countries conclude that inequality leads to property and/or violent crime (see, e.g., the survey by Demombynes and Ozler 2005).[15] Findings in these cross-sectional studies, however, may be subject to an omitted variable bias problem, as they do not control for unobserved fixed effects that are specific to the cross-sectional unit and possibly correlated with the unit's inequality. When panel data models with fixed effects are considered, on the other hand, evidence is somewhat weak and mixed. Lee (1993, cited in Freeman 1996) regresses changes in crime in metropolitan areas between 1970 and 1980 against changes in inequality and finds insignificant coefficient estimates. Doyle *et al.*'s (1999) first-differenced model also produces insignificant coefficients of the Gini index. On the contrary, on the basis of international panel data, Fajnzylber *et al.* (2002) report significantly positive coefficients of inequality for both homicide rates and robbery rates even after country-specific fixed-effects are controlled for.

The best way to measure the income inequality incentive to commit crime has been one of the central issues in this literature. One reason why studies differ is which part of the income distribution is used to measure the degree of income inequality (e.g., Bourguignon *et al.* 2003). Some researchers use the Gini coefficient (e.g., Ehrlich 1973; Blau and Blau 1982; Fajnzylber *et al.* 2002), some use the proportion of the population below a certain percentage of the median income (e.g., Bourguignon *et al.* 2003), while the other exploits the mean log deviation as a special case of generalized entropy measure (e.g., Demombynes and Ozler 2005).

Unlike these studies, Lee and Shin (2011) emphasize the bipolarization aspect of the income distribution as a determinant of individual crime behavior. They argue that, from both the economic and the psychological perspectives, it is not inequality per se but polarization that matters in the crime model. From a dynamic viewpoint, other things being equal including the probability of detection, even a low income earner at a point of time would not have high crime incentive if she/he had better prospects in the future: if one had higher expectation of upward income mobility, then his expected lifetime income would be high and so be the marginal cost of crime. Put differently, income distance itself, which is represented by the conventional inequality measures at a point in time, could be either the net gain of crime or the net gain of labor supply, depending on income mobility. On the contrary, phenomenon of the disappearing middle class and formation of two segregated income classes, which are reflected in bipolarization indices, are directly related with the concept of income mobility.

To test the aforementioned hypotheses effectively, Lee and Shin (2011) develop a generalized bipolarization index by allowing for asymmetric degrees of alienation feeling between the low- and the high-income classes, as in Equation (5). Their index considers both monetary incentive–disincentive generated by income mobility and asymmetric antagonism between different income groups as its elements of crime incentive. Based on panel data sets at the country level and the US state level, their fixed-effects Generalized Method of Moments estimates suggest that, when both the Gini and the bipolarization indices are included in the regression model, bipolarization significantly raises the crime rates, whereas the Gini index does not. It is also found that the explanatory power of the generalized bipolarization index is greater when a heavier weight is placed on the alienation feeling of the lower income class.[16]

We investigate the labor supply–bipolarization and the crime–bipolarization relationships using Korean data. As previously found in Table 5.1, the mobility from the low to the middle class is negatively correlated with changes in bipolarization. We attempt to explain variation in the property crime rate and labor supply using the bipolarization index, and to determine which one of the bipolarization and the Gini index better predicts their variations. For the purpose of highlighting differences between inequality and bipolarization indices in their effects on crime and labor supply generated by their mobility aspects, not psychological aspects, we use the index suggested by Esteban *et al.* (1999).

To ensure enough degrees of freedom, we also analyze the polarization–crime and the polarization–labor supply association by region and year. First, the NSO reports various crime-related statistics by the region-by-year cell for the 1999–2003 period. As the entire country is divided into 15 regions, excluding Jeju island, the total number of region-year observations is 75. The NSO also supplies labor force participation rates by region and year. When we explain the crime rate, we include measures of the regional unemployment rate, men's share of the region's population, average age, and region dummies as well as the bipolarization and Gini indices.[17] The same explanatory variables are used to explain the regional labor force participation rate, except that in this case the gross regional domestic product (GRDP) is used in place of the local unemployment rate.

While our previous analysis has been mainly based on the KLIPS data, the yearly sample size of the KLIPS is not great enough to provide reliable regional data. Accordingly, we adopt the *Occupational Wage Survey* (OWS) data to compute the EGR polarization and the Gini indices for 15 regions from 1999 through 2003. While the OWS focuses on labor income of those who have permanent jobs, and therefore, understates the overall importance of bipolarization and inequality, each year's sample size of approximately 500,000 individuals provides reliable data at the region-by-year level. GRDP, men's share of the region's population, and average age are used as additional control variables in the participation equation. The crime equation has the same specification except that the regional unemployment rate is used in the place of GRDP.

Table 5.2 reports the estimation results. Focusing on the participation equation, when region dummies are excluded from the equation, the elasticity of the participation rate with respect to the EGR polarization index is −0.064, statistically significant at the 1 percent significance level (column 1). When the polarization index is replaced by the Gini index, the estimated coefficient of the Gini also remains significant (column 2), although less so than that of the bipolarization index. When the two variables are included in the participation equation, the coefficient of the polarization index is precisely estimated and has the negative sign, while that of the Gini becomes insignificantly positive. These results remain when regional fixed dummies are included in the equation, though the absolute values of the estimated coefficients are substantially reduced.

Turning to estimation results of the crime equation in the lower panel in Table 5.2, the coefficients are imprecisely estimated, although, with region dummies excluded from the equation, the estimated coefficient are greater for the bipolarization index than for the Gini index. This result is somewhat disappointing considering that Lee and Shin (2011) observed stronger effects in US data.

To compare the current results with those of the United States, Table 5.3 replicates Table 5.2 based on the US data. Data used in Table 5.3 runs from 1991 through 2004 for 51 states, and the *Current Population Survey* (CPS) data are used to compute the bipolarization and the Gini indices by region and year. Even after the regional income inequality is controlled for, labor supply is greatly reduced when the distribution is more bipolarized. In fact, it is polarization, and not inequality, that has negative effects on labor supply. In addition, this tendency is stronger when regional fixed effects are not controlled for. In the case of the United States, the estimation results of the crime equation are also more supportive of the bipolarization theory. In the absence of the region dummies the bipolarization index significantly increases the property crime rate whether entered separately or with the Gini index while the coefficient of the Gini coefficient is imprecisely estimated and even has a negative sign. Inclusion of the region dummies, however, removes the significance of the EGR index and produces a negative coefficient on the Gini coefficient.

The CPS data is used to compute the bipolarization and the Gini indices for 51 states from 1991 through 2004. Gross state product (GSP), the share of the region's population who are men, white, and young (under 35) are used as additional control variables in the participation equation. The crime equation has the same specification except that the regional unemployment rate is used in the place of GSP.

A comparison of Table 5.2 and Table 5.3 reveals some similarities and differences between the two countries' estimates. First, estimates are generally less significant for Korea than for the United States, presumably because the number

Table 5.2 Bipolarization, labor supply and property crime: Korea

	Without region dummies			With region dummies		
Log(participation rate)						
log(EGR)	−0.064*** (0.018)	–	−0.078** (0.031)	−0.014* (0.008)	–	−0.026** (0.012)
log(Gini)	–	−0.089** (0.036)	0.031 (0.060)	–	−0.005 (0.018)	0.035 (0.026)
Log(per capita property crime)						
log(EGR)	0.076 (0.169)	–	0.275 (0.292)	0.128 (0.161)	–	0.056 (0.243)
log(Gini)	–	−0.037 (0.315)	−0.455 (0.544)	–	0.288 (0.333)	0.202 (0.504)

Table 5.3 Bipolarization, labor supply and property crime: United States

	Without region dummies			With region dummies		
Log(participation rate)						
log(EGR)	−0.250*** (0.020)	—	−0.309*** (0.034)	−0.020** (0.010)	—	−0.038*** (0.014)
log(Gini)	—	−0.313*** (0.039)	0.134** (0.062)	—	0.002 (0.017)	0.044* (0.023)
Log(per capita property crime)						
log(EGR)	0.360*** (0.089)	—	0.627*** (0.207)	−0.071 (0.047)	—	0.038 (0.070)
log(Gini)	—	0.496*** (0.163)	−0.541 (0.379)	—	−0.220** (0.088)	−0.272** (0.131)

of observations is smaller for Korea (75) than for the United States (714). Second, for both countries, estimates are less precise from the crime equation than from the participation equation. The bipolarization measure is strongly associated with labor participation in Korea and the US but weakly with the crime rate measure. One possible explanation for Korea is that, while the theory predicts directly the reduction of labor supply following bipolarization of the income distribution, those who choose not to supply labor in the legal paid market have alternatives other than crime behaviors such as home production or suicides. Another reason underlying the results for Korea is that individuals' reports of regions are subject to measurement error. The OWS classifies individuals' regions based on the location of the regional labor office they belong to, which is often not their actual residence. The limitation of the OWS to only part of the workforce may provide another important source of measurement error in the computed bipolarization and inequality indices. Measurement errors in the polarization and inequality indices tend to attenuate corresponding estimated coefficients for both crime and participation equations.

VI Summary and implications

One of the main purposes of this chapter is to explore how the income distribution has evolved since the recent financial crisis. Analysis based on the *Korean Labor and Income Panel Survey* for the 1997–2004 period indicates that the distribution of total household income has become much more bipolarized than unequal for the entire sample period. For example, while the Gini coefficient has increased by 6 percent in 2004 relative to its 1997 level, the bipolarization index has more than doubled for the same sample period. The strong upward trend in the bipolarization index persists even in the presence of the unemployment rate or the growth rate. The increase in polarization in Korea exceeds that in other OECD countries. We also find that the distribution of labor earnings exhibits only a weak tendency of bipolarization relative to the distribution of the total income. Finally, mobility from the low to the upper class is reduced as the distribution becomes more bipolarized and the size of the middle class shrinks.

The current chapter also investigates economic and social consequences of bipolarization of the income distribution. Extensions of Becker (1968) would suggest that, as the expected lifetime income is reduced by the decreased upward mobility, which is induced by bipolarization, both the marginal cost of crime and the incentive to supply labor in the legal labor market go down. Evidence from Korea and the United States shows that labor force participation rates are lower in more polarized regions, other things being constant. Property crime rates are higher in more polarized regions, but this relation does not hold up in the presence of regional fixed effects. Variations of regional participation rates, as well as regional property crime rates, are better explained by the bipolarization index than by the Gini index.

Overall, the findings support the hypothesis of a centrifuging society which is characterized by the disappearance of the middle class and the formation of two poles, and which is observed in the United States and the United Kingdom, among others. That the United States and the United Kingdom have the most flexible labor market system among OECD countries and that, during late 1990s, the Korean government introduced various measures to make the labor market flexible make us suspect the possible connection between labor market flexibility and income bipolarization, which may deserve some attention.

Given that non-labor income plays a major role in bipolarization of the income distribution, measures for mitigating the bipolarization should be sought primarily outside of the labor market. While more comprehensive and in-depth research is needed on the causes of bipolarization of the income distribution, evidence accumulated so far may be enough to alert that anti-polarization or resurrection of the middle class should be at the top of all policy measures before it is too late.

Notes

* This chapter extends Shin (2008) by adding more recent years of observations in the sample and by including most up-to-date research in the discussion of economic and social consequences of income polarization.
** Shin is the corresponding author.
1 See International Labour Organization (2003) for example.
2 While the issue of bipolarization is of more importance in wealth than income, the current chapter focuses on bipolarization of income distribution mainly due to the lack of reliable data on assets.
3 Although Wolfson (1994) proposes an alternative bipolarization measure, we prefer the ER-type measures to the Wolfson index mainly because, while the latter is derived purely based on the shape of income distribution and focuses on how the distribution centrifuges from the median, the ER measure is based on group behavioral functions so that overall changes in the measure are easily understood in terms of between-group and/or within-group changes. In addition, Esteban *et al.* (1999) show that the Wolfson index can be treated as a special case of their extended index.
4 An income distribution may be polarized around more than two poles, and how to choose the number of groups is still under development. The current chapter, however, focuses on the case of bipolarization for the following reasons. First, most existing research has been dealing with bipolarization of income distribution presumably because most researchers have been preoccupied with the historical event of the disappearing middle class. Second, the very reason we are interested in polarization is that we want to know the degree of social unrest, and according to Esteban *et al.* (1999), the degree of social tensions tends to be great when the society is divided into a small number of significantly sized groups, presumably two groups. Third, focusing on two poles is desirable for the purpose of communicating with another popular bipolarization measure developed by Wolfson (1994). As previously noted, the EGR measure is proven to incorporate the Wolfson measure as its special case when the number of poles is two. Finally, the current policy debates in Korea are mostly centered on bipolarization of individuals' attributes.
5 It is easy to see that $EGR\ (\alpha,\ 0)=ER(\alpha)$. That is, the degree of bipolarization is upwardly biased by the simple ER bipolarization index.
6 As noted by Lee and Shin (2011), the $EGR\ (\alpha,\ \beta)$ index could be negative or violate one of Esteban and Ray's (1994) axioms. The index could even decrease when the between-group distance increases (Lasso de la Vega and Urrutia 2006). In contrast, the generalized index of Equation (5) satisfies all axioms in Esteban and Ray (1994), as the structure of the index remains the same. To facilitate statistical inferences, they

also derive the asymptotic distribution of the generalized index, and provide an easy-to-implement jackknife variance estimation algorithm. See Lee and Shin (2011) for details of the generalized index.

7 See Park (2000) as an example.

8 In deriving size- and age-adjusted family income, Shin (2007) applies "the OECD equivalence scale," which assigns a value of 1 to the first household member, of 0.7 to each additional adult and of 0.5 to each child. Using alternative methods such as "the OECD modified scale" or "the square root scale" makes little difference in the final conclusion.

9 Figures 5.3 and 5.4 are directly imported from Shin and Shin (2007).

10 The bipolarization measure computed from the OWS sample may understate the true degree of bipolarization in the earnings distribution of representative workers, as the sampled workers of the OWS includes only permanent workers, but excludes workers from small-scale establishments. On the contrary, as long as men's and women's earnings are not perfectly correlated, the level of bipolarization revealed by the distribution of "individual" earnings in the OWS tends to be higher than that by the distribution of earnings at the "household" unit in the KLIPS, other things being constant. Consideration of these factors, however, would make little difference in the trend.

11 We borrow the materials in this subsection from Shin and Shin (2007) and extend them by including more recent years of observations. Since this issue is about statistics, not psychological aspects of bipolarization, they used the original EGR measure, *EGR* (1.3, 1.0), to compute the bipolarization index.

12 For the 1997–2003 period, Shin and Shin (2007) adopted a somewhat different definition of the middle income class, and found that the respective sample correlations of changes in the bipolarization index and mobility from the middle- to the low-income class, from the middle- to the high-income class, and from the low- to the middle-income class are 0.081, 0.071 and −0.067.

13 Much of the discussion of the current section is borrowed from Lee and Shin (2011).

14 Since Becker (1968), many economists have established successfully a robust link between property crime behaviors and incentives generated by economic conditions (Corman *et al.* 1987; Pyle and Deadman 1994; Sjoquist 1973). According to these studies, people choose the optimal level of time and effort to invest in crime behaviors in an effort to maximize the expected utility that puts appropriate weights on the revenue and the cost of crime. Empirical investigation has focused on the effects of the criminal justice system and economic activities on crime rates. These studies found generally that property crime rates are countercyclical.

15 For example, Krohn (1976) found that the Gini index predicts national homicide rates better than the unemployment rate, implying that it is relative than absolute deprivation that has the greater effect on crime. Similar findings were made by Blau and Blau (1982), Krahn *et al.* (1986), Gartner (1990), and Chiu and Madden (1998).

16 It is interesting to note that, using the generalized bipolarization index developed by Shin and Shin (2011), Chang and Shin (2010) found that suicide rates are better explained by bipolarization than rising inequality, other things being held constant.

17 Unfortunately, crime deterrent effort variables such as the police size or the arrest rate were not available.

References

Becker, Gary S., "Crime and Punishment: An Economic Approach," *Journal of Political Economy*, vol. 76, pp. 169–217, 1968.

Blau, Judith and Peter Blau, "The Cost of Inequality," *American Sociological Review*, vol. 47, pp. 114–129, 1982.

Bourguignon, Francois, Jairo Nunez and Fabio Sanchez, "What Part of Income Distribution Does Matter for Explaining Crime? The Case of Columbia," DELTA Working Paper no. 2003–04, 2003.

Chang, Jiyeun and Donggyun Shin, "Sodeuk Yanggeukhwawa Jasal [Income Bipolarization and Suicide]," *Sahoebojangyongu* [*Study of Social Security*], vol. 26, no. 2, pp. 1–21, 2010.

Chiu, W. Henry and Paul Madden, "Burglary and Income Inequality," *Journal of Public Economics*, vol. 69, pp. 123–141, 1998.

Choi, Heegab, "Woewhan Wuigiwa Sodeuk Bunbaeeui Yanggeukwha [Financial Crisis and Bipolarization of the Income Distribution]," *Gukje Gyeongje Yeongu* [*Study of International Economy*], vol. 8, no. 2, pp. 1–20, 2002.

Corman, Hope, Theodore Joyce, and Norman Lovitch, "Crime, Deterrence, and the Business Cycle in New York City: A VAR Approach," *Review of Economics and Statistics*, vol. 69, pp. 695–700, 1987.

Demombynes, Gabriel and Berk Ozler, "Crime and Local Inequality in South Africa," *Journal of Development Economics*, vol. 76, pp. 265–292, 2005.

Doyle, Joanne, Ehsan Ahmed and Robert Horn, "The Effects of Labor Markets and Income Inequality on Crime: Evidence from Panel Data," *Southern Economic Journal*, vol. 65, no. 4, pp. 717–738, 1999.

Duclos, Jean-Yves, Joan Esteban and Debraj Ray, "Polarization: Concepts, Measurement, Estimation," *Econometrica*, vol. 72, pp. 1737–1772, 2004.

Ehrlich, Isaac, "Participation in Illegitimate Activities: A Theoretical and Empirical Investigation," *Journal of Political Economy*, vol. 81, pp. 521–65, 1973.

Esteban, Joan, and Debraj Ray, "Conflict and Polarization," *Journal of Economic Theory*, vol. 87, pp. 379–415, 1999.

Esteban, Joan and Debraj Ray, "On the Measurement of Polarization," *Econometrica*, vol. 62, pp. 819–851, 1994.

Esteban, Joan, Carlos Gradin and Debraj Ray, "Extensions of a Measure of Polarization with an Application to the Income Distribution of five OECD countries," Mimeo, Instituto de Analisis Economico, 1999.

Fajnzylber, Pablo, Daniel Lederman and Norman Loayza, "Inequality and Violent Crime," *Journal of Law and Economics*, vol. 45, pp. 1–39, 2002.

Foster, James E. and Michael C. Wolfson, "Polarization and the Decline of the Middle Class: Canada and the US," mimeo, Vanderbilt University, 1992.

Freeman, Richard, "Why Do So Many Young American Men Commit Crimes and What Might We Do About It?" *Journal of Economic Perspectives*, vol. 10, pp. 25–42, 1996.

Gartner, Rosemary, "The Victims of Homicide: A Temporal and Cross-National Review," *American Sociological Review*, vol. 55, pp. 92–106, 1990.

Gradin, Carlos, "Polarization and Inequality in Spain: 1973–1991," *Journal of Income Distribution*, vol. 11, pp. 34–52, 2002.

Gradin, Carlos and Maximo Rossi, "Income Distribution and Income Sources in Uruguay," *Journal of Applied Economics*, vol. 9, pp. 49–69, 2006.

International Labour Organization, *Employment Stability in an Age of Flexibility. Evidence from Industrialized Countries*, edited by Auer, Peter and Sandrine Cazes, International Labour Organization, Geneva, 2003.

Kelly, Morgan, "Inequality and Crime," *Review of Economics and Statistics*, vol. 82, pp. 530–539, 2000.

Keum, Jae-Ho and Joonmo Cho, *Sileopgujoeui Byeonwhawa Jeongchaek Gwaje*

[*Changes in the Unemployment Structure and their Policy Implications*], Hankuk Nodong Yeonguwon [Korea Labor Institute], 2000.

Korea Development Institute, *Medium- and Long-Term Prediction of Gross Domestic Product and the Employment-GDP Ratio by Industry*, 2002.

Krahn, Harvey, Timothy F. Hartnegel and John W. Gartrell, "Income Inequality and Homicide Rates: Cross-National Data and Criminological Theories," *Criminology*, vol. 24, pp. 269–295, 1986.

Krohn, Marvin D., "Inequality, Unemployment, and Crime: A Cross-national Analysis," *Sociological Quarterly*, vol. 17, pp. 303–313, 1976

Lasso de la Vega, Casilda and Ana Marta Urrutia, "An Alternative Formulation of Esteban–Gradin–Ray Extended Measure of Polarization," *Journal of Income Distribution*, vol. 15, pp. 42–54, 2006

Lee, David, "An Empirical Investigation of the Economic Incentives for Criminal Behavior," BA thesis, Harvard University, 1993.

Lee, Yoonseok and Donggyun Shin, "Income Polarization and Crime: A Generalized Index and Evidence from Panel Data," unpublished manuscript, University of Michigan, 2011.

Lee, Yoonseok and Donggyun Shin, "What Aspect of the Income Distribution Matters in the Crime Model?" unpublished manuscript, University of Michigan, 2007.

Levy, Frank and Richard J. Murname, "US Earnings Levels and Earnings Inequality: A Review of Recent Trends and Proposed Explanation," *Journal of Economic Literature*, vol. 30, pp. 1333–1381, 1992.

Park, Seongjoon, "Geumyoongwuigi Ihu Sodeuk Bulgyundeunge Daehan Yeongu [Study on Income Inequality After the Recent Financial Crisis]," *Nodong Gyeongje Nonjip* [*Korean Journal of Labor Economics*], vol. 23, no. 2, pp. 61–80, 2000.

Pyle, David J. and Derek F. Deanman, "Crime and the Business Cycle in Post-War Britain," *British Journal of Criminology*, vol. 34, pp. 339–357, 1994.

Shin, Donggyun, "Inequality, polarization, and Social Unrest," in *Beyond Flexibility: Roadmaps for Korean Labor Policy*, edited by Freeman, Richard, Sunwoong Kim and Jae-Ho Keum, Korea Labor Institute, Korea, 2008.

Shin, Donggyun, "Woewhan Wuigi Ihu Sodeuk Bunbae Yanggeukwhaeui Chui, Wueonin, Mit Jeongchaekjeok Sisajeom [Bipolarization of the Income Distribution after the Recent Financial Crisis: Trends, Causes, and Policy Implications]," *Gyeongjehak Yeongu* [*Study of Economics*], vol. 55, no. 4, pp. 503–548, 2007.

Shin, Donggyun and Byungyu Cheon, "Sodeuk Bunpoeui Yanggeukwha Chui [Trends in the Bipolarization of the Income Distribution in Korea]" *Nodong Gyeongje Nonjip* [*Korean Journal of Labor Economics*], vol. 28, no. 3, pp. 77–109, 2005.

Shin, Donggyun and Kwanho Shin, "Sodeuk Bunpo Yanggeukwhaeui Teukseonggua Gyeongje Sahoejeok Yeonghyang [Characteristics of Income Bipolarization and Its Economic and Social Consequences]," *Hankoog Kyeonjaeeui Bunseok* [*Analysis of Korean Economy*], vol. 13, no. 1, pp. 63–111, 2007.

Sjoquist, David L., "Property Crime and Economic Behaviors: Some Empirical Results," *American Economic Review*, vol. 63, pp. 439–446, 1973.

Wolfson, Michael C., "Divergent Inequalities: Theory and Empirical Results," *Review of Income and Wealth*, vol. 43, pp. 401–421, 1997.

Wolfson, Michael C., "When Inequalities Diverge," *American Economic Review*, Papers and Proceedings, vol. 84, pp. 353–358, 1994.

6 Institutional insecurity and dissipation of economic efficiency from the labor market flexibility in the Korean labor market

Joonmo Cho

I Introduction

Labor market flexibility is intrinsically linked to institutional security. As with institutional security in non-labor institutions, institutional security in the labor field comes from the coherence and transparency of the institutional framework. Lack of coherence and transparency paves the way for opportunism on the part of employers or employees, raises transaction costs in the labor market and dissipates economic efficiency. Uncertainty about the rules governing institutions or about implementation provides essential loopholes that enable employers to exploit or evade their legal obligations. These loopholes, a poor monitoring system and ill-defined legal terms create the ground for dual labor markets.

This chapter examines two cornerstones in the Korean government's policies on labor market flexibility; the deregulation of dismissal law and the liberalization of the legal restraints for hiring irregular workers. The deregulation of dismissal law was introduced to relax limitations on employers' use of discretion in relation to employment adjustment. We demonstrate that the disorderly and ill-coordinated manner in which this change was introduced may have led to a higher transaction cost in the labor market. The other cornerstone in government policy for labor market flexibility was the liberalization of the legal restraints for hiring irregular workers. Institutional insecurity in Korean irregular employment provides loopholes that enable employers to exploit or evade their legal obligations.

The analysis of the Korean situation may be useful in helping developing countries choose flexibility policies. Any institutional insecurity may cause unintended negative effects and lessen efficiency gains expected as a result of labor market flexibility. Section II assesses the flexibility in the Korean labor market. Section III displays the dualistic recovery of Korean labor market since the financial crisis. Section IV addresses institutional insecurity associated with institutional insecurity in relation to irregular employments and examines court cases concerned with unjust dismissal.

II Flexibility and dualism in Korean labor market

OECD Employment Outlook (2006) pointed out that there is duality in the labor market: labor inflexibility in core sectors and insecurity in peripheral areas. While conglomerates score low in terms of both numerical flexibility and functional flexibility, small and medium-sized enterprises (SMEs) are struggling with deteriorated productivity and lack of workers due to employment insecurity. Social policies have been designed to help workers reinforce the duality in the labor market while social safety net policies and active labor market policies (ALMPs) are doing poorly to better-balance flexibility and security in the labor market (Cheon 2006a).

OECD (2004) compared the level of employment protection regulations among nations based on the levels of flexibility in: (a) regular worker dismissal; (b) temporary forms of employment; and (c) collective dismissals. Among the 28 OECD member nations, Korea ranked third in collective dismissals, sixteenth in regular worker flexibility and seventeenth in temporary employment flexibility, making the overall ranking for Korea twelfth, indicating a slightly above-average level of flexibility. However, as OECD's comparison of labor market flexibility does not reflect internal flexibility, wage flexibility and functional flexibility, its ratings understate the inflexibility of the Korean labor market, reflected in the seniority wage scheme, or in the strong bargaining power of labor unions in conglomerates.

In Table 6.3, the average monthly turnover of a conglomerate is 1.57, and that of an SME is 2.64. In Table 6.4, the percentage of workers in a conglomerate with a union who have held their job for four years is 60 percent, while that of workers in an SME without a union is only 35.9 percent. The percentage of workers dismissed after four years of service is 11.7 percent and 19.3 percent, respectively in the union conglomerate and in the SME – another wide gap.

Table 6.5 compares tenure between Korea and the United States. In comparison to the United States, the percentage of workers with four years' service in a well-organized Korean conglomerate is 63.0 percent, which is higher than the US figure of 55.1 percent, and especially in the case of youth workers the rate is significantly higher than that of the United States.

Figure 6.1 compares mobility in Korea with that in other OECD countries. It shows that the percentage of workers moving from an irregular job position to a regular job position within one year is around 15 percent in Korea compared to over 40 percent in countries with flexible labor markets such as Denmark and Ireland. In the Korean labor market, the chances of moving from irregular employment to regular employment is so limited that the common example of labor mobility is not moving from regular to irregular but moving back and forth between irregular job employment and irregular employment/unemployment/ economically inactive states, showing a pattern of repeated unemployment or repeated economic inactivity.

Table 6.6 shows that the percentage of low-wage workers is only 0.8 percent among regular workers in unionized conglomerates but 38.1 percent among

Table 6.1 Flexibility in the Korean labor market

	Flexibility		Security		
	Numerical flexibility	Functional flexibility	Employment protection	Social safety net	Active labor market policy
Key areas (manufacturing, conglomerates, regular employment)	Rigid	Rigid	Relatively high	Ineffective	Inefficient
Peripheral areas (service industry, SME, irregular employment)	High labor mobility and employment insecurity	None	Blind spot	Blind spot	Blind spot

Source: cited from Byung You 2006.

Table 6.2 Indicators of the strictness of employment protection regulations (2003)

	Regular employment		Temporary employment		Collective dismissals		Total EPL Version 1		Version 2	
	Score	Rank	Score	Rank	Score	Rank	Score	Rank	Score	Rank
Sweden	2.9		1.6		4.5		2.2		2.6	
Germany	2.7		1.8		3.8		2.2		2.5	
Korea	2.4	16	1.7	17	1.9	3	2.0	16	2.0	12
Japan	2.4		1.3		1.5		1.8		1.8	
Denmark	1.5		1.4		3.9		1.4		1.8	
United States	0.2		0.3		2.9		0.2		0.7	

Source: OECD, *Employment Outlook*, 2004.

Note
Version 1 includes only regular employment and temporary employment. Version 2 also includes collective dismissals.

Table 6.3 Job accession rate and job separation rate trends

	Total (10 or more)		SME		Conglomerate	
	Accession	Separation	Accession	Separation	Accession	Separation
2005	2.40	2.41	2.55	2.64	1.84	1.57
2004	2.13	2.27	2.29	2.47	1.67	1.66
2003	2.34	2.42	2.62	2.74	1.58	1.52
2002	2.46	2.44	2.80	2.77	1.43	1.45
2001	2.26	2.52	2.34	2.55	1.41	1.69
2000	2.84	2.63	2.89	2.66	2.03	1.81
1999	2.64	2.43	2.75	2.51	1.66	1.65
1998	1.78	2.68	2.06	2.88	1.09	2.16
1997	2.32	2.65	2.67	2.99	1.53	1.88
1996	2.77	2.86	3.15	3.27	1.90	1.92
1995	2.84	2.86	3.06	3.09	2.13	2.02
1994	2.90	2.85	3.31	3.27	2.04	1.96
1993	3.01	3.14	3.51	3.62	2.04	2.20

Source: Ministry of Labor, *Monthly Labor Statistics Survey*.

Note
Small and medium-sized company is between ten to 299 employees and a conglomerate is 300 or more employees.
However, from 1999 a small and medium-sized enterprise is defined as a company employing between five and 299 workers.

non-union irregular workers in SMEs. Once a worker leaves a regular job position in a conglomerate, it is highly likely that the worker will fall into poverty even if he/she finds another job.

Since the 1997 financial crisis, continuous efforts have been made to expand the social safety net such as unemployment benefits and national basic livelihood security. More resources were invested in active labor market policies. However,

Table 6.4 Percentages of tenure (2000–2004)

	2 years' tenure	4 years' tenure	Dismissal after 2 years	Dismissal after 4 years
Total	54.7	42.7	13.0	16.7
Conglomerate				
w/union	67.8	59.3	9.2	11.7
w/o union	65.1	55.4	10.3	13.4
SME				
w/union	57.2	42.6	8.9	11.7
w/o union	48.9	35.9	15.1	19.3

Source: *Employment Insurance Database*.

Table 6.5 Comparison of tenure between Korea and the United States (males)

	United States (1991–1994)	Korea (2000–2004)	Korea (unionized conglomerates) (2000–2004)
Ages 15 to 24	29.6	26.1	45.5
Ages 25 to 39	58.0	45.0	65.8
Ages 40 to 54	68.3	49.9	62.1
Age 55 and up	45.7	30.0	22.6
Total	55.1	44.3	63.0

Source: United States: Neumark *et al.* 1999; Korea: *Employment Insurance Database*.

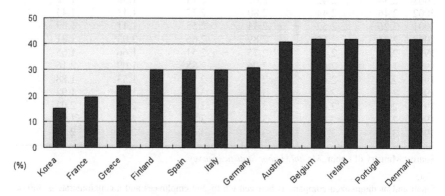

Figure 6.1 Comparison of mobility in Korea to other OECD countries (source: National Statistical Office, *Secondary Survey of the Economically Active Population*, 2003–2004; for other nations, OECD 2006a).

the measures have not been successful enough to protect workers from the risk of dropping out of the flexible and dual-structured labor market. The social programs are mostly targeted at regular workers of conglomerates. As of 2005, the percentages of workers covered by social insurances including employment insurance, health insurance, national pension and corporate benefits including

Table 6.6 Percentage of low-wage (less than 60 percent of the mean wage) workers

	Total	Conglomerate		SME	
		w/union	w/o union	w/union	w/o union
Total	17.9	2.3	7.0	6.6	22.8
Regular worker	8.6	0.8	2.4	3.2	11.8
Irregular worker	34.1	10.8	19.8	16.0	38.1
Temporary worker	28.9	9.8	19.2	14.7	33.0

Source: Korea National Statistical Office, *Secondary Survey of the Economically Active Population*, 2005.

Note
Mean wage of the total wage is 1.3 million won.

severance pay, bonus and paid leaves are about 80 percent for regular workers of conglomerates and around 20 percent for regular workers in SMEs. In terms of wage workers' participation in vocational training, 15 percent of regular workers and 2.3 percent of irregular workers received training.

III Dualistic recovery from the 1998 financial crisis

This section analyzes the changes in the time series data of the two-year job retention rate for the four periods 1995–1997, 1997–1999, 1999–2001 and 2001–2003. It aims to assess the changes in job stability before and after the financial crisis, and track the progress in job stability to check whether or not there has been a structural change in Korea's labor market.

Figure 6.2 and the third column of Table 6.8 display the two-year job retention rate distributed across tenure. They show that the two-year retention rate fell for all tenures in 1997–1999 following the outbreak of the crisis, particularly the rate for long-tenured workers over nine years. In the period 1995–1997 preceding the crisis, the job retention rate showed a monotonic increase over tenures. However, the rate drew a plateau-shaped curve with a peak at 65.9 percent of the 9–15-years' tenure in 1997–1999. This means that short-tenured workers of under two years and long-tenured workers of nine years and over experienced a deeper job stability compared to those of a tenure between two and nine years. In particular, we should pay due attention to those with a tenure of 15 years and over where the job retention rate dropped the most.

In the periods 1999–2001 and 2001–2003 after the impact of the financial crisis dissipated, the two-year job retention rate increased by a large amount over all tenures with the exception of short-tenured workers of fewer than two years. The two-year retention rate for long-tenured workers of nine years and over, in particular, recovered its pre-financial crisis level of the period 1995–1997. However, short-tenured workers are still exposed to job instability despite the economic recovery. These results indicate that there is a growing disparity between short- and long-tenured workers in terms of job stability. The significant

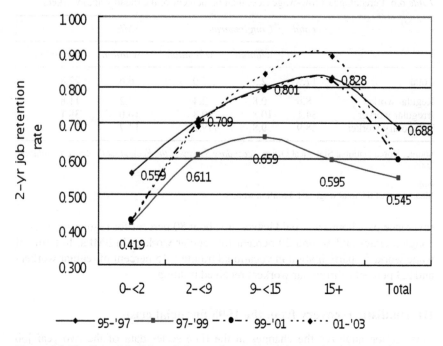

Figure 6.2 The financial crisis and changes in two-year job retention rate per tenure.

drop in the job retention rate of long-tenured workers due to the financial crisis is in line with the change in the retention rate for different age groups in Table 6.7. The retention rate increases with age and then falls after peaking at the 45–55 age group, drawing a plateau-shaped curve, and declines the most for the higher age groups which indicates that the financial crisis took a huge toll on employment for the those workers over 55.

Also, just as the two-year job retention rate of long-tenured workers recovered considerably in the periods 1999–2001 and 2001–2003 after the shock of the financial crisis subsided, the two-year job retention rate of middle-aged workers recovered a great deal in comparison to younger age groups. This is displayed in Figure 6.3 where the two-year job retention rate for workers under 40 shows no particular change after 1999 but the retention rate for workers in their forties and fifties increased significantly.

With regard to gender, the two-year job retention rate for women dropped from 58.2 percent in the period 1995–1997 to 46.2 percent in the period 1997–1999, and recovered slightly to 49.9 percent and 51.3 percent in the periods 1999–2001 and 2001–2003, respectively, but failed to recover completely to pre-financial crisis levels. The two-year job retention rate for men also showed a similar trend. If we examine the changes in the job retention rate for men and women across different tenures, the job stability of long-tenured men took the hardest hit from the financial crisis but also showed a relatively swift recovery since 1999.

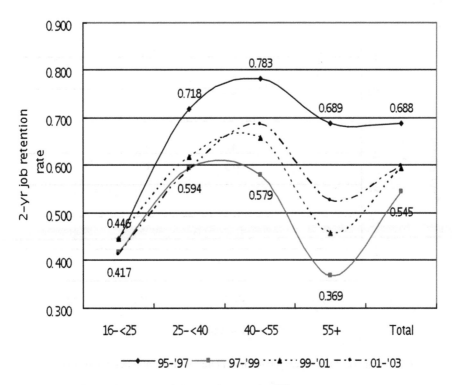

Figure 6.3 Changes in two-year job retention rate for different age groups.

Meanwhile, the two-year job retention rate for men with a tenure of under two years did not show any particular signs of improvement after 1999, causing concern that the job instability had become a fixed and continuing phenomena. While a similar trend was found for women, the recovery in the two-year job retention rate for long-tenured workers was more pronounced among men.

Examining the job retention rate for different forms of employment, note that there was no marked difference in the two-year job retention rate for regular and irregular workers in the period 1995–1997. However, in the period 1997–1999, the job retention rate for irregular workers plummeted to 41.3 percent while the rate for regular workers recorded 58.2 percent. This reconfirms the fact that the instability for irregular workers worsened after the financial crisis. The job stability of regular workers recovered relatively quickly during the recovery period after 1999, whereas the job instability of irregular workers with a tenure of less than nine years showed slow improvement. Thus the gap between the subgroups of different employment type result in job stability has widened (Figure 6.4).

In summary, while all subgroups were adversely affected by the financial crisis the job retention rate declined most for long-tenured workers of nine years or 15 years and over. Labor market stability deteriorated most for irregular

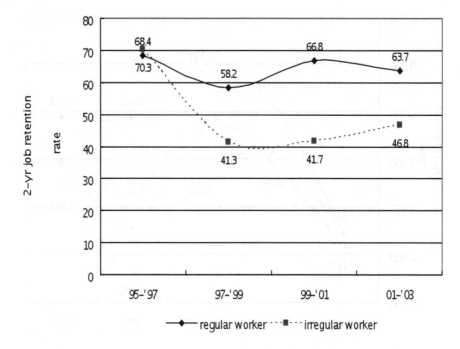

Figure 6.4   Changes in two-year job retention rate for different types of employment.

workers, the older age groups, and blue-collar workers and those in sales in services. In the recovery since 1999 long-tenured workers tended to rapidly recover
their job stability regardless of their job type, but the recovery was greater for
long-tenured blue collar workers and those employed in services and sales.
While long-tenured workers of nine years and over in almost all job types
regained their 1995–1997-level job retention rate by the period 2001–2003,
short-tenured workers were unable to make such a recovery.

IV Institutional insecurity in the Korean labor market

A *Korean irregular employment: law-dodging practices and poor social security coverage*

The data in this section come from *The Survey of the Economically Active Population of Korea* in 2005 (hereafter, the survey) produced by the Korea National
Statistical Office.[1] The definition of irregular workers follows the survey criteria.
Workers must satisfy two criteria. The first criterion is that the contractual duration is one year or less, and the second criterion is that they do not receive the
retirement grant and bonus on completion of the contract. Irregular workers are
composed of temporary workers and daily hired workers. Temporary workers
are those with contractual duration periods of less than one year, and daily hired

Table 6.7 Changes in two-year job retention rate: gender, employment type, age (%)

Tenure	1995–1997	1997–1999	1999–2001	2001–2003
Total				
0–<2	55.9	41.9	42.4	42.3
2–<9	70.9	61.1	69.7	69.0
9–<15	80.1	65.9	79.0	83.7
15+	82.8	59.5	81.9	88.8
Total	68.8	54.5	59.5	59.9
Gender				
Women	50.2	34.9	37.4	38.0
0–<2	60.6	55.9	64.6	65.0
2–<9	75.9	57.7	68.8	79.2
9–<15	79.5	62.5	80.0	89.1
15+	58.2	46.2	49.9	51.3
Total	61.0	48.7	47.6	46.6
Men	76.9	64.2	73.1	71.7
0–<2	81.3	68.6	82.2	85.2
2–<9	83.3	59.0	82.2	88.7
9–<15	74.5	59.3	65.9	65.9
15+				
Total				
Employment type regular wage worker[1]				
0–<2	56.9	45.3	51.1	45.4
2–<9	69.8	63.6	71.2	70.4
9–<15	79.0	69.7	80.7	85.7
15+	82.9	64.7	83.5	89.8
Total	68.4	58.2	66.8	63.7
Irregular wage worker[2]				
0–<2	52.0	31.3	31.7	35.1
2–<9	76.1	49.6	61.2	62.7
9–<15	85.2	51.2	70.9	67.7
15+	82.6	43.3	73.5	82.1
Total	70.3	41.3	41.7	46.8
Age group				
16–<25	44.6	41.7	44.7	41.2
25–<40	71.8	59.4	61.7	59.1
40–<55	78.3	57.9	65.8	68.7
55+	68.9	36.9	45.8	52.7
Total	68.8	54.5	59.5	59.9

Notes
1 Workers who are working in the same workplace more than one year or workers who are working in the same workplace as long as she/he wants to work.
2 Workers who are not regular workers.

workers are workers with contractual duration periods of less than three months. The criterion relating to receipt of retirement and bonus is important in evaluating law-dodging practice. Under the Korean Labor Standards Act, firms having more than five employees are legally obliged to provide the retirement grant for those employees who have maintained an employment relationship with that particular employer for at least one year.

Employment arrangement can be divided into two categories: direct employment and indirect employment. Direct employment is the traditional employment arrangement. Indirect employment is an arrangement where the labor user is not in fact the employer. In some cases a triangular relationship exists between the employer, the labor user and the employee. The indirect employment arrangement operates in the case of contract company work and that of temporary help work. Contract company workers are those who are employed by one particular company and then assigned to work under contract at a customer's work site.

Table 6.8 displays the distribution of employment arrangement in large and small firms and for the various employment contracts. In 2005, 52.7 percent of the total working population was employed in irregular employment. In firms with five or fewer employees, irregular employment stood at 88.5 percent, whereas it was only 37.0 percent in firms with more than five employees. This demonstrates that irregular employment was concentrated in small firms. In the main, irregular workers were employed under a direct employment arrangement. The percentage of irregular employees under an indirect employment arrangement was slightly higher in large firms than in small firms.

In Table 6.9, the labor contracts are classified into a form of matrix according to employment type and contract duration. Contract duration is divided into fixed term and indefinite contract. Each box matches employment type and contract duration. The lower-left figure in each box denotes the percentage for large firms and the upper-right percentage is the figure for small firms. For example, in box A, regular workers with indefinite contract duration who are the core workers in the Korean labor market represent 53.2 percent of workers employed in firms with over five employees and 10.8 percent of the workers employed in firms with five or fewer employees. Box A represents workers who are subject to human resource regulations and are entitled to retirement grants and a bonus on completion of the contract, the duration of which is not fixed (this category includes long term contracts which have an age limit).

Box B represent the kernel of problem of irregular employment in Korea. It refers to irregular workers whose contractual duration is longer than a year. This occurs as a consequence of the repetitive signing of short term contracts over that length of time.[2] It includes instances where the contract duration is decreased to a critical 364 days in order to bypass liability to pay retirement grants to workers with contracts of longer than one year's duration. In some cases, the employer falsifies the legal documents to achieve the same end. In this manner, any legal responsibilities associated with the employment of regular workers are fraudulently averted. These irregular workers in box B do not receive a retirement grant or bonus on completion of the contract. Under the Korean Labor

Table 6.8 Firm size and distribution of employment type and arrangement

Firm size	Employment type	Total		Direct employment arrangement		Indirect employment arrangement	
		Person	%	Person	%	Person	%
All firms							
Total		26,083	100.0	25,109	96.3	974	3.7
Regular		13,704	52.5	13,311	97.1	393	2.9
Temporary		8,411	32.2	7,986	94.9	425	5.1
Daily-hire		3,968	15.2	3,812	96.1	156	3.9
Firms with up to five employees	Total	5,320	100.0	5,157	96.9	163	3.1
	Regular	613	11.5	574	93.6	39	6.4
	Temporary	2,909	54.7	2,831	97.3	78	2.7
	Daily-hire	1,798	33.8	1,752	97.4	46	2.6
Firms with over five employees	Total	20,763	100.0	19,952	96.1	811	3.9
	Regular	13,091	63.0	12,737	97.3	354	2.7
	Temporary	5,502	26.5	5,155	93.7	347	6.3
	Daily-hire	2,170	10.5	2,060	94.9	110	5.1

Source: Korean National Statistics Office, *the Survey on Economically Active Population of Korea*, August 2005.

Table 6.9 Composition of employment type and contract duration in large and small firms (%)

	Regular employment	Irregular employment (temporary, daily-hired)	
		Contractual duration over one year	Contractual duration under one year
Firms with up to five employees: labor contract duration			
Contract of indefinite period	A 53.2	B 30.2	C 3.9
Fixed term contract	D 5.4	E –	F 7.3
Firms with over five employees: labor contract duration			
Contract of indefinite period	A 10.8	B 63.3	C 11.3
Fixed term contract	D 0.9	E –	F 13.7

Source: Korean National Statistics Office, *the Survey on Economically Active Population of Korea* (August, 2005).

Standards Act, firms with more than five employees have a liability to provide retirement grants and bonuses in cases where the duration of employment contract is one year or more. The percentage in box B represents the proportion of irregular workers employed under repetitive short-term contracts, which allow law-dodging. Typically, temporary and daily hired workers are hired under such conditions and thus denied legally mandated retirement grants and bonuses.

Boxes C and F represent irregular workers whose contractual durations are one year or less. Like irregular workers in box B, those in boxes C and F do not receive the retirement grant and bonus on completion of the contract. Contractual terms in box C are indefinite as a consequence of the repetitive signing of short term contracts over that length of time, which is similar to that in box B. The contractual term in box F is fixed but the termination period is yet to come. Box E is blank because the contractual duration for irregular workers with fixed term contracts is less than one year by definition.[3]

Providing other conditions remain constant, what might happen if the repetitive hiring of persons in temporary and daily hired positions was restricted to suppress social security related law-dodging practices as in box B. One of the most likely scenarios is that these practices would move to firms with five or fewer employees so employers could continue to bypass the Korean Labor Standards Act. Firms with five or fewer employees are not subject to the Korean Labor Standards Act. These firms provide a hotbed for unlawfulness and little or no protection of the rights of those in irregular employment. Another scenario is that the higher transaction costs associated with the establishment of these law-dodging contracts may destroy job opportunities.

Table 6.10 documents the social security coverage rate by employment type in large and small firms. This is affected by employment type and firm size. In the case of employment type, the coverage rate for irregular workers is markedly lower than that for regular workers. In fact, only 0.5–9.4 percent of irregular workers is covered under the social security system. The situation becomes even more pronounced for small firms. In firms with five or fewer employees, the coverage rate for regular workers decreases to 8.0–8.9 percent, implying that even regular workers face a lack of social security coverage in small firms.

1 Typical cases for law-dodging practice in Korean irregular employment

Under Korean labor law, temporary help refers to an ordinance by which an agency dispatches employees to another company where they engage in work in compliance with that company's directions and orders (the Korean Act on Protection for Temporary Help Employees came into force on February 20, 1998 and will hereafter be referred to as the temporary help law). Under these circumstances, an agency first hires workers and then dispatches them to affiliated companies for a specific period of time. Employees work under affiliates' directions or orders, and the affiliate companies pay the dispatch (service) charge to the temporary help agency rather than to the employees. A typical dispatching contract in Korea is shown in Figure 6.5. The problem is that temporary help is not used to cope with uncertainty of demand in fields requiring professional skill but to replace those in regular employment, primarily in low-income and low-skill areas.[4]

Social security related law-dodging is frequent where temporary help is employed. It occurs when affiliate employers use temporary help workers to dodge social security related laws. For example, the Korean temporary help law states no explicit social security obligation to which temporary help agencies

Table 6.10 Social security coverage for irregular employment (%)

Firm size	Employment contract	National pension	Medical insurance	Unemployment insurance
All firms	Regular	51.1	51.5	42.7
	Temporary	9.3	9.4	8.6
	Daily-hire	0.6	0.5	0.5
Firms with up to five employees	Regular	8.9	8.9	8.0
	Temporary	7.0	6.9	6.4
	Daily-hire	0.4	0.4	0.3
Firms with over five employees	Regular	61.9	62.4	51.6
	Temporary	9.9	10.1	9.1
	Daily-hire	0.6	0.5	0.5

Source: Korean National Statistics Office, *Survey on Economically Active Population of Korea*, August 2005.

Figure 6.5 Korean temporary help contract.

must conform during periods when workers are not dispatched. In many cases, the temporary help agencies referred to in this study do not pay wages during these periods and hence the placement of temporary help workers represents illegal job placement. Furthermore, the law contains no article on who should be under obligation to pay the legally mandated social security benefits such as national pension, national medical insurance and unemployment insurance etc. The current temporary help law in Korea details the obligations of affiliate employers and temporary help agencies in Articles 2 and 3. Article 2 states the obligations of temporary help agencies to provide appropriate social security benefits for their employees. Article 3 states that affiliate employers should use temporary help in an appropriate manner but does not define "appropriateness." There is no article that outlines the means of monitoring or enforcing such directions, or of imposing penalties for breach of Articles 2 and 3. The law's ambiguously wording allows affiliate employers to avoid their social security obligations to temporary help employees. This ambiguity allows temporary help agencies to avoid the obligations of substantial employers and to concentrate solely on receiving brokerage fees for the provision of labor exchange.

In some other cases, workers maintain their legal status as temporary help employees while performing duties for affiliate companies though the particular jobs they occupy are not legally approved. In such cases, and during the two-year legal limit of the dispatch, workers are more accurately described as regular employees but they do not receive any social security benefits. The most exemplary case of this practice in Korea is that of D-Industries.[5] In D-Industries, there is no substantial employment relationship between the temporary help agency and dispatched employees, and recruitment or dismissal is performed by the affiliate companies. Other cases of social security law-dodging are associated with the legal limit of a two-year dispatch period.[6] In many cases, the temporary help employees are forced to take unpaid leave at the expiration of the dispatch period or the contractual terms between the temporary help agency and the employees are established to coincide with the dispatching period, so that the temporary help agency can avoid social security liabilities.

2 Sub-contact company work

In Korea, when company A (the contract company) subcontracts labor to company B (the order company); the tasks performed by employees in company

A is subcontract work and company A is the subcontractor. There is some difference between subcontract and temporary help contract. The contract company not only bears the liability of social security but also directs their own workers while the temporary help agency does not direct or order their workers during the dispatch periods. In fact, there is no substantial employment relationship existing between the order company (company B) and workers of subcontractor (company A) because the order company does not tell the workers how to do the job and does not even monitor their labor intensity. The order company only evaluates overall quality or completeness of tasks by the subcontractor.

Figure 6.6 represents the subcontract. Here there are two forms of contract which allow law-dodging in relation to social security obligations. One occurs when the subcontractor places any person (not necessarily their employees) in the workplace of the order company. The subcontractor then receives most of the contract payment but does not pay the due amount to workers. In some extreme cases, most of the payment the subcontractor receives is for the stated purpose of covering wages but the subcontractor does not pay the due amount, then the subcontractor fraudulently exploits the workers.[7]

The second type of law-dodging contract occurs when the employment relationship between subcontractor and worker is very loose. In this case, the purchaser of the service plays a substantial role as an employer and at the same time avoids his/her legal obligations as mandated by Korean social security. Such obligations include the national pension, medical insurance and industrial injury insurance. A case which exemplifies this form of social security law-dodging is that of a particular subcontract worker in an SK-company[8] where the subcontractor was the branch company of SK, and the substantial employer was the SK-company. The subcontracted workers formed a union to demand that the company comply with their obligation in relation to the payment of social security benefits. The SK-company threatened to terminate their contracts. Another example of this form of law-dodging is seen in the case of D-Foods. This company established a camouflaged subcontracting company (S-Industrial), while D-Foods remained effectively in charge of that company's operations. This enabled D-Foods to avoid social security liabilities even though a substantial employment relationship existed between itself and the subcontracted workers.[9]

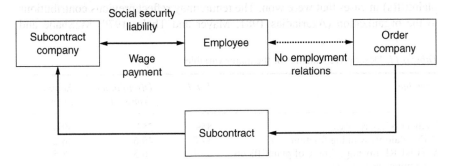

Figure 6.6 Subcontract work.

B Effect of dismissal law on the rate of unjust dismissal

1 Data: survey of court cases

The data were obtained via the content-analysis of all known court cases concerning unjust dismissals for the period of 1987–2000. Court cases were identified via online database searches using the Lex, Kingsfield, and Net-Law databases, and by reviewing all relevant decisions in the case collections of the Korean Labor Relations Commission (hereafter, the KLRC), the District Court, the Higher Court, and the Korean Supreme Court. Between March 1987 and November 2000, a total of 859 court cases addressed unjust dismissals. Two avenues were open to employees who sought protection from unjust dismissal. The first avenue involved the submission of a remedial application for unjust dismissal to the KLRC. The plaintiff or defendant could appeal to the courts to reverse the KLRC's adjudication. Among the 859 cases, 434 selected this option. The other avenue was to follow the litigation procedure through a civil lawsuit. Here, employees could proceed directly to the district court. These cases could later be appealed in a higher court. Parties in the other 425 cases selected this route. In all, 591 out of the 859 cases were appealed in higher courts. Cases at lower levels of the KLRC or in lower courts were excluded from the final data set in order to prevent any double-counting.

We use the court adjudication rate of unjust dismissal as a proxy variable for the rate of unjust dismissal. This is an imperfect measure of unjust dismissals because certain institutional factors affect the court adjudication rate of unjust dismissal, but do not influence the genuine rate of unjust dismissals. For example, institutional changes in the litigation process may influence the litigation probability of unjust dismissal. These changes include more accessible proceedings, support for claimants, or public recognition of remedies. We utilize the evidence on the KLRC dummy to ameliorate these factors. The probability of unjust dismissal is relatively low for KLRC cases because the more trivial cases are sent to the KLRC as opposed to the courts.

Table 6.11 summarizes the descriptive statistics of the proxy variables for unjust dismissals. WIN is the number of unjust-dismissal cases won as a percentage of the total of cases brought. WTENURE is the average tenure of the plaintiff(s) in cases that were won. The tenure may reflect previous contributions to the organization (Azariadias 1981; Mayer and Thaler 1979; McShane and

Table 6.11 Descriptive statistics of the major variables

Variable	Total	Disciplinary dismissal	Economic dismissal
Number of court cases	859	557	69.0
WIN (plaintiff winning fraction, %)	37.8	40.6	36.2
WTENURE (average tenure of plaintiffs on winning cases, year)	6.1	6.5	8.5

McPhillips 1987).[10] Korean courts have traditionally used tenure, age, and the number of family members as important criteria for establishing the justness of dismissal.[11]

Two factors should increase WTENURE. The first of these is that employers dismiss long-tenured employees with far-fetched interpretations of the deregulation of dismissal laws. Such cases are more likely to be adjudged as unjust dismissals. Under the seniority-based compensation scheme in the majority of Korean firms, changes in wages depend on the employee's tenure rather than productivity (Cho 2005; Cho and Keum 2004). Since the increase in productivity is less than the increase in the wage scale, employers have an incentive to dismiss these employees to reduce their costs. Second, socio-economic factors that affect court adjudication of the dismissal of long-tenured employees beyond the merits of particular cases may also increase WTENURE. For example, when the labor-market weakens for workers, diminishing their bargaining power, employers' incentive for dismissing long-tenured employees will increase, leading to a greater number of such dismissals. Preempting this incentive, the court may rule in the direction of protecting long-tenured employees during an economic downturn (Cho and Lee 2006).

Figure 6.7 shows the variation in WIN by period in the unjust-dismissal cases from 1987 to 2000. WIN showed a declining tendency between 1988 and 1990, reaching its nadir in 1990, at just 24.6 percent. In 1991, when the Supreme Court made its final adjudication in *Dongbu Chemical Corp* v. *Choi*, this downward trend was reversed and WIN increased to 38.9 percent in 1992. It subsequently stabilized at approximately 35–40 percent, where it remained until 1998. However, during the economic crisis and the subsequent IMF rescue package in 1999, this stable trend was disrupted, and the WIN soared to 59.5 percent. We seek to determine whether these changes could be attributed to judicial changes.

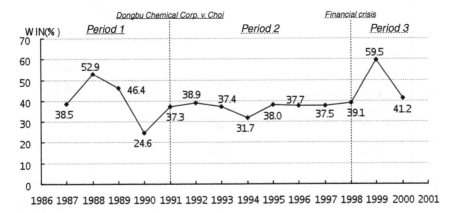

Figure 6.7 Time-trend of the percentage of winning plaintiffs for unjust dismissals, 1987–2000 (source: classified from the original resource of Cho and Lee 2006, 2007).

2 Empirical investigation by sub-period

For analytical purposes, we divided the court cases into three sub-periods. This allowed us to analyze longer-term trends in employers' unjust dismissals and any possible influence on them by changes to the law. The first period encompasses the period from 1987 to 1990, during which the Korean civil movement for democratization fostered a dramatic increase in labor disputes: 115 of the 859 cases occurred during this period. The second period encompasses the years between 1991 and 1997, during which the Supreme Court's decision on *Dongbu Chemical Corp.* v. *Choi* broadened the scope of possible just reason for economic dismissal, in spite of the Korean labor law's strictly prohibition of any economic dismissal. During this period, 662 cases of unjust dismissal were brought. Finally, the third period encompasses the years from 1998 to 2000, during which the financial crisis began to be resolved and the deregulation of the dismissal law went into effect. Specifically, it was during this time that Article 31 of the Labor Standards Act was revised in order to relax the limits on employers' discretion in terms of employment adjustment. This was implemented at the time of the onset of the economic crisis in Korea resulting from the Asian financial crisis. There were 82 cases brought during this period.[12]

Unlike disciplinary dismissals, economic dismissals are predicated purely on an economic rationale and, by definition, depend far less heavily on employee conduct. Taking this fact into consideration, we hypothesize that the increase in WIN with regard to economic dismissals is more likely to reflect an increase in the employer's rate of unjust dismissals.

In Figure 6.8, the trend in WIN for disciplinary dismissal is stable over all three periods, moving only slightly from 40.9 percent in the first period, to 40.0

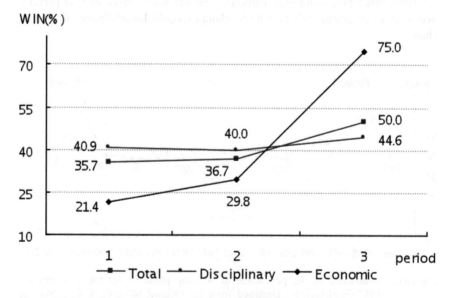

Figure 6.8 Variation in the fraction of winning plaintiffs by period.

percent in the second period, and to 44.6 percent in the third period. By way of contrast, the rising WIN for economic dismissal over the third period is substantially higher than in the case of disciplinary dismissal, and is also more prominent when compared with that for the total number of dismissal cases. It was 21.4 percent in the first period, and 29.8 percent in the second period, before rising dramatically to 75 percent in the third period, which subsumes the adoption of the new dismissal law.

C The effect of the 1998 dismissal law on contemporary court adjudications and on management practices

Court adjudications from 1998 to 2001 strictly interpreted four prerequisites. However, since 2002, when the Supreme Court's adjudication resulted in a partial relaxation of the rigidity of the statutory requisites, the requisites for dismissal justification have been continually loosened. More specifically, in 2002, the Supreme Court[13] regarded the urgent needs of management as a sufficiently objective reason for workforce downsizing, in order to address not just the crisis facing Korea at that time, but also any future ones. Since then, the court has accepted this reason as just, even if the firm did not engage in prior consultation or if consultation was effectively meaningless in the face of strong objections from the labor union against dismissal due to an insufficient consultation period (Cho 2004).

One interpretation of these phenomena would be that the court recognized the excessive rise in the rate of unjust dismissals by employers in the course of law enforcement from 1998 to 2002, when the law that had been intended to render the labor market more flexible in 1998 was technically interpreted and applied, and therefore the court relaxed the rigidity of the law to some extent to fulfill market demand for flexibility.

Furthermore, in 2006, the court undertook to explicitly relax the effect of the 1998 dismissal law. It shortened the prior consultation period, one of the prerequisites for dismissal, from the previously existing 60 days to 50 days.[14] However, this action brought about only limited changes in the rigidity of the dismissal system, and thus large establishments officially made a request in 2006 to render the dismissal system even more flexible in the pledges of the 2006 presidential election (Korea Employers Federation 2002, 2007).

In 1998, the enactment of the dismissal law caused employers to expect that dismissal would be permitted under certain conditions, rather than being banned outright. However, the effect of the law did not allow for easy or flexible dismissal. After several years of enforcement, companies concluded that the dismissal law failed to contribute to flexibility and began requesting further flexibility in the dismissal system.[15] Since 2000, employers have sought management strategies excusing them from hiring new standard workers who are difficult to fire, and replacing standard workers, if possible, by non-standard ones including short-tenured workers,[16] as well as outsourcing internal operations to minimize human resource management costs incurred on account of the rigidity of the law

V Conclusion

This chapter provides an empirical examination of two key aspects of the Korean government's policies for labor market flexibility; the deregulation of dismissal law and the liberalization of legal restraints for hiring irregular workers. Our results demonstrate that the 1998 dismissal law failed to achieve its intended effect of increased flexibility after 2000, and that the courts have gradually moved to make the law more flexible while employers have bypassed the rigidity of the law both by hiring non-standard workers and by outsourcing. The experience with the 1998 Korean dismissal law highlights the problem in sustaining a legal change that is incongruent with the needs of the market as reflected by employers. Any mismatch between institutional and legally required behavior on the one hand, and the changing opportunity structure as well as shifting behavioral dispositions of economic agents on the other, can result in institutional failure.

The empirical evidence the second aspect of the Korean government's policies for labor market flexibility, liberalization of legal restraints for hiring irregular workers, confirmed that one reason employers take on irregular workers is the enticement to avoid the social security obligations imposed on them. Of course, such illegal practices were overlooked in part because of government policies that took measures to exclude small businesses from social security related regulations and because of weak law enforcement. The experience highlights the issues for the government in expanding social security for irregular workers. Even if the social security system expands, the elimination of the informal sector may take a long time as the market norm of law-dodging in the informal sector dies hard in the short run. The risk aversion of the Korean government may make it hesitant to adopt the policies due to uncertainty regarding their effect on the growth of employment and income in the formal sector. The government may prefer to focus the enforcement in the formal sector until the enforcement capacity increases or the majority of the informal sector members seek to cooperate with the government in obeying the regulations. But this will preserve a social security system which excludes irregular workers for the foreseeable future. The analysis of the Korean situation contained in this chapter may provide useful guidelines for other developing countries that seek to choose flexible policies. Any institutional insecurity paves the way for opportunism on the part of either employers or employees, raising transaction cost and dissipating economic efficiency.

Notes

1 The survey includes questions concerning the respondent's employment type, employment duration, employment arrangement and whether the respondent is covered by the social security system. The social security related categories include items concerning whether the respondent is covered by the retirement grant, the national pension plan, medical insurance and unemployment insurance.

2 Box C where the substantial contractual duration is less than a year may also occur as a consequence of the repetitive signing of short term contracts over that length of time.

3 Temporary workers are those with contractual duration periods of less than one year and daily hired workers are workers with contractual duration periods of less than three months.

4 Entering into a complex "triangular relationship" involving the affiliate firm, the temporary help agency and the worker, the temporary help worker have little leverage to negotiate. When given an assignment, the temporary help worker lacks essential knowledge about pay scales and work requirements. Gonos (1997) reports that the average mark-up of the temporary help agency (the difference between what a temporary help agency charges an affiliate firm to provide temporary help work, and what it pays the temporary worker for that work) in the United States is 30–50 percent of wages for every hour worked.

5 See the Working Voice website, online, available at: www.workingvoice.net.

6 In the Korean temporary help work market, the dispatch period should not exceed one year, except in the event of agreement between a dispatch agency, dispatch employer and dispatched worker. In this case, the duration can be extended beyond one year; however, even then it is only allowable on one occasion. In addition, it is prescribed that the temporary help agency and the affiliate company do not treat the dispatched worker in a disadvantageous manner in providing social security benefits when compared to other employees undertaking similar tasks (Article 6, The Korean Act on Protection for Temporary Help Employees).

7 The reduced amount could represent economic value the subcontractor provides in reducing search costs, facilitating a better employment match etc. However, Cho investigated the Korean metal industry and reported that the workers of subcontractors receive 50 percent lower average wages than workers in other companies even if they perform the same jobs (Cho 2004a). In some cases, the workers of subcontractors are assigned to jobs inferior to those of the workers in the order company. The discrimination in job assignment between subcontractor workers and workers in order companies are well explained by the Korean Tripartite Commission (2004).

8 See the Working Voice website, online, available at: www.workingvoice.net.

9 An atypical example of this was a case where a company that had originally signed employees to irregular contracts tried to transfer these employees to alternative contracts which would have rendered them subcontract workers. The company's motive was to avoid its obligations to temporary workers under the Korean social security laws. These efforts were illegal since direct management was performed by the mother company even after it became the contractor.

10 McShane and McPhillips (1987) used the tenure variable in their empirical study concerning Canadian court cases. In Canada, when an employee has been dismissed unjustly, the courts decide the length of reasonable notice that should have been provided and award severance pay in lieu of that notice. McShane and McPhillips determine that the tenure variable is the strongest predictor of the court's determination.

11 See Korean Supreme Court 96NU8031 and Korean Supreme Court 92DA34858.

12 As 30 cases involving government-owned firms, 25 for hospitals, 25 for nonprofit organizations, and 40 cases for educational institutes were excluded from the 859 cases, 739 cases of profit-making firms were examined in order to characterize the trends of differently-sized firms.

13 As particulars regarding worker dismissal in the interests of the management of a company are not final or fixed, but rather flexibly determined on the basis of the satisfaction of other prerequisites in a specific case, the decision as to whether the dismissal in the specific case of a managerial reason satisfies all the prerequisites and is justifiable should be made after comprehensive evaluation of the individual condition of each prerequisite of the above (Korean Supreme Court, 09.05.2002, 2001DA29452; Korean Supreme Court, 13.11.2003, 2003DU4119, etc.).

14 The principal objective of the activity in 2006 was to truncate the consultation period under the existing law and to more flexibly manage the period, given company

conditions, the number and the percentage of people to be fired, etc. in order for the company to achieve a quick turnaround through dismissal, because a long consultation period is applied indiscriminately, regardless of any special situations or company turnaround.

15 In its "Doing Business" report, the World Bank ranks Korea 110th out of 175 countries in terms of hiring and firing (World Bank 2006). All indices in Korea, including difficulties in hiring, the rigidity of working hours, and difficulties in firing, were higher than the average indices among East Asian countries and OECD members, thus implying that Korea is relatively more rigid. The cost of firing someone is 91 times the average weekly wage, and this ratio is almost triple the average ratio of 31.3 times among average workers in OECD member countries.

16 The rise in the number of non-standard workers since 2000 is as follows: It was 26.8 percent in 2001 and 27.4 percent in 2002 and then rose significantly to 32.6 percent in 2003. Then, it maintained high rates of 37 percent in 2004, 36.6 percent in 2005, 35.5 percent in 2006, 35.9 percent in 2007, 33.8 percent in 2008 and 34.9 percent in 2009 (National Statistical Office; an annual statistical survey on the economically active population).

References

Auer, Peter and Cazes, Sandrine, "The Resilience of the Long-term Employment Relationship: Evidence from the Industrialized Countries," *International Labor Review*, 139(4) 2000, pp. 379–408.

Azariadis, C., "Self-Fulfilling Prophecies," *Journal of Economic Theory*, 25, 1981, pp. 380–396.

Bernhardt, A., Morris, M., Handcock, Mark S. and Scott, Marc A., "Trends in Job Instability and Wages for Young Adult Men," *Journal of Labor Economics*, 17(4) 1999, pp. 65–90.

Boisjoly, Johanne, Duncan, Greg J. and Smeeding, Timothy, "The Shifting Incidence of Involuntary Job Losses from 1968 to 1992," *Industrial Relations*, 37(2) 1998, pp. 207–231.

Cheon, Byung You, "A Study of Regional Employment Growth Differentials in Korea," *Regional Industry-mix with Regional Industrial Policies*, 68, 2006a, pp. 205–235.

Cheon, Byung You, "Labor Market Flexicurity in Korea and Labor Market Policy Tasks," Proceedings for International Symposium on the National Employment Strategy and its Vision for Job Creation, 2006b.

Cho, Joonmo, *An Empirical Evaluation on the Working Conditions in Korean Metal Industry*, Korean Labor Institute, 2004a.

Cho, Joonmo, "Flexibility, Instability and Institutional Insecurity in Korean Labor Market," *Journal of Policy Modelling*, 26(3) 2004b, pp. 315–351.

Cho, Joonmo, "Human Resource Management, Corporate Governance and Corporate Performance: A Comparative Study of Japan, US and Korea," *Japan and the World Economy*, 17(4) 2005, pp. 417–430.

Cho, Joonmo and Jae-Ho Keum, "Job Instability in the Korean Labor Market: Comparison before and after the 1997 Financial Crisis," *International Labour Review*, 143(4) 2004, pp. 373–392.

Cho, Joonmo and Lee, K.Y., "Deregulation of Dismissal Law and Unjust Dismissals in Korea," International Review of Law and Economics, 27(4) 2007, pp. 409–422.

Cho, Joonmo and Park Sungjae, "The Effect of Corporate Governance on Labor Adjustment," *Korean Journal of Industrial Relations*, 17(2) 2007, pp. 39–66.

Cho, Joonmo, Kim Giseung and Tahee Kwon, "Employment Problems for Irregular Workers in Korea," *Pacific Affairs*, 81(3) 2008.08, pp. 407–426.

Cho, Joonmo, Lim Chanyoung and Lee, Jaeseong, "Gender and Job Turnover in the Dual Labor Market: A Korean Perspective," *Asian Journal of Women's Studies*, 16(1) 2010, pp. 91–124.

Collins, Hugh, "The Meaning of Job Security," *Industrial Law Journal*, 20(4) 1991, pp. 227–239.

Diebold, Francis X., Neumark, David and Polsky, Daniel, "Job Stability in the United States," *Journal of Labor Economics*, 15(2) 1997, pp. 206–233.

Farber, Henry S. "The Changing Face of Job Loss in the United States, 1981–1995," *Brookings Papers on Economic Activity: Microeconomics*, 1997.

Fehr, Ernst, Erich Kirchler, Andreas Weichbold and Simon Gächter, "When Social Norms Overpower Competition: Gift Exchange in Experimental Labor Markets," *Journal of Labor Economics*, 16(2) 1998, pp. 324–350.

Gonos, George, "Never a Fee!! The Miracle of the Postmodern Temporary Help and Staffing Agency," State University of New York at Potsdam, Paper presented at the Meetings of the Industrial Relations Research Association, New Orleans, 1997.

Gottschalk, Peter and Moffit, Roberts, "Changes in Job Instability and Insecurity Using Monthly Survey Data," *Journal of Labor Economics*, 17(4) 1999, pp. 91–126.

Hall, Robert, "The Importance of Lifetime Jobs in the US Economy," *American Economic Review*, 72(4) 1982, pp. 716–724.

Idson, Todd, "Employer Size and Labor Turnover," in: Polachek, Solomon (ed.), *Research in Labor Economics*, Greenwich: JAI Press, 1996.

Idson, Todd and Robert G. Valletta, "Seniority, Sectoral Decline, and Employee Retention: An Analysis of Layoff Unemployment Spells," *Journal of Labor Economics*, 14(4) 1996, pp. 654–676.

Jaeger, David A. and Stevens, Ann Huff, "Is Job Stability in the United States Falling? Reconciling Trends in the Current Population Survey and Panel Study of Income Dynamics," *Journal of Labor Economics*, 17(4) 1999, pp. 1–28.

Koike, Kazuo, "Japan's Industrial Relations: Characteristics and Problems," *Japanese Economic Studies*, 7(3) 1978, pp. 42–90.

Korea Employers Federation, *Problems of Irregular Workers*, 2003.

Korea Employers Federation, R*esearch on 2007 Work Competency Evaluation of New Employees*, 2007.

Korean Ministry of Labor, International Comparison of Employment Protection Legislation, 2001.

Korean Ministry of Labor, *The Survey of National Union Organization*, Korea, 2000.

Korean Tripartite Commission, *Social Agreement on Job Creation*, 2004

Ku, Gunsuh, *The Labor Law and Industrial Relations in Korea*, Korea: Central Economy Press, 1999.

McShane, Steven and McPhilips, David, "Predicting Reasonable Notice in Canadian Wrongful Dismissal Case," *Industrial and Labor Relations Review*, 41(1), 1987, pp. 108–117.

Mayers, David and Thaler, Richard, "Sticky Wages and Implicit Contracts: A Transactional Approach," *Economic Inquiry*, 17(4), 1979, pp. 559–564.

Neumark, David, Polsky, Daniel and Hanse, Daniel "Has Job Stability Declined Yet? New Evidence for the 1990s," *Journal of Labor Economics*, 17(4) 1999, pp. 29–64.

OECD, "Addressing Labor Market Duality in Korea," OECD Report for Joint MOL/OECD Seminar On Labour Market Duality in Korea: An International Perspective, 2006a.

OECD, *OECD Employment Outlook*, 2004.

OECD, *OECD Employment Outlook – Boosting Jobs and Incomes*, 2006b.

OECD, *Employment Outlook*. Paris: OECD Publication, 1999, pp. 129–132.

Park, Dukjae, "A Comparison of Korea's Redundancy System with that of the UK," Korean Industrial Relations Association, Proceedings for 2002 Summer Conference, 2002.

Valletta, Robert G., "Declining Job Security," *Journal of Labor Economics*, 17(S4) 1999, pp. 170–197.

World Bank, *Doing Business in 2006: Creating Jobs*, 2006.

Wyneth, Pitt, "Justice in Dismissal: A Reply to Hugh Collins," *Industrial Law Journal*, 22(4) 1993, pp. 251–268.

7 Youth employment measures

Jae-Ho Keum

I Introduction

Among the biggest victims in a weak job market are young people. As of 2009, unemployment among youths aged 15–29 stood at 8.1 percent, more than double the overall rate of 3.6 percent. The number of unemployed youths, at 347,000, takes up 39.0 percent of all unemployed. Moreover, the number of employed youths has continued to decline ever since 2000, following demographic changes, job shortages and rising enrollment in higher education.

Youth unemployment often causes long-term loss of income throughout one's life, as it deters the accumulation of human capital in the early stage of one's career. In particular, with the low labor market flexibility in Korea, it also leads to a stigma effect, further raising the cost of youth non-employment. According to Gang-Woo Park and Seung-Jae Hong (2009), one-year non-employment by a 25-year-old youth would incur 37 million Korean won of short-term loss in income, but if the long-term effect is accounted for, the present value of income loss amounts to around 280 million won.

II Recent trends in youth employment and unemployment

The number of unemployed youths aged 15–29 fell from 4.879 million in 2000 to 3.957 million in 2009, an 18.9 percent drop (see Figure 7.1). It also brought down the youth employment/population rate to 40.5 percent in 2009, which is almost identical with the number during the Asian financial crisis. Since most of the 15–19 population are in school,[1] if the scope is limited to 20–29, the employment/population rate in 2008 goes up to 58.2 percent, as seen in Table 7.1. This is still the lowest since 2000, although higher than the 57.4 percent in 1998. In particular, the period after 2006 appears to have been especially challenging for the youth. The cumulative effect of the job market crisis in the past few years was further exacerbated by the 2008 global financial crisis.

The higher unemployment rate among youths is not a phenomenon specific to Korea, but common to almost all OECD countries. In fact, compared to the major OECD countries, Korea's is low (see Figure 7.2). But Korea has both a low unemployment rate and a low employment/population ratio. The

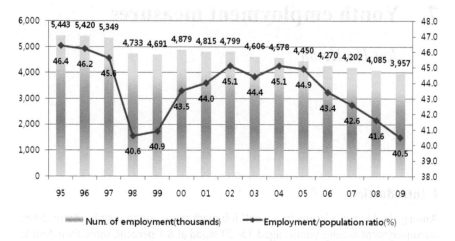

Figure 7.1 Trends in youth employment/population ratio (age 15–29) (source: National Statistical Office, *Economically Active Population Survey,* each year).

Table 7.1 Trends in youth employment: age 20–29 (thousands, %)

Year	Population	Number of employed	Employment/ population ratio	Number of unemployed	Unemployment rate
1980	6,051	3,512	58.0	310	8.1
1985	7,178	4,068	56.7	310	7.1
1990	7,153	4,442	62.1	231	4.9
1995	7,910	5,022	63.5	226	4.3
1996	7,862	5,021	63.9	232	4.4
1997	7,770	4,964	63.9	280	5.3
1998	7,669	4,401	57.4	568	11.4
1999	7,542	4,340	57.5	489	10.1
2000	7,474	4,490	60.1	341	7.1
2001	7,401	4,457	60.2	333	7.0
2002	7,315	4,486	61.3	302	6.3
2003	7,203	4,334	60.2	345	7.4
2004	7,070	4,320	61.1	351	7.5
2005	6,874	4,207	61.2	334	7.4
2006	6,741	4,061	60.2	321	7.3
2007	6,653	3,992	60.0	285	6.7
2008	6,584	3,894	59.1	278	6.7
2009	6,496	3,779	58.2	323	7.9

Source: National Statistical Office, *Economically Active Population Survey,* each year.

employment/population ratio among the 15–24 youth group in 2008 stood at 23.8 percent, around half of the OECD average of 43.7 percent. Such a low employment/ population ratio reflects the high enrollment rate in higher education and shortage of job opportunities. In addition, in a culture where the parents are expected to bear the brunt of the tuition and living costs, not many students find part-time jobs.

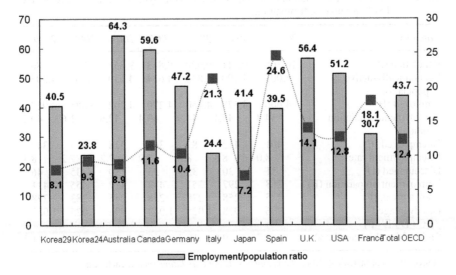

Figure 7.2 15–24 Youth employment/population ratio and unemployment rate in major countries (15–29), 2007 (source: OECD, *OECD Employment Outlook*, 2008).

Notes
Korean 29 is unemployment and employment/population ratios for age 15–29, Korean 24 is for age 15–24.

The youth unemployment rate in Korea is low compared to other OECD countries, but the official unemployment rate does not reflect the job challenges that they experience. Table 7.2 shows the 347,000 unemployed youths in 2009. In addition to the unemployed youths, there were 46,000 discouraged jobseekers, 411,000 youths in "employment preparation" and 278,000 "taking a break" for no apparent reason. Classifying all of these persons as employment disadvantaged gives a number of 1.082 million, which is 3.1 times the number unemployed and 11.1 percent of the 15–29 population.

Table 7.3 shows the continuing and significant rise in the employment disadvantaged since 2003, while the unemployment rate falls. The reasons appear to be the rise in the absolute number and share of young people who choose to be in "employment preparation" instead of job-seeking. It shows that there are many more youths suffering from difficulties in finding jobs than shown by the official unemployment rate. This is a problem that can undermine the growth potential of the economy and lead to under-utilization of human resource.

By age, the 25–29 group has the highest number of employment disadvantaged at 592,000 (as of 2009), or 15.4 percent of that age group. By gender, men are likelier to suffer from non-employment than women. As of 2009, 9.5 percent of women were experiencing job challenges but among men, it was 12.7 percent. By education level, the highly educated (four-year university degree or higher) had the highest number of employment disadvantaged, hinting that the overall rise in educational attainment is one of the main causes of the youth job crunch.

Table 7.2 Changes in the number of employed and employment-disadvantaged in the 15–29 group (%, thousands)

Category	2003	2004	2005	2006	2007	2008	2009
Population (A)	10,368	10,141	9,920	9,843	9,855	9,824	9,780
Economically-active population	5,007	4,990	4,836	4,634	4,530	4,400	4,304
Employed (B)	4,606	4,578	4,450	4,270	4,202	4,085	3,957
Employment/population ratio	44.4	45.1	44.9	43.4	42.6	41.6	40.5
Unemployed (C)	401	412	387	364	328	315	347
Unemployment rate	8.0	8.3	8.0	7.9	7.2	7.2	8.1
Discouraged (D)	31	30	32	33	30	35	46
Employment preparation (E)	268	297	351	413	417	455	411
Took a break (F)	225	258	278	258	245	283	278
Disadvantaged (C+D+E+F)	906	978	1,025	1,043	996	1,025	1,082
Ratio of disadvantaged (%)	8.7	9.6	10.3	10.6	10.1	10.4	11.1

Source: National Statistical Office, *Economically Active Population Survey*, each year.

Notes
Discouraged workers are those among the economically inactive who are willing and capable of working but are not currently seeking jobs due to labor market reasons and who have job-seeking experience in the past one year. The employment-challenged is the percentage calculated by using the youth population as the denominator and the employment-challenged as the numerator.

Even within the youth group as a whole, there are considerable changes in the unemployment and employment/population ratios by age, with the younger population experiencing a higher unemployment rate and lower employment/population ratio (see Table 7.3). By gender, women exhibit a lower unemployment rate than men. In the case of employment/population ratio, it is higher for women before the age of 25, but there is a reversal afterwards, with men showing a higher employment rate. The main contributors to such sharp rise in men's employment/population ratio in accordance with age are military service and advancement to higher education. In other words, many men aged 20–24 are not able to participate in the labor market due to compulsory military service and/or school enrollment.

By education, high school graduates experience not only the highest unemployment rate but also low employment/population ratio, a telltale sign that their unemployment problem is more severe than highly educated youths. High school graduates tend to move in and out of jobs, mostly low-skilled, low-pay and/or non-standard ones, which result in a high unemployment rate and low employment/ population ratio. Moreover, the lower the educational attainment, the higher the share of non-standard employment. The problem is, non-employment among the low-educated youths continues well after their thirties. Figure 7.3 shows that for the high school graduates of 30–32 aged the non-employment rate was 33.4 percent. This suggests that the low-educated youths are at the risk of going back and forth between non-standard employment and non-employment without settling down in the labor market, not only in their twenties but also after their thirties.

Table 7.3 Employment status among youths by gender and age, 2009 (thousands, %)

Description	15–29	15–19	20–24	25–29
Overall				
Economically active population	4,305	203	1,305	2,797
Employed	3,957	178	1,182	2,598
Employment/population ratio	40.5	5.4	44.6	67.6
Unemployed	347	25	124	199
Unemployment rate	8.1	12.3	9.5	7.1
Employment disadvantaged	1,082	68	423	876
Economically inactive population	5,477	3,082	1,346	1,049
Men				
Economically active population	2,076	85	495	1,497
Employed	1,872	72	439	1,362
Employment/population ratio	39.0	4.2	39.1	69.4
Unemployed	203	13	56	135
Unemployment rate	9.8	15.1	11.4	9.0
Employment disadvantaged	608	35	188	582
Economically inactive population	2,722	1,629	628	465
Women				
Economically active population	2,229	118	810	1,300
Employed	2,085	106	743	1,236
Employment/population ratio	41.8	6.7	48.6	65.6
Unemployed	144	12	68	64
Unemployment rate	6.5	10.3	8.3	4.9
Employment disadvantaged	474	33	235	294
Economically inactive population	2,755	1,453	718	584

Source: National Statistical Office, *Economically Active Population Survey*, each year.

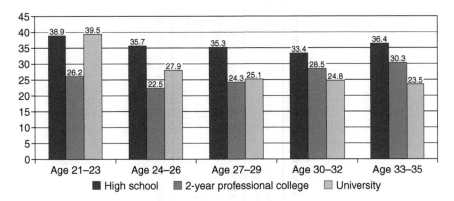

Figure 7.3 Share of unemployment by education and age, 2009 (source: National Statistical Office, *Economically Active Population Survey*, 2009).

Notes
The values are estimated for out-of-school population only.

Table 7.4 Post-school time required until first employment: wage workers (1,000, %)

	Youth with job experience	Wage worker	0–3 months	3–6 months	0.5–1 year	1–2 years	2–3 years	3 + years	Average
May 2009	4,322	4,194 (100.0)	2,243 (53.5)	502 (12.0)	397 (9.5)	461 (11.0)	224 (5.3)	368 (8.8)	11 months
May 2008	4,513	4,383 (100.0)	2,281 (52.1)	549 (12.5)	429 (9.8)	499 (11.4)	232 (5.3)	393 (9.0)	11 months

Source: National Statistical Office, *Economically Active Population Survey: Supplementary Survey on Youth*, May 2009.

III Other indicators of the labor market outcome of the youth group

The youth group tends to take a longer time until first employment. As shown in Table 7.4, the time until first employment after graduating or dropping out of the school is 11 months as of May 2009, due to such reasons as insufficient career counseling, inadequate labor market functions and mismatch in the job market. By gender, men take longer than women to find employment, with eight months of post-school time being required for women and 14.5 months for men. By education, the higher the education, the shorter the time until employment. For high school graduates, 14.8 months is required until first employment, for college graduates 8.2 months and university graduates 8.1 months.

The time until employment differs by employment type. In the case of jobs with a shorter than one-year contract term or temporary jobs with no contract term, the time until employment is 12.4 months, which is 1.7 months longer than the 10.7 months for continuous jobs. This is an indirect indicator of the frequent tendency among youths to first look for secure jobs like standard employment, then, upon failing to find one, getting a fixed-term contract job (with shorter than one-year term). In a similar vein, when the first job is part-time, the time required is 11.5 months, again longer than the 10.5 months for full-time jobs.

It was found that young workers have a higher risk of job turnover compared with other age groups. Table 7.5 below is the result of the "two-year job retention rate"[2] estimated using the KLIPS (*Korean Labor and Income Panel Study*) to understand the possibility of maintaining the same job for the next two years. The rate for those aged 16–29 in 2003–2005 is 51.4 percent, lower than in other age groups. Within the youth group, those aged 16–24 show 43.7 percent of two-year job retention rate, indicating that more than half of the wage workers in that age group are likely to leave the current job within the next two years. This shows that young workers, even after getting employed, are highly likely to leave the job due to job insecurity or dissatisfaction.

By education, it was found that the lower the education, the higher the possibility of leaving the job within two years. Thus it is construed that both the

Table 7.5 Age distribution and trends in two-year job retention rate: wage workers

Age	1995–1997	1997–1999	1999–2001	2001–2003	2003–2005
16–29	54.3	49.1	49.6	46.9	51.4
16–24	44.6	41.7	44.7	41.2	43.7
25–29	63.3	55.1	54.0	51.5	56.3
30–39	76.9	61.7	64.9	62.8	67.6
40–49	79.1	59.9	66.7	69.0	68.7
50–59	75.0	44.4	56.0	65.4	69.1
60 or older	54.2	33.3	46.1	45.0	49.0
Total	68.6	54.3	59.5	59.9	63.3

Source: Korea Labor Institute, *Korea Labor and Income Panel Study (KLIPS)*, each year.

Table 7.6 Reasons for leaving the first job: May 2009

Category	Dissatisfied with working conditions	Major/skill mismatch	No future	Personal/family reasons	Contract expired	Company reasons	Honorary retirement, dismissal	Close-down, bankruptcy
Men	43.6	6.8	12.2	13.4	5.5	3.9	1.4	4.3
Women	39.1	6.7	8.0	26.4	5.5	3.4	1.7	3.5
Total	41.0	6.7	9.9	20.7	5.5	3.6	1.6	3.9

Source: National Statistical Office, *Economically Active Population Survey: Supplementary Survey on Youth*, May 2009.

high unemployment rate and the low employment/population ratio among low-educated youths are due to the job insecurity that they often experience. In comparison, university graduates were found to find employment out of school much quicker and have a higher probability of maintaining the job.

The supplementary survey to the *Economically Active Population Survey* also shows that as of May 2009, only 26.8 percent stayed in the same job, indicating that the rest already left their first job. Highly educated men have a higher probability of staying in the first job, while only 12.7 percent of high school graduates stayed in the first job. Among the young workers who left the first job, their average time at the first job is 21.3 months. Reasons for leaving the first job were, in the order of frequency: "dissatisfaction with working conditions" and "personal or family reasons" such as children rearing, household work, health, marriage or education. In addition, "no future at the current job or work" also accounted for 9.9 percent. Compared to women, more men cited the reasons of working conditions and lack of career future.

The *Supplementary Survey* in August 2008 shows 1.421 million won as the average monthly wage for youth workers. But there are significant differences by age, with the wage level sharply rising with age: the 15–19 group earned only 622,200 won, the 20–24 group 1.132 million won, and 25–29 group 1.624 million won. Meanwhile, for overall wage workers, the average monthly wage for three months from June to August 2006 was found to be 1.846 million won.

By gender, men earned an average of 2.226 million won per month, while women earned 1.318 million, or only 59.2 percent of what men earned. Also in case of men, the wage level goes up in accordance with age, peaking at 45–49.

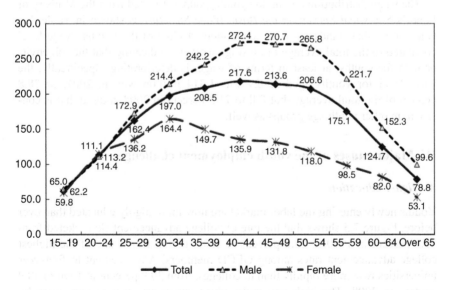

Figure 7.4 Age distribution of monthly average wage in June–August 2008 (source: National Statistical Office, *Economically Active Population Survey: Supplementary Survey*, August 2008).

Table 7.7 Wage level of employed youths: workplaces with five or more employees (1,000 won/month, %)

Year	Age			
	15–19	*20–24*	*25–29*	*All*
2000	755 (45.3)	971 (58.2)	1,314 (78.8)	1,668
2001	891 (50.9)	1,032 (58.9)	1,384 (79.0)	1,752
2002	958 (49.2)	1,112 (57.1)	1,498 (76.9)	1,948
2003	992 (46.6)	1,189 (55.9)	1,601 (75.3)	2,127
2004	1,073 (47.6)	1,269 (56.3)	1,688 (74.9)	2,255
2005	1,179 (49.0)	1,362 (56.7)	1,824 (75.9)	2,404
2006	1,322 (52.0)	1,452 (57.1)	1,883 (74.1)	2,542
2007	1,369 (51.0)	1,478 (55.1)	1,911 (71.2)	2,683
2008	1,044 (37.2)	1,462 (52.0)	2,004 (71.3)	2,810

Source: Ministry of Employment and Labor, *Survey on Wage Structure* and *Working Conditions by Employment Type*, each year.

Notes
Total wage = fixed pay + overtime pay + annual special pay of the previous year/12. Numbers in parentheses are the wage ratio compared to all wage workers.

But for women, it peaks at 30–34, and then continues to decline with age. As a result, although the wage gap is small between men and women in their youth, it widens after the thirties and continues thereafter: the wage ratio by gender reaches 0.767 at 30–34 and 0.444 at 55–59.[3]

The wage distribution among the youth group, estimated from the Ministry of Labor's *Statistical Survey on the Basic Wage Structure* is shown in Table 7.7. One feature that stands out is the continuous decline of the youths' wage level compared to the total average of all wage workers, indicating that the job environment for youths, at least in terms of wage, is deteriorating. Specifically, the wage level for youths aged 25–29 was 1.314 million won in 2001, or 78.8 percent of the total average, but fell to 71.3 percent in 2008, a trend that is consistent in other youth age groups as well.

IV Major causes of the youth employment challenge

A Higher education

Youths newly entering the labor market are now more highly educated than ever before. Figure 7.5 shows that the rate of college advancement skyrocketed from 33.2 percent in 1990 to 83.8 percent in 2008, giving Korea one of the highest college advancement rates among OECD members. Advancement to four-year universities rose more rapidly than to colleges, from 20.9 percent in 1990 to 58.9 percent in 2008. The high university advancement rate was accompanied by lower quality of education and subsequent deterioration in productivity. College graduates' preference for "decent jobs" and high reservation wages, end up

Table 7.8 Major-job match in the latest job: May 2009 (%)

Category	Highly mismatched	Somewhat mismatched	Somewhat matched	Highly matched
Gender				
Men	39.4	15.3	26.1	19.1
Women	34.3	15.6	28.7	21.5
Education				
High school or lower	52.0	19.2	23.5	5.3
2-year college	33.8	13.6	26.8	25.8
University or higher	21.5	12.8	32.6	33.1
Age				
15–19	68.4	9.7	14.8	7.0
20–24	41.1	16.0	23.7	19.2
25–29	35.2	15.4	29.1	20.3
Number of jobs				
One	24.8	14.1	31.2	30.0
Two	36.2	15.8	29.7	18.4
Three	40.9	17.2	26.4	15.5
Four or more	51.5	15.6	20.4	12.5
Total	36.7	15.5	27.5	20.4

Source: National Statistical Office, *Economically Active Population Survey, Supplementary Survey on Youths*, May 2009.

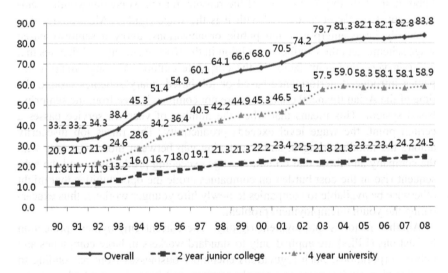

Figure 7.5 Trends in college advancement rate (source: Ministry of Education, Science and Technology, *Annual Report on Educational Statistics*, each year).

prolonging the time required to become employed. Most highly-educated youths prefer professional or office positions in large companies or public organizations rather than in SMEs with non-competitive working conditions and low social recognition. Many of those who fail to get a job of their choice delay employment before downward-adjusting their expectations and accepting a less-than-desired job.

B Gap between education and industrial demand

Another cause of the severe deterioration in youth unemployment can be found in the gap between school education and industrial demand. Industrial structure has changed rapidly but formal education, rigidly tied to enrollment quota by major and outdated curriculum, fails to keep up with the changing demand in human resources. As Table 7.8 shows, 36.7 percent of employed youths responded that their major and job description were "highly mismatched," with only 20.4 percent agreeing that they were "highly matched." No difference by gender was discerned, but by educational level, there was a higher rate of mismatch among the low-educated (high school or lower). The younger the respondent, the likelier the mismatch. In addition, the probability of the mismatch increased as the number of job turnovers grew.

C Labor market rigidity

Labor market rigidity is also one of the reasons for the worsening youth unemployment. One factor associated with it is the wage rigidity. Most companies, especially large enterprises and public organizations, apply a seniority-based wage scheme, and the Confucian tradition in the Korean society still dictates that age is a very important factor in the corporate culture. Although many companies introduced performance-based or job-based salary schemes around the time of the Asian financial crisis, they are not completely free from the seniority-based system. This means that when the number of years in service passes a certain point, the wage level exceeds productivity. This raises job insecurity among the middle/old-aged, and a widening gap between those who stay with the company and those that do not. A wage exceeding productivity and the subsequent rise in the cost burden on companies erode the opportunities that might otherwise be available to companies to newly hire younger workers, thus exacerbating the youth unemployment problem.

Another factor is employment rigidity. The current employment protection legislations (EPLs) are applied only to standard workers in large companies and public corporations. Such regulations encumber businesses from responding to the changing environment in a timely manner, and keep the standard workers' wage cost higher than their productivity. Thus many businesses opt for low-wage non-standard workers or outsource part of their production process as a way of cost control. The contractors that perform the outsourced work provide workers with low wage and low employment protection. At the same time, the youth jobseekers fresh out of university would avoid low-wage non-standard positions, leading to a longer job-seeking period and higher unemployment.

D Inadequate information and intermediary market institutions

Inadequate information about the labor market and employment services also negatively affects the challenges facing the youths. There is a gap in market information between groups and individuals, particularly between core workers with high education and skills and marginal workers with low education and skills. Mechanisms to resolve the supply–demand mismatch in the labor market through intermediaries are inadequate. The practice of employment services is relatively new, and there is insufficient availability of information or other services that could aid informed decision-making on both the demand and supply side of the labor market. What is missing is systematic information or career education that can help youths to seek the right career path, without which many youths fail to manage their expectations and become unemployed. Even when they do get employed, lack of information can result in mismatched jobs, leading to voluntary or involuntary job displacement. This not only negatively affects their career development/management and human resource development, but also keeps down the youth employment/population ratio and drives up unemployment.

Aside from these, unstable industrial relations exacerbate the youth unemployment problem. On the surface, industrial relations have stabilized lately but companies still harbor anxiety that they might flare up again in the future. This makes companies reluctant to hire new workers. In addition, economic growth in Korea has largely been driven by manufacturing, export and large companies, but their growth – compared to growth of the service industry, domestic demand and SMEs – contributes less to job growth. This has resulted in low employment elasticity of economic growth in Korea compared to other countries, and even now it is undergoing a trend decline. As "jobless growth" becomes reality, it is the youths who are hit the hardest.

E Imbalance in corporate size – the economy's weak middle tier

The imbalance in corporate size, which makes the Korean economy weak in the middle, is another cause of the worsening youth unemployment. While the big companies preferred by young jobseekers have reduced their hiring, mid-level (or mid-sized) companies that could serve as the alternative option do not have a large enough presence in the market. As shown in Figure 7.6, 67.1 percent of workers, or over two-thirds, are employed in small enterprises with less than 50 employees. In comparison, 12.9 percent are in large companies with 300 or more employees, meaning that less than 20.0 percent work in mid-sized companies with 50–299 employees.

Thus, young people who fail to get into a large company would opt to delay employment to try again or take a different path altogether rather than join an

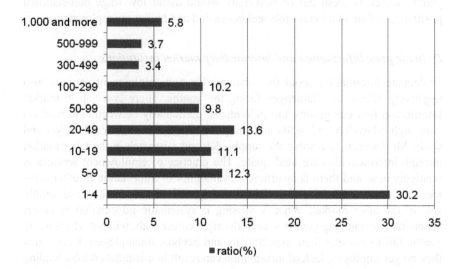

Figure 7.6 Distribution of wage workers by company size (excl. agriculture, forestry and fishery) (source: National Statistical Office, *Survey on Businesses*, 2007).

SME with a low wage and a tenuous future. In particular, the widening gap between the two types in terms of productivity and financial capacity have led to a growing discrepancy in wage level and working conditions, further exacerbating the problem. As seen in Figure 7.7, if the wage level at businesses with 10–29 employees is 1.000, the wage level at large companies with over 500 employees was 1.383 in 1997, but rose sharply to 1.690 in 2007. The same is

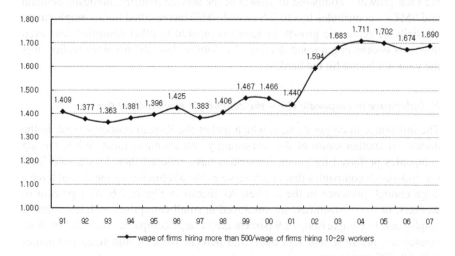

Figure 7.7 Relative wage between large (500 and more workers) and small (10–29 workers) firms (source: Ministry of Employment and Labor, *Monthly Labor Survey Report*, each year).

true for employee benefits: the larger the company, the more generous they are. And the occupational accident rate is higher among smaller companies, likely to leave a sense of relative deprivation to their workers.

V Youth employment policy

Because of the strong socio-political pressure, the government has made extensive efforts to resolve the job crunch among the youths, but approximately 100 policy initiatives implemented so far have yielded little success. Keum *et al.* (2007) found that the lack of visible success is mainly due to the lack of clear labor market policy objectives, inadequate policy implementation, and some structural problems of the Korean economy.

A Formulating sound public policy objectives

Most of the youth employment measures consist of programs for labor market supply and infrastructure, leaving much to be desired in terms of developing policies to increase demand for youth labor. Programs targeting the demand side have proven to be ineffective, such as "overseas job placement," "SME job placement," and "business start-up support." Only the programs related to "provision of short-term jobs" are reaping visible results, but they are mostly for non-standard positions and do not present a fundamental solution to the youth unemployment situation. Also, there is not enough research and policy development to strengthen the correlation between economic growth and youth employment, or to increase new hiring by companies.

Policies should focus more on demand for youth labor. Namely, (temporary) easing of EPLs to promote hiring of youths, providing consulting service to support corporate efforts to increase new hiring, and installation of a council with participants from labor, management, government, and private institutions at the regional or industrial level as a possible option. The impact of strict EPLs on youth unemployment has not been addressed. There should be more detailed analysis of the impact that elements of the labor market environment, such as "stable industrial relations," "innovation in the wage/job scheme," and "implementation of the Non-standard Workers Protection Act," can have on youth unemployment.

There is much anxiety in Korea about starting a business because of the self-employment crisis. But it is important to encourage competent young people to start their own business, especially in new growth service sectors not overly crowded by self-owned businesses (such as wholesale/retail, hotels/restaurants, manufacturing or personal services) to breathe in new vibrancy and competitiveness. As things stand today, business start-up is still considered as merely a backup plan in case of failure to secure a "decent job," which increases the risk of failure. There should be adequate preparation at the individual and government level to make sure that they start their business fully ready. To help well-prepared business start-up, there should be a systemic support mechanism.

It should be a comprehensive package of support including financial support, consulting service regarding business ideas and information and even training opportunities. More specifically, there should be efforts to develop and disseminate programs to promote new growth industries, support students' business start-up clubs and provide more related information. In particular, there should be a "business start-up support" section under job information websites such as WorkNet.[4]

Currently the SMBA (Small and Medium Business Administration) is in charge of business start-up support, but much more should be done. As young entrepreneurs' businesses would start out small, it is important for the local government, the entity with the administrative jurisdiction, to get involved, but they lack expertise in the area. To provide the kind of systemic support needed for young would-be entrepreneurs, there should be cooperation and well-designed division of roles between school, private specialists, the central government and local governments.

Overall in order to ease youth unemployment, it is necessary to ensure wage flexibility. The rapid aging of the population requires striking a balance between job security for the middle/old-aged and new jobs for the young. One way of doing that is the innovation of company pay structure so that the wage would be more in line with productivity. If wage is always consistent with productivity, companies would have no reason to dismiss their workers. Thus enabling more flexibility in the wage system is a way to protect jobs and enhance corporate competitiveness, thus creating more jobs. Innovation of the wage system would also lead to higher productivity thanks to rationalization of human resource management, which would not only help ease youth unemployment but also reduce the gap between standard and non-standard workers and union members and non-members. In addition, by realigning the pay structure, official retirement age can be applied for the middle/old-aged workers,[5] to allow them to better prepare for post-retirement life.

Second, the labor market functions have to be strengthened. More flexibility in the labor market would heighten motivation for corporate investment and thus help increase growth potential, which in turn would help ease the youth job crunch and resolve the dual structure in the labor market. The relevant laws and institutions would have to be improved to make sure that the market functions efficiently. In particular, a new type of employment may be considered where wage and other working conditions are on par with other jobs, only with lower job security. This would ease the burden on companies when hiring new workers and likely to increase employment opportunities for the youth.

Finally, for the labor market to function properly, information must be provided adequately. Effective provision of information about career, employment, education and training to young jobseekers would enable timely and appropriate decision-making. Providing information and services regarding the labor market to the youth, thereby strengthening market functions, is what employment service is about. But given that such service in Korea is significantly inadequate compared to developed countries, it is necessary to increase investment to strengthen its role. Such investment should be made in a way that ensures balanced development of the different components: employment service at university level, private employment service and public employment service (PES). And it is also necessary to improve the content and quality of such services by reinforcing the PES' manpower and organization,[6] increasing employment assistance at schools, improving labor market information systems, strengthening career counseling, and reinforcing the expertise of the counselors.

B *Improving implementation*

Despite the importance of creating jobs, such policies still do not command high priority. The Ministry of Employment and Labor,[7] Ministry of Education, Science and Technology, Ministry of Knowledge Economy and SMBA (Small and Medium Business Administration) are each making and implementing policies of their own but they are more driven by the policy-makers' expedience than the users' demand. The same shortcoming is witnessed in the activities of local governments. They not only lack both awareness and capability for employment policies, but also tend to include job creation programs as part of welfare policy, not employment policy.

The cooperation between local governments and central government needs to be improved. Most local governments, although concerned and interested in youth unemployment, lack the policy tools, financial resources and policy capability to tackle the issue. The central government should work together with local governments to design and implement youth employment policies suitable to each locality's needs. Such cooperation would also improve the effectiveness of such policies by enhancing the structure and efficiency of the delivery system.

Currently, the youth employment policy includes a multitude of programs with different purposes and descriptions, blurring the fundamental goals of the policy. With over 100 programs in place, it becomes a challenge merely to implement the policy in an integrated and consistent manner. Around half of these programs were found to have little direct relevance with addressing youth unemployment.

The government needs to reduce the number of policy tasks as much as possible and impose a systemic management scheme under the principle of "select and focus." This would strengthen the planning, coordination and evaluation functions for youth employment measures and integrate the many components that are currently scattered in different ministries. In addition, the purpose, implementation process and performance analysis of each program should be put into a better structure, and performance evaluation and progress monitoring should be reinforced. There should also be clear evaluation criteria for programs that can be included into the youth employment policy.

The time lag between implementation and actual impact was found to be quite long. Thus, it is necessary to place the focus on building the infrastructure and human resource development to promote youth employment with a mid/long-term vision. Many programs had adequate implementation mechanism but no follow-up management. Particularly for programs providing direct support to the youth group, often there was no clear accountability as to who is responsible for what. And there was also a lack of capability in follow-up.

C Addressing long-term structural issues

At the heart of the youth job crunch is a lack of "decent jobs" that meet their expectations. This will become even more apparent as low birth rate and aging of the population deepen.[8] It is necessary to create decent jobs with the high pay, high skills and standard status preferred by highly educated youths by developing newly growing industries, knowledge-based industries and restructuring the services industry. One aim should be to ameliorate highly educated young people's aversion to SMEs by improving their competitiveness and working environment. Also, there should be stronger efforts to create local jobs for those graduating from local universities, and the school-to-work transition should be strengthened to minimize the time between graduation and employment. To that end, job education should be strengthened and school education should be qualitatively improved, so as to be able to develop the talent needed by the industry.

Higher expectations among young jobseekers who are graduating from universities at a higher rate than any time before are one of the factors that exacerbate the youth unemployment problem. Many jobseekers go into "preparation for employment" to get a decent job because if they fail to enter a large company or public corporation they may be relegated to join an SME with unfavorable working conditions and a precarious future. And the discrepancy between university education and industrial needs is also worsening young people's employment opportunities.

Against this backdrop, it is necessary to improve the education system. If the quality of labor is described in three skills level, or high, medium and low, Korean education is mostly focused on developing medium or lower skills. It inevitably leads to shortage of high skills and oversupply of medium skills. One key challenge to address the education problem of Korea is to improve the system itself so as to improve the quality of education. To that end, the system must be altered in a way that minimizes government intervention and maximizes the private sector's (such as university's) capability.

Universities should be given more freedom, from student selection to operation of academic affairs, to create an environment where universities would compete with each other to improve the quality of their education. To stem potential ill effects of such freedom, the universities should also be held more accountable. Their accountability lies in meeting the needs of the users of education (students) and users of labor (businesses). The schools should be encouraged to improve their education programs to bolster their students' employability, as well as their curriculum to meet the labor demands of the industry, and it should be left to the end users of labor to judge their efforts.

In order to shorten the job-seeking period and find the best-suited job, it is important to have some form of job experience in advance. Figure 7.8 shows that

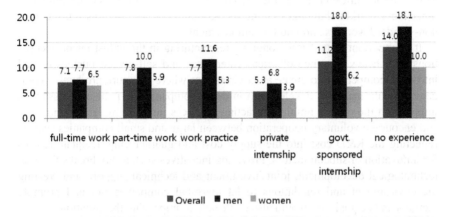

Figure 7.8 Job experience and job-seeking period (until first employment after graduation) (source: National Statistical Office, *Economically Active Population
Survey, Supplementary Survey on Youth*, May 2009).

having job experience during school years considerably reduces the job-seeking
period after graduation. The youths with no job experience took 14 months to
find first employment, while those with internship experience took only 6.83
months.

It was also found that having job experience increases the chances of finding
a standard job. In all job experience programs except for part-time or
government-sponsored programs, it was found that job experience increases the
likelihood of finding standard employment. Thus, it is necessary to increase job
experience opportunities for the student currently in school or on leave of
absence, while at the same time trying to improve the effectiveness of the existing government-sponsored job experience programs.

There is also a need to develop mid-tier companies that the employees can be
proud of by implementing ongoing restructuring and productivity improvement
in the sectors dominated by micro enterprises and the self-employed. As for
large companies and public corporations, greater transparency should be required
while regulations are eased to further free up their activities in the market and
encourage them to compete with multinationals in the global market. Policies to
develop mid-tier companies would also have the added benefit of improving the
Korean economy's structural weakness, which is that its share of small businesses is very high compared to developed economies.

As the majority of workers are employed in small companies with an insecure
financial position and high risk of bankruptcy, many of them are not adequately
protected by labor laws (such as the Labor Standards Act) or social insurance.
Moreover, the smaller the company, the higher the share of non-standard
workers. By developing mid-tier companies, de facto coverage of labor laws
such as the Labor Standards Act would be expanded, as well as social insurance
programs such as employment insurance, national pension and health insurance.

More vibrant mid-tier companies would also make positive contributions to other labor market challenges facing the Korean economy such as job security, non-standard workers and youth unemployment.

It is important to undertake ongoing restructuring in the industries or occupations with heavy presence of micro enterprises and self-owned businesses and introduce competition to create an environment where the more productive companies would naturally develop into mid-tier companies. It is also necessary to improve on the current unfair contracting practices imposed by large companies and encourage voluntary cooperation between large and small companies such as reflecting the R&D cost into the supply cost and guaranteeing adequate returns for innovation of subcontractors. Providing incentives such as tax breaks for joint technological development, joint investment and technical support, and creating the environment and regulations to let marginal companies fail and promote mergers and acquisitions would also contribute to improving the situation.

Developing mid-tier companies in manufacturing is in the same vein as developing the parts and materials industry. In addition, it is important to design policies to develop the service industry (particularly wholesale/retail, hotels/restaurants, transportation, real estate lease, personal services, and social services) which remains underdeveloped compared to advanced nations' service sector and other domestic industries like manufacturing, and which is mostly led by SMEs and self-owned businesses. This will require a set of finely segmented and highly refined policies to develop the industry and individual companies.

In the end, it is the companies that create jobs, and the intensity of job creation will depend on how hard they work. In this respect, although the government's effort to improve the environment to do business is important, at least as important is the companies' effort to increase flexibility in its internal labor market by maintaining good industrial relations with labor. To that end, workplace innovation should be actively pursued, as a means to improve both industrial relations and productivity.

Workplace innovation involves not only installing a learning organization within the company, but providing a total consulting service encompassing the overall human resource management (HRM) and industrial relations of the company. Such effort is also in line with job-sharing, and there is a need to conduct research to find ways to improve corporate productivity and create jobs at the same time (by using more part-time work, revising the wage system, etc.). This would ultimately help ease youth unemployment by enhancing job creation capability of the business sector.

Notes

1 As of 2009, 91.1 percent of the 15–19 age groups were in school.
2 "Two-year job retention rate" is one of the most commonly used indicators of job stability.
3 The wage ratio by gender at all age groups is as follows: 0.767 at 30–34, 0.618 at 35–39, 0.499 at 40–44, 0.487 at 45–49, 0.444 at 50–54, 0.444 at 55–59, 0.538 at 60–64, and 0.533 at 65 or older.

4 WorkNet is a portal site for jobseekers and companies operated by the Ministry of Employment and Labor.
5 In reality, many employees leave their job earlier as the companies, suffering from the high burden of wage payment, are reluctant to keep employees until the mandatory retirement age.
6 The most important public employment service (PES) institution is the job center administrated by the Ministry of Employment and Labor. Currently the ministry is operating 71 job centers nationwide.
7 To emphasize the importance of employment, the Ministry of Labor changed its name to the Ministry of Employment and Labor on July 1, 2010.
8 The youth population (age 15–29) is decreasing both in sheer number and share in overall population. By 2012, the number is expected to have decreased by 608,000 from the 2007 level. If economic growth remains on par with targets, the number of employment disadvantaged youth population (currently around one million) should fall sharply. As a result, there is likely to be an acute shortage of young workers in low-wage, low-productivity and 3D (difficult, dangerous, and dirty) jobs. Thus the youth employment policies should also take into account the labor market situation in 5–10 years' time.

References

Keum, Jae-Ho and Yi, Insill, "Income and Sales of Self-employed," mimeo, February, 2009.

Keum, Jae-Ho, Kim, Jong-Sook and Kim, Han-Joon, "Policy Evaluations on Youth Employment," Ministry of Employment and Labor, December, 2007.

Korea Labor Institute, *Korean Labor and Income Panel Study*, each year.

Ministry of Education, Science and Technology, "Annual Report on Educational Statistics," each year.

Ministry of Employment and Labor, *Survey on Wage Structure and Working Conditions by Employment Type*, each year.

Ministry of Employment and Labor, *Monthly Labor Survey Report*, each year.

National Statistical Office, *Economically Active Population Survey*, each year.

National Statistical Office, *Economically Active Population Survey: Supplementary Survey on Youth*, May, 2009.

National Statistical Office, *Survey on Businesses*, 2007.

OECD, *OECD Employment Outlook*, 2008.

Park, Gang-Woo and Hong, Seung-Jae, "Changes in Employment Environment and Policies for Youth Unemployment," Bank of Korea, February, 2009.

8 Not in education, employment, or training (NEET) youth

Jaeseong Lee and Kwangho Woo

I Introduction

In the 2000s, youth unemployment[1] has received keen policy attention in Korea with the prevalent risk of growth without employment. Worse yet, the latest global economic crisis that began in September 2008 exacerbated the decreasing youth employment of those aged 30 or younger. Unemployment among the age group between 15 and 29 averages twice the overall unemployment in the economy for the past 20 years.[2] Youth unemployment accounts for 40–50 percent of overall unemployment. But the youth unemployment rate does not fully reflect the labor market problems of young persons.

In Figure 8.1, the youth unemployment rate has maintained at around 7–8 percent since 2006 while the youth employment has decreased on a quarterly basis, which suggests a greater gap between the unemployment rate and the employment rate. Youth unemployment is no longer effective as a measure of youth employment. In this chapter we examine an alternative measure of the problems of young persons in the job market: NEET, which is an acronym for "not in education, employment or training". It was first used in the United Kingdom in 1999. In Japan, the definition expanded to include people between

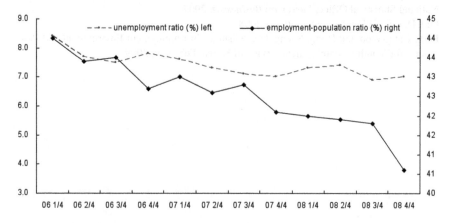

Figure 8.1 Youth unemployment rate and employment rate.

15 and 34, who are generally referred to as youth in non-employment, and from 2004 formal statistics for the group have been released. NEET means not only a state where people are not working, but also a situation where they do not participate in any education or training to participate in productive activities.[3]

Youth and their parents are acutely aware that youth have run into a serious difficulty in finding a job. The government has implemented various measures to counter the issue. However, as long as youth unemployment is an important indicator that the government has in place to assess policy direction, the measures have inherent limits in that they are results of the shaky assumption of low youth unemployment. In this light, it is required that NEET in Korea, as a policy indicator that reflects what the true labor market in Korea genuinely looks like, and its variables should be well defined.

II NEET in Korea

Major empirical studies on NEET in Korea include Jae-Ryang Nam (2006) and Bu-Hyung Lee (2005). Jae-Ryang Nam (2006) defines NEET in Korea (a) during the previous one week, (b) unemployed persons who are between 15 and 34, (c) who are single without partners, and (d) who are neither engaged in housework or child care, nor commute to formal schools, preparatory schools, or vocational training facilities. According to the definition that this study adopts, NEET in Korea refers to individuals who are between 15 and 29 year old, excluding the following:

1 Employees
2 Commuters to regular schools or preparatory schools
3 Individuals who are engaged in child care, under mental or physical strain, waiting to join the military service, or preparing for marriage.

However, those who participate in training for employment or are engaged in other activities for employment are included in NEET. Similar to NEET is the disadvantaged in employment group. The Ministry of Labor (2004) has expanded into the youth group the concept of the disadvantaged in employment group, which generally focused on women, the older and the disadvantaged, by examining the difficulty in getting a job as not only an unemployment issue but also a pattern of the labor market. Byung-Hee Lee (2004) estimated the number of the youth group disadvantaged in employment to be approximately 690,000 to 930,000 as of June 2004, and classified those who have finished regular education and try to enter the labor market as the most disadvantaged in employment group. Jae-Ryang Nam (2006) and Min-Hong Oh (2007) recognized that the main characteristics of NEET was their unwillingness to work, but still broke down NEET into the jobseeker NEET (the unemployed who are willing to work and engaged in job-seeking activities) and the non-jobseeker NEET (inactive population who are not engaged in job-seeking activities). They reported that jobseeker NEET responded to economic cycles and that non-jobseeker NEET were less sensitive to economic cycles and grew in size. In Korea, men, high school graduates or those in their twenties rather than in teens take a greater share in non-jobseeker NEET. NEET in Korea is classified into jobseeker NEET who express a desire to be employed and are engaged in job-seeking activities, and non-jobseeker NEET. In Korea unlike other countries, there is a higher percentage of NEET who prepare for government official exams for an extended period of time or who are engaged in family labor, paid or unpaid. These have to be taken into account in adjusting the definition of NEET that genuinely reflects the trend of the labor market in Korea.

III Data sets

For college and university graduates, this study collected quantitative information using the *Graduates Occupational Mobility Survey* (GOMS) conducted by the Korea Employment Information Service and an additional survey for a qualitative cause and effect analysis on youth unemployment and youth NEET. For those with high school diploma, quantitative data in GOMS was used in conjunction with Sungkyunkwan University's (SKKU) YES (*Youth Employment Survey for High School Graduates*) data to build a data set that allows for comparison by the type of group (*Youth Works Survey*).

Table 8.1 illustrates the subdivisions of schools, number of graduates, employment rate, employment rate by big companies, and average monthly income used in the analysis. The high schools have been divided into academic and vocational schools, and the universities into liberal arts, social studies, education, engineering, natural science, medical, and art and sports majors. Each of the subdivision data for the number of graduates, employment rate, employment rate by big companies, average monthly income are shown. The number of graduates in each subdivision recorded in August 2004 and February 2005, shows 228,336 for colleges and 268,833 for universities. The average employment rate for colleges was 82.8 percent while the rate was 77.0 percent for universities. The employment rate by big companies (with a scale of 300 or more employees) was 17.5 percent for colleges and 27.4 percent for universities, showing that unlike the average employment rate, universities had a 10 percentage point higher employment rate by big companies than colleges. The table shows that the employment rate by big companies is much lower than the average employment rate. The table also shows that the medical and engineering majors in both colleges and universities had high employment rates overall by big companies. Even though the employment rate by major companies is overall very low, most of the college or university graduates are waiting to enter big companies.

IV NEET and unemployment rate of high school graduates

This section compares and evaluates unemployment rates of the jobseeker NEET, non-jobseeker NEET, total NEET for graduates from different types of schools. Before discussing the main body, the definition of each statistics must

Table 8.1 The subdivision of schools, colleges and universities

Division of school	Major	Specific major	1	2	3	4
High school	Academic	Liberal arts, foreign language, science	—	—	—	—
	Vocational	Art and physical education, commercial, technical	—	—	—	—
College	Liberal arts	Japanese language, English language, library and information	12,159	72.9	19.2	152.7
	Social	Business administration, economics, law	54,576	82.7	17.9	165.6
	Education	Early childhood education, special education	10,226	85.2	3.6	121.9
	Engineering	Heating, ventilating and air conditioning, electric	74,349	84.2	20.8	168.7
	Natural science	Agriculture and fisheries, biology	17,177	82.1	14.7	151.9
	Medical	Nursing, healthcare, rehabilitation	21,515	88.7	26.8	151.5
	Art and sports	Industrial design	38,334	79.4	9.3	143.7
	Total		228,336	82.8	17.5	158.0
University	Liberal arts	Language studies, library and information, religious studies	39,258	74.4	21.1	157.1
	Social studies	Economics, law, sociology	69,926	79.4	27.7	189.9
	Education	Educational studies, language education	14,632	72.3	7.3	170.1
	Engineering	Heating, ventilating and air conditioning, automotive engineering, advanced materials engineering	69,419	77.9	39.5	201.5
	Natural science	Agriculture, environment, mathematics	36,441	68.1	23.7	159.5
	Medical	Medical, nursing, rehabilitation	12,466	87.5	41.9	220.4
	Art and sports	Industrial design, applied art	26,691	82.5	12.1	145.2
	Total		268,833	77.0	27.4	180.5

Source: Korea Employment Information Service.

Notes
1 The number of graduates.
2 Employment rate.
3 Employment rate by big companies (300+).
4 Average monthly income (10,000 won).

be clarified. First, the jobseeker NEET rate has been calculated by combining the family labor NEET (type A) and youth unemployment NEET (type B). Among the people who are working unpaid for family for 18 hours or less, family labor NEET includes unpaid workers seeking employment and those looking for jobs while engaged in housework such as child rearing. The NEET rate is defined by the NEET population rate of each cohort. The youth unemployment NEET refers to the traditional youth unemployment concept of youth ranging from 15 to 29.

The non-jobseeker NEET rate has been calculated by combining the "trap" NEET (type C), which includes those who do not seek jobs but study for government official exams or public enterprises by attending preparatory schools, institutions or by studying alone; the "escaping from reality" NEET (type D), defined as non-jobseekers who are not engaged in any social activity. They include those who answered in the survey as the following:

- There seems to be no adequate job for my major or career record,
- There seem to be no jobs with the income or working conditions I want,
- There seem to be no jobs nearby,
- I don't have the education, skills, or experience,
- The employer will think that I am too young or too old,
- I sought employment before but could not find one.

This is the Japanese type NEET concept that does not include leave of absence, waiting for an appointment, preparing for school entrance, suffering from physical and mental fatigue, waiting to serve military duty, and preparing for marriage etc. The NEET rate was calculated by combining both the jobseeker and non-jobseeker NEET, and the unemployment rate is the same concept as the youth unemployment NEET among jobseeker NEET.

Table 8.2 illustrates the subdivisions of high school and NEET rate and youth unemployment rate. The overall high school graduate NEET rate was 23.01 percent which was over 2.5 times that of the 9.03 percent unemployment rate. Among high school graduate jobseekers, the NEET for academic high schools was 0.11 percentage point higher than the vocational high schools. Among non-jobseekers the NEET rate for academic high schools was 6.55 percentage points higher than for vocational high schools. The academic non-jobseeker NEET rate (25.47 percent) was higher than the vocational non-jobseeker NEET rate (19.07 percent).

Table 8.2 Estimate of NEET and youth unemployment rate of subdivision of high schools (%)

Subdivision	Major	Job-seeker NEET	Non-job-seeker NEET	NEET	Unemployment
High school	Academic	9.51	16.22	25.74	8.94
	Vocational	9.40	9.67	19.07	9.15
	All	9.47	13.74	23.01	9.03

By contrast, academic high schools recorded 8.94 percent in the unemployment rate while vocational high schools recorded 9.15 percent. In other words, the academic high school graduate unemployment rate, when considering the relatively high NEET rate, does not adequately reflect the unemployment problem of academic high school youth. Most of the academic high school youth NEET consist of non-jobseeker NEETs. In the case of academic high school graduates, the rate of non-jobseeker NEET is at least 1.5 times that of jobseeker NEETS. This means that many of the academic high school graduates who did not enter college have become "trap" NEETS or "escaping from reality" NEETs. Perhaps giving academic high school students greater options to transfer to vocational high schools or for vocational training or acquirement of certificates could reduce these problems.

In the case of vocational colleges, it is easy to acquire an industrial worker certificate that is acknowledged in the market, but in the case of vocational high school graduates, the certificates and work skills that they acquire are not as effective in the market. Vocational high schools were modeled after Germany's dual system where students study at technical high school for two years then get on-site experience for one year, thereby providing cheap labor for one year, but the rate that they turn into regular workers is low, which exacerbates the NEET phenomena shown in the above table. The dual system of vocational high schools is not functioning according to its original purpose, with the company strongly viewing these graduates as free-lunch eaters or disposable workforce. Vocational high school interns, on their part, start to form an aversion to SMEs after they have experienced working in an SME. Such phenomenon is reflected in the high non-jobseeker NEET rate of vocational high school graduates.

V NEET and unemployment rate of vocational college and university graduates

In order to estimate the NEET and youth unemployment rate of university graduates, the GOMS (*Graduates Occupational Mobility Survey*) was used to calculate the NEET and youth unemployment rate of each major in both vocational colleges and universities. The NEET rate of vocational college graduates was 12.58 percent and 13.91 percent for university graduates, which was lower than the high school graduate NEET rate of 23.01 percent. The youth employment rate of vocational college graduates and university graduates was 5.49 percent and 4.54 percent respectively which was lower than the 9.03 percent of high school graduate unemployment rate.

Regarding the rate of jobseeker NEET and non-jobseeker NEET, in the case of high school graduates, the non-jobseeker NEET rate was 13.74 percent and the jobseeker NEET rate was 9.47 percent. The gap between vocational college graduate jobseeker and non-job seeker NEET was also not very big, but in the case of university graduates, the non-job seeker NEET rate, which was relatively high at 9.25 percent, and the jobseeker NEET rate was around twice that of the non-jobseeker NEET rate, which was relatively higher compared to high school graduates and vocational graduates.

Disaggregating the jobseeker NEET rate, we find that the vocational college graduate NEET is 5.74 percent, which exceeds the university graduate NEET rate of 4.66 percent. The non-jobseeker NEET rate was 6.84 percent for college graduates and 9.25 percent for university graduates. This implies that there were more vocational college graduate jobseeker NEETs than university graduates, but it was the other way around for non-jobseeker NEETS. Also, concerning the overall NEET rate, vocational colleges recorded 12.58 percent and universities 13.91 percent. Considering the fact that the unemployment rate of college graduates was 5.49 percent while the number of university graduates was 4.54 percent, the underlying problem of youth unemployment among college and university graduates is much bigger, the problem being more severe for university graduates.

The high non-jobseeker NEET rate among university graduates indicates that there are many people preparing for government official exams and public enterprises, and also many "escaping from reality" NEETs. Those people are not seeking jobs and therefore are not included in the economically active population, and thus not reflected in the unemployment rate. In the case of people preparing for government official exams or public enterprises, if their status is maintained for a long time, they will miss the appropriate age opportunity to find jobs and can turn into "escaping from reality" NEETs more than others. So in their case, the possibility that they might remain part of the NEET population is high.

Table 8.3 Estimate of NEET and youth unemployment rate of vocational college and university/major (%)

Division of school	Major	Job-seeker NEET	Non-job-seeker NEET	NEET	Unemployment
College	Liberal arts	6.69	8.05	14.74	6.69
	Social	5.97	7.76	13.73	5.80
	Education	1.66	4.47	6.13	1.29
	Engineering	6.13	6.89	13.02	5.83
	Natural science	6.82	7.13	13.95	6.22
	Medical	2.99	5.27	8.26	2.29
	Art and sports	6.82	6.69	13.51	6.34
	Total	5.74	6.84	12.58	5.49
University	Liberal arts	5.20	10.45	15.65	4.99
	Social	4.82	12.02	16.84	4.72
	Education	3.19	14.15	17.34	2.99
	Engineering	4.50	6.47	10.97	4.38
	Natural science	6.14	9.03	15.17	6.05
	Medical	1.55	4.30	5.85	1.40
	Art and sports	4.28	6.54	10.82	4.20
	Total	4.66	9.25	13.91	4.54

VI Conclusion

Taking into account NEETs, the youth jobless problem is more serious than indicated in the unemployment data. This chapter has used GOMS for vocational college and university graduates and a separate survey for high school graduates, in order to analyze Korea's youth employment and youth NEET phenomena, and the causes behind them. In the case of high school graduates, quantitative data in GOMS was used in conjunction with survey (SKKU YES) data to establish three comparable data for each group.

The overall high school graduate NEET rate was 23.01 percent, which was greater than 2.5 times that of the 9.03 percent unemployment rate. The overall NEET rate was 12.58 percent for college graduates and 13.91 percent for university graduates, which was lower than the 23.01 percent of the high school graduate NEET rate. The youth unemployment rate of vocational college and university graduates were 5.49 percent and 4.54 percent which was lower than the 9.03 percent of high school unemployment rate. In the case of academic high schools, the higher non-jobseeker NEET rate could be caused by the lack of information and training, and absence of psychological counseling service. High school graduates might have relatively higher stress levels because of their young age, the psychological vacuum of having to face the workforce market. Therefore, customized design of psychological services is needed for the selection and concentration of counseling given to individuals because different grades have different group psychologies. Also, allowing the transfer of academic high school students who have given up on their plans to enter college to vocational schools and introducing vocational training programs may be a good solution to prevent these graduates from joining the NEET ranks.

In the case of academic high school, graduates join the labor market without any specific ability, which means that psychological counseling and vocational training as well as information on finding employment must be provided at the same time to prevent students from joining the NEET population. Students need an institutional design that allows them to develop the career they want early on. This will be made possible through the strengthening of training and information provision given to students from the time they enter academic high schools, or by keeping a separate track, or having a transfer system between academic and vocational high schools. On the other hand, the NEET rate of vocational high school graduates shows an overall failure, calling for a fundamental reform of the vocation high school. Current vocational high school plays a larger role as a stepping stone to enter college rather than fostering skilled workers and although they are supposed to have a program that helps graduates find jobs, their support is hardware-centered, and does not provide the help that vocational high schools were designed for.

However, in the case of vocational college and university graduates, when looking at the overall NEET rate, vocational colleges recorded 12.58 percent and universities 13.91 percent. When considering that the unemployment rate was 5.49 percent for vocational college graduates and 4.54 percent for universities, it can be inferred that vocational college and university graduate youth unemployment is an especially big problem that has not been uncovered yet, and that the problem was more serious in universities. The fact that the university graduate non-jobseeker NEET rate is high, shows that the factors composing it, i.e., people who prepare for government official exams or public enterprises, and "escaping from ability" NEET are numerous. Among university graduates, education, social studies, and liberal arts majors had the highest NEET rate in the said order. In the case of liberal arts graduates, they have a harder time than other majors in finding employment, not to mention there are government policies for stipends and scholarships for when they continue on to graduate schools, so many university graduates give up their search for employment and extend their education. In this case, if the graduate schools are serving as a hideout from the labor market for liberal arts graduates, then it might exacerbate the problem and make them into lifelong NEETS, so support for graduate schools and the number limit of students should be considered from the employment aspect. In the case of education majors, the only characteristic found was that they prepared for teacher certification examinations. Engineering, natural science, medical, art and sports majors were similar to liberal arts majors in that graduates decided to further their education, and their graduate schools had the problem of serving as a hideouts from the labor market.

In order to resolve the severe youth NEET problem, government policies such as establishing customized youth support, enhancing the efficient management of employment service infrastructure, expanding investment on employment services, reestablishing the function of vocational high schools and colleges etc, should be put in place to create jobs that youth want and so encourages youth to actively seek jobs.

Notes

1 OECD defines youth unemployment based on the age between 15 and 24. However, in Korea the population aged between 25 and 29 should be included since the majority of male college graduates who are unemployed after completing military services fall into the age bracket. In this study, youth unemployment should be defined on a basis of age between 15 and 29.

2 Youth unemployment (age between 15–29), having peaked at 12.2 percent in 1998 immediately after the financial crisis, decreased and recorded 6.6 percent in 2002, which was close to the level of 5.7 percent recorded in 1997 prior to the financial crisis. The economic recession that began in 2003 pushed the youth unemployment rate upward to 7.9 percent in 2004 and the number of the unemployed to 390,000. The youth disadvantaged numbers a whopping 700,000 if those in preparation for employment are included. This is translated that 14 percent of the total youth are faced with difficulties in finding a job. Cross-country comparison reveals that Korea's youth unemployment rate, which is 2.7 times higher than the total unemployment rate, is over 1.9 times the OECD average.

3 The labor economic white paper released by the Ministry of Health, Labor and Welfare of Japan defines youth NEET as inactive population (not reported as being employed or unemployed) aged between 15 and 34, who already finished schools, are single, and are neither engaged in housework nor commuting to school. However, the research arm

of the Cabinet Office defines youth NEET as those who "do not commute to regular schools including high schools and colleges, college entrance exam prep schools, or trade schools, are single without a partner, and are aged between 15 and 34 without regular income." According to Ki-Hun Kim (2005), the white paper excludes housework completely, but the Cabinet Office's research body on youth employment recommends that women who are not employed, single and taking care of housework should be included. The former reported that there are 520,000 young persons who were NEET in 2003; the latter estimated youth NEET at 850,000, which stands for 6.3 percent of the age group in 2002.

References

Arcidiacono, P., "Ability Sorting and the Returns to College Major," *Journal of Econometrics*, 121(1–2) 2004, pp. 343–375.

Becker, G.S., *Human Capital: A Theoretical and Empirical Analysis with Special Reference to Education*, Chicago, IL: University of Chicago Press, 1975.

Blau, P.M. and Duncan, O.D., *The American Occupational Structure*, NY: Wiley, 1967.

Byung-Hee, Lee, "The Structure Change of Youth Labor Market," Korea Labor Institute, 2004.

Ellwood, D.T., "Teenage Unemployment: Permanent Scars or Temporary Blemishes?," in Freeman, R.B. and Wise, D.A.(eds.), *The Youth Labor Market Problem: Its Nature, Causes, and Consequences*, Chicago, IL: University of Chicago Press, 1982.

Goo-Mook, Chai, "An Analysis of the Realities and Causes of Youth and New College Graduate Unemployment," *Korean Journal of Social Welfare*, 56(3) 2004, pp. 159–181.

Hwang, Yeo-jung and Byoung-bu Baek, "Determinants of Employment Status of University Graduates Youth," *Vocation Development Review*, 11(2) 2008, pp. 1–23.

Keane, Michael P. and Wolpin, Kenneth I., "The Career Decisions of Young Men," *Journal of Political Economy*, 105(3) 1997, pp. 473–522.

Keum, Jae-Ho, Cho, Joonmo and Young-il, Jeon, *An Empirical Evaluation on Korean NEET: Categorizing Various Cohorts of Korean NEET*, Korea: Ministry of Employment and Labor, 2007.

Lee, Bu-Hyung, "Increase the 'NEET' in Korea," Hyundai Research Institute, 2005.

Nam, Jae-Ryang, "The Determinant of Youth NEET," Eighth Korean Labor Income and Panel Study Conference, Korea Labor Institute, 2006.

OECD, *Education at a Glance*, Paris: OECD, 2006.

Oh, Min-Hong, "Young People Not in Education, Employment, or Training in Korea," Korea Employment Information Service, 2007.

Rees, Albert, "An Essay on Youth Joblessness," *Journal of Economic Literature*, 24(2) 1986, pp. 613–628.

Social Exclusion Unit, *Bridging the Gap: New Opportunities for 16–18 Year Olds Not in Education, Employment, or Training*, 1999.

9 The relationship between research performance and teaching outcome

Evidence from higher education in South Korea

Cheolsung Park and Young Lee

I Introduction

Korea achieved very rapid expansion of university education over the past 30 years, and now 82 percent of high school graduates enter universities and colleges. This rapid increase in the number of students has increased the unemployment rate of university graduates. In the meantime, universities in Korea and the government place stronger emphasis on research completed by faculties, and provide various incentives for research. Strong emphasis on research is commonly observed in most of the high ranked universities in the world. Does emphasis on research help or hinder labor market performance of students?

The relationship between the faculty research output and the teaching outcome in higher education has attracted much interest. The relationship is theoretically ambiguous. Hattie and Marsh (1996) outline the theories by education researchers that can lead to a negative, a positive, or an independent relationship between the two. For example, a negative relationship can arise since the two activities compete for the faculty member's limited time, while a positive relationship can arise since the abilities underlying the success of the two activities is similar. Thus the direction and the size of the relationship should be studied empirically. Hattie and Marsh (1996) survey empirical studies of the relationship and conduct a meta analysis of the correlations between research outcomes such as the number of publications, citations, or grants and teaching effectiveness, mostly measured by student evaluations published in 58 studies in education. They find that the weighted average of the correlations is slightly positive, about 0.06 and conclude that the relationship is zero. In a follow-up study, Marsh and Hattie (2002) reach the same conclusion using data from a university in Australia.

Most of these studies are, however, based on small samples and measure the teaching outcome by subjective student or peer evaluations that may have only a tenuous link to the labor market performance of graduates. To overcome the limits of the previous studies, in this chapter we use a large sample that covers the high education sector for the entire country and measure the teaching outcome by objective measures of success: (a) the proportion of graduates who have secured a regular full-time job, or (b) who advance into post-graduate study. These two measures are likely to be more directly related to the human capital augmented by higher education than the subjective student evaluations.

We find that the raw association between the faculty research output and student achievements in the labor market or advance into post-graduate studies is strongly positive and statistically significant, but that the association is explained mostly by departmental characteristics, student quality and university fixed effects. Given these factors, the association between the research output and the percentage of the graduates who have found regular employment becomes almost zero and statistically insignificant. The association between the research output and the percentage of graduates pursuing post-graduate study is also reduced after those factors are controlled for, but in the sciences and engineering sector it is still statistically significant.

The rest of this chapter is organized as follows. In Section II we provide an overview of the university system in Korea and the employment performance of university graduates. In Section III we discuss the model and explain the data used in this study. In Section IV we present the estimation results. In Section V we summarize the findings and conclude the chapter.

II Overview of the university system in Korea

Korea achieved an unprecedented rapid expansion of tertiary education in the 30 years from 1980 through 2010. The number of university and college students more than quintupled from 650,000 in 1980, to 3,600,000 in 2009. As of 2009, the entrance ratio of high school students to colleges and universities was 82 percent, which is the highest rate in the world. The corresponding figure for the United States is 69 percent, for Japan 68 percent, and for Germany 43 percent. The introduction of the graduation quota system in the early 1980s and the deregulation of establishment of universities in the mid-1990s greatly increased the number of university students.

In Korea, private colleges/universities play a significant role in education and research. Private colleges/universities educate three-quarters of students and carry out around half of government supported research. However, government subsidies for education at private universities, and government scholarships and student loans have been very small. As a result, private universities are heavily dependent on tuition for their revenue and some face financial difficulties. There

Table 9.1 Students and teachers in universities/colleges of Korea, 1980–2009

	1980	*1990*	*2000*	*2005*	*2007*	*2009*
Number of schools	237	265	372	419	408	407
Number of students	647,505	1,691,681	3,363,549	3,548,728	3,558,711	3,591,088
Number of teachers	20,662	42,911	56,903	66,862	70,957	75,469

Source: Korea Education Development Institute.

is near consensus as to the need for expansion of government finance for universities, but the form of government support has been controversial. In early 2010 the Korean government introduced income-contingent loans for university students, which require a very large amount of government subsidies. The Korean government also increased research grants to researchers in universities. Though not as large as student loans or research grants, the government offers various institutional-level and program-level financial support to universities.

The rapid expansion of tertiary education in Korea was mainly financed by private expenditure. More than half of the expenditure of Korean private universities comes from tuition fees, while the comparable figure for the United States is less than 20 percent. Compared to universities in advanced countries, the financing sources for the Korean universities are less diversified.

As the number of university students increased, the problem of youth unemployment became severe. In 2005, the unemployment rate of those aged 15–24 in Korea was 10.2 percent which is almost three times as large as the overall unemployment rate at 3.7 percent. The youth unemployment rate in Korea is lower than that in European countries but higher than that in Japan and Singapore.

Now more and more students advanced to graduate schools. The number of new PhDs from Korean universities increased from 513 in 1980 to 9,912 in 2009. The research performance of universities in Korea also improved. The number of publications increased from 21,000 in 2003 to 35,500 in 2008. The rapid improvement of research performance was due to strong financial support from the Korean government and emphasis on research performance in personnel management for faculties.

III Model and data

We are interested in estimating the relationship between the research output of the faculty members and achievement (e.g., employment) of the students taught by the faculty. We assume that the achievement of student i studying for a degree in department j of university k is determined as follows:

$$y_{ijk} = \beta_0 + \beta_1 r_{jk} + \alpha_k + \delta_j + \gamma_{jk} + \eta_{gk} + u_{ijk}$$

where r_{jk} is the department faculty members' research output, α_k is the university characteristics, δ_j is the departmental characteristics, γ_{jk} is the faculty members'

Table 9.2 Research performance of universities in Korea

	2003	2004	2005	2006	2007	2008
Number of publications	21,107	22,674	27,797	28,316	27,284	35,569
World ranking	14	12	11	11	12	12

Notes
Ranking in 2008: first United States (340,638); second China (112,804); third United Kingdom (91,273); fourth Germany (87,424).

characteristics other than the research output, η_{ijk} is the student's characteristics, and u_{ijk} is the error term with zero conditional mean. It should be noted that δ_j is the characteristics of the department or the major that are common across different universities such as the labor market condition for those graduated with a degree in the same major.

Since we have data only at the department level, we consider the model aggregated at the departmental level. By taking the means at the department level, we get

$$y_{ijk} = \beta_0 + \beta_1 r_{jk} + \alpha_k + \delta_j + \gamma_{jk} + \eta_{gk} + u_{ijk}$$

Our aim is to estimate the coefficient β_1 in the equation. To estimate β_1 consistently we have to deal with the correlations between the research output and the characteristics of the university, the department, the faculty members, and the student. We control for the university characteristics by treating it as the fixed effect and estimate the model using the "within" variations. Department dummies control for the departmental characteristics that are likely to produce different outcomes. The size and the composition of the faculty control for faculty characteristics. The average SAT score by the students is included to control for the student characteristics that are likely to be correlated with the faculty members' research output.

We use the data posted on the University Information Web (UIW).[1] Since 2008 all the primary, secondary, and post-secondary educational institutions in South Korea, except for some exempted by national security reasons, are required by law to submit information and statistics regarding the rules of the institution, students, facilities, teaching staff, financial status, and the like to be shared with the public through the Internet. Visitors to the website can search for a specific piece of information for one institution or compare it across different institutions, as well as view some overall performance indexes for each institution. The website is managed by the Korean Educational Development Institute (KEDI) under the supervision of the Ministry of Education, Science and Technology. We use the data for years 2008 and 2009 provided to us by the KEDI.

We limit the sample to the undergraduate departments of universities only. Departments in medicine, performing and fine arts and sports are excluded from the sample, since the career paths of the graduates from those departments are likely to differ greatly from those of the graduates in the other fields. The faculty members' research outputs are measured by the average number of papers per full-time faculty member published in international journals listed in international research indexes such as the Science Citation Index (SCI), the SCI Expanded, and the Social Science Citation index (SSCI), the Arts and Humanities Citation Index (A&HCI), and the Scopus printed in the previous year.[2] For convenience we call the variable "per capita SCI publication."

We measure student achievements using the statistics of employment and post-graduate study of those who graduated in August in the previous year or in February in the current year. The universities report statistics as of April 1 each year. We use two outcome measures: the net regular employment rate and the net post-graduate study rate. If an individual is gainfully employed and works for 18 hours or more in a week, he or she is considered to have regular employment. The net regular employment rate refers to the percentage of graduates with regular employment among the graduates, excluding foreign nationals and those pursuing a post-graduate or a second degree, serving in military, emigrated, deceased, institutionalized or disabled. The net post-graduate study rate is the percentage of graduates pursuing a post-graduate or second degree, excluding foreign nationals and those serving in military, emigrated, deceased, institutionalized or disabled.

We also control for the number of male graduates, the number of female graduates, the numbers of tenured professors (full professors) and non-tenured professors (associate professors, assistant professors, and the full-time lecturers), and the first-year tuition fee. We distinguish the graduates by gender, because the labor market conditions faced by men are likely to differ from those faced by women. We separate the tenured professors from the non-tenured professors because the two groups are likely to differ in experience in and motivation for teaching and research. The tuition fee is included because it is likely to be positively correlated with the educational expenses spent for the students.

We use the data of the average SAT scores collected by a private institution providing a university counseling service. We use the scores of the cohorts admitted in 2003 for both 2008 and 2009. The cohorts admitted in 2003 roughly match the graduates in 2007 and 2008. Furthermore, the average SAT scores are not likely to change much from one cohort to the next. The average SAT score data set is merged with the UIW data set based on the names of the departments. Due to changes over time in the structure of some universities and incompleteness of the SAT score data, the matches are not perfect. The numbers of successful matches are 2,536 out of 3,452 departments in the UIW 2008 data set and 2,185 out of 2,868 departments in the UIW 2009 data set.

Table 9.3 shows the sample means and the standard deviations of the variables. The statistics are shown for the entire sample and separately for humanities and social sciences and for sciences and engineering. The average net regular employment rate is 45 percent in 2009 and 39 percent in 2008, while the net post-graduate study rate is 10 percent in 2008 and 11 percent in 2009 across all departments. Both rates are much higher in the sciences and engineering field than in humanities and social sciences field. The per capita SCI publication is based on a weighted average of papers that gives greater weight to single-authored or corresponding authored papers than for being a co-author in another position on a multi-authored paper. The per capita SCI publication has increased slightly from 0.15 per faculty member in 2008 to 0.18 in 2009. There is a substantial difference in the number of SCI publications between the two fields.

The average number of graduates is about 47 in 2008 and 45 in 2009. While the gender ratios of the graduates differ substantially between the fields, the average numbers of the graduates do not. The number of tenured professors is about 4.5 and the number of untenured professors about 3.5 in both years. The

Table 9.3 The sample means of the variables

	All fields	Humanities and social sciences	Sciences and engineering
(I) 2008			
Net regular employment rate	45.3[a] (22.7)	40.4[a] (21.2)	51.9 (23.0)
Net post-graduate study rate	9.9 (12.0)	7.6 (9.8)	12.9 (13.9)
Per capita SCI publication	0.15 (0.35)	0.02 (0.08)	0.33 (0.48)
Number of male graduates	24.3 (35.8)	19.3 (28.6)	31.1 (42.7)
Number of female graduates	22.9 (20.8)	27.4 (22.3)	16.9 (16.7)
Number of tenured professors	4.5 (4.7)	4.0 (3.8)	5.2 (5.7)
Number of untenured professors	3.6 (3.7)	3.6 (4.1)	3.5 (3.2)
Tuition (million won)	5.8 (2.4)	5.4 (2.0)	6.4 (2.8)
Average SAT score	256.9 (56.9)	262.8 (54.6)	249.1 (59.0)
Number of observations	2,536	1,452	1,084
(II) 2009			
Net regular employment rate	38.6[a] (22.4)	33.3 (19.9)	44.8[a] (23.5)
Net post-graduate study rate	10.9 (13.0)	7.8 (10.3)	14.4 (14.8)
Per capita SCI publication	0.18 (0.39)	0.02 (0.08)	0.36 (0.51)
Number of male graduates	23.8 (34.6)	19.1 (28.1)	29.3 (40.3)
Number of female graduates	21.4 (18.6)	25.3 (19.7)	16.9 (16.2)
Number of tenured professors	4.4 (4.7)	3.8 (3.5)	5.2 (5.6)
Number of untenured professors	3.3 (3.3)	3.3 (3.5)	3.3 (3.1)
Tuition (million won)	5.7 (2.6)	5.3 (2.1)	6.1 (3.0)
Average SAT score	259.3 (58.3)	266.1 (54.9)	251.3 (61.0)
Number of observations	2,185	1,174	1,011

Notes
The sample standard deviations are in parentheses.
a The statistics are computed with one missing observation.

departments in sciences and engineering retain about one more tenured professor on average than the departments in humanities and social sciences. The average first-year tuition fee is about six million won and the average SAT score is about 260. Although the average SAT score is lower in the sciences and engineering field than in the humanities and social sciences field, the scores are not comparable between the fields since the subjects taken by the applicants usually differ substantially by the field of their choice.

Figure 9.1 shows XY-scatter diagrams between the per capita SCI publication of the faculty members and the two measures of student achievements: the net regular employment rate and the net post-graduate study rate, for year 2008 for all fields of study. The two charts show that the two measures are strongly positively correlated with the number of publications by the faculty. The slopes of the fitted lines are 7.3 (robust s.e. = 1.27) and 15.1 (robust s.e. = 0.98) in charts (A) and (B) respectively.

Figure 9.2 shows the same charts for humanities and social sciences in the left and science and engineering in the right. In humanities and social sciences the net regular employment rate of the graduates is strongly and positively correlated with the faculty's research output; but in science and engineering not so.

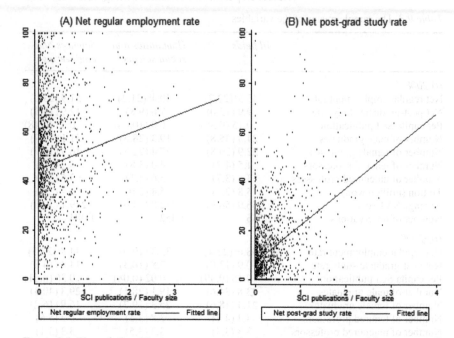

Figure 9.1 The relationship between research output and students' achievements, all fields, 2008.

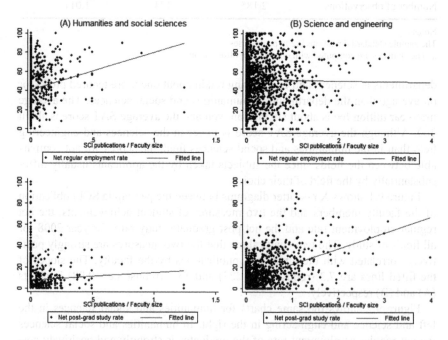

Figure 9.2 The relationship between the research output and the students' achievements, by fields, 2008.

In science and engineering the net regular post-graduate study rate of the graduates is strongly and positively correlated with the faculty's research output; but in humanities and social sciences far less so.

The charts of Figures 9.1 and 9.2 suggest a strong relationship between the faculty's research output and the incidences of the students' employment or advancement to further studies, but the simple correlations may be biased due to the effect of other variables on both research and student performance.

Such correlations are strong. Table 9.4 shows the pairwise sample correlations among the net regular employment rate, the net post-graduate study rate, the per capita SCI publication of the faculty, and the average SAT score of the students separately by the field. All correlations are positive and mostly significant. The average SAT score is strongly correlated with the outcomes and the number of SCI publications. The correlations between the SCI publications and the student outcomes in Figures 9.1 and 9.2 are thus likely to be explained partly, if not entirely, by the positive correlation between the research output of the faculty and the quality of the students. Disentangling the effect of student quality from the effect of the faculty research output on the student outcome is the task we undertake in the next section.

IV Estimation results

We estimate the coefficient of the faculty research output, or per capita SCI publication under four specifications labeled A, B, C, and D with an increasing number of control variables. Under the simplest specification A, the student outcome variable is regressed only on the research output variable and the constant to estimate the degree of raw association between the two variables. Specification B includes measures for the salient departmental characteristics such as

Table 9.4 Pairwise sample correlations and their *p*-values, humanities and social sciences in the lower triangle and sciences and engineering in the upper triangle

	Net regular employment rate	Net post-graduate study rate	Per capita SCI publication	Average SAT score
(I) 2008				
Net regular employment rate		0.01 (0.733)	0.01 (0.76)	0.13 (0.000)
Net post-graduate study rate	0.12 (0.000)		0.50 (0.000)	0.38 (0.000)
Per capita SCI publication	0.18 (0.000)	0.07 (0.006)		0.36 (0.000)
Average SAT score	0.01 (0.661)	0.25 (0.000)	0.19 (0.000)	
(II) 2009				
Net regular employment rate		0.07 (0.02)	0.07 (0.03)	0.20 (0.000)
Net post-graduate study rate	0.16 (0.000)		0.56 (0.000)	0.43 (0.000)
Per capita SCI publication	0.17 (0.000)	0.11 (0.000)		0.36 (0.000)
Average SAT score	0.18 (0.00)	0.30 (0.000)	0.25 (0.000)	

Note
The *p*-values are in parentheses.

the number of graduates by gender, the numbers of tenured and non-tenured professors, the first-year tuition fee, and the department dummies. Specification C
augments specification B with the average SAT score of the students admitted in
2003 and its square. Specification D additionally controls for the university fixed
effect. If a university has more than one campus in different areas, each campus
is treated as if it is an independent university.

Tables 9.5 and 9.6 show the estimation results using the data of all departments for 2008 and 2009 respectively. The tables have two panels and four
columns in each panel. Panel (I) shows the results for the net regular employment rate and panel (II) for the net post-graduate study rate. The four columns
correspond to the four specifications used for estimation.

The estimation results in column (A) indicate that the faculty's research
output is positively and significantly associated with the net regular employment
rate and the advance rate to graduate study. In 2008 an increase of the per capita
SCI publication by one standard deviation ($\cong 0.35$) is associated with an increase
of the net regular employment rate by 3 percentage points or one-eighth of the
standard deviation. An increase of the per capita SCI publication by one standard
deviation is also associated with an increase of the net post-graduate study rate

Table 9.5 Estimation results, all fields, 2008

	(A)	(B)	(C)	(D)
(I) Dependent variable: net regular employment rate (n = 2,535)				
Per capita SCI publication	8.70 (6.15)	4.10 (2.53)	0.38 (0.25)	0.67 (0.42)
No of male graduates		0.04 (2.62)	0.05 (3.39)	0.03 (1.11)
No of female graduates		−0.07 (3.21)	−0.06 (2.74)	−0.09 (3.42)
No of tenured professors		0.20 (1.58)	−0.11 (0.89)	−0.05 (0.30)
No of untenured professors		0.43 (3.28)	0.14 (1.09)	0.12 (0.90)
Tuition		0.56 (3.62)	0.45 (3.01)	−0.17 (0.67)
Average SAT score			−0.51 (8.19)	−0.20 (2.09)
Average SAT score squared			0.001 (9.29)	0.00 (2.21)
R^2	0.02	0.40	0.44	0.41
(II) Dependent variable: net post-graduate study rate (n = 2,536)				
Per capita SCI publication	14.76 (13.97)	9.51 (9.05)	6.58 (6.98)	6.04 (5.97)
No of male graduates		−0.05 (4.56)	−0.04 (4.08)	−0.03 (2.33)
No of female graduates		−0.03 (2.32)	−0.03 (3.27)	−0.03 (2.00)
No of tenured professors		0.54 (6.04)	0.32 (4.07)	0.17 (1.63)
No of untenured professors		0.37 (4.48)	0.17 (2.19)	0.13 (1.98)
Tuition		0.09 (1.08)	0.07 (0.91)	−0.02 (0.13)
Average SAT score			−0.12 (3.69)	0.08 (1.70)
Average SAT score squared			0.0004 (5.23)	−0.0001 (1.42)
R^2	0.19	0.39	0.45	0.34
Department dummies	Not included	Included	Included	Included
University fixed effect	Not controlled	Not controlled	Not controlled	Controlled

Note
The absolute heteroskedasticity-robust t-values are in the parentheses.

Table 9.6 Estimation results, all fields, 2009

	(A)	(B)	(C)	(D)
(I) Dependent variable: net regular employment rate (n = 2,184)				
Per capita SCI publication	9.73 (6.64)	4.92 (2.66)	0.10 (0.06)	−0.09 (0.07)
No of male graduates		0.03 (1.50)	0.05 (2.65)	0.06 (2.75)
No of female graduates		−0.07 (2.44)	−0.06 (2.26)	−0.06 (2.60)
No of tenured professors		0.56 (3.63)	0.11 (0.77)	0.02 (0.14)
No of untenured professors		0.46 (2.90)	0.06 (0.45)	−0.19 (1.41)
Tuition		0.31 (2.08)	0.16 (1.15)	−0.05 (0.23)
Average SAT score			−0.59 (9.07)	−0.22 (2.17)
Average SAT score squared			0.001 (10.71)	0.0005 (2.62)
R^2	0.03	0.43	0.51	0.47
(II) Dependent variable: net post-graduate study rate (n = 2,185)				
Per capita SCI publication	16.66 (13.72)	10.57 (7.84)	7.67 (6.78)	5.63 (6.03)
No of male graduates		−0.08 (5.23)	−0.07 (5.48)	−0.04 (3.00)
No of female graduates		−0.04 (2.73)	−0.05 (3.44)	−0.03 (1.51)
No of tenured professors		0.76 (6.92)	0.49 (5.23)	0.26 (2.17)
No of untenured professors		0.72 (6.15)	0.49 (4.88)	0.30 (3.40)
Tuition		−0.20 (2.15)	−0.26 (3.00)	−0.38 (2.69)
Average SAT score			−0.18 (5.22)	0.05 (1.06)
Average SAT score squared			0.0005 (6.99)	−0.00007 (0.74)
R^2	0.25	0.48	0.55	0.42
Department dummies	Not included	Included	Included	Included
University fixed effect	Not controlled	Not controlled	Not controlled	Controlled

Note
The absolute heteroskedasticity-robust t-values are in the parentheses.

by 5 percentage points or two-fifths of the standard deviation. In 2009 the associations are estimated to be slightly stronger. Judging from R^2 of the regressions, the variation in the per capita SCI publication alone explains surprisingly well the variation in the net post-graduate study rate.

The results in column (A) of Tables 9.5 and 9.6 suggest that the faculty research output is positively correlated with the students' performance in the labor market; the faculty research output has much greater association with the student's choice into post-graduate studies. In column (B) we control for departmental characteristics, and it is clear that a substantial part of the association between the per capita SCI publication and the students' outcome can be explained away by the departmental characteristics. The estimated size of the coefficient of per capita SCI publication is reduced by about one-half in panel (I) and by about one-third in panel (II), although the coefficient is still statistically significant at the 2 percent level.

An increase of the faculty size is associated with an increase of the net regular employment rate and of the net post-graduate study rate. This appears to suggest that an increase of the faculty–student ratio has a positive effect on both student outcomes. An increase of female graduates is estimated to decrease both rates, possibly because some female graduates marry and become homemakers soon after graduation. On the other hand, an increase of the number of male graduates is associated with an increase of the net regular employment rate but with a decrease of the net post-graduate study rate.

The amount of tuition has a positive association with the net regular employment rate, but it is estimated to have an insignificant and even a negative association with the net post-graduate study rate. Since the amount of tuition tends to be positively correlated with the amount of educational expenses spent by the department or university, the latter result is somewhat surprising. We conjecture that it is because some elite national universities in South Korea charge lower tuition than the average and the graduates from those universities are more likely to undertake post-graduate studies than those from other universities.

In column (C) we control further for student quality, by controlling for the average SAT score and its square. Now we find that in panel (I) of both Tables 9.5 and 9.6 the per capita SCI publication no longer has significant association with the net regular employment rate. The size of the coefficient is very close to zero. This implies that the apparently positive correlation between the faculty research output and the graduates' performance in the labor market results from their correlations with departmental characteristics and, most importantly, student quality.

In panel (II) we also find that controlling for student quality decreases the coefficient size of the per capita SCI publication, but not by much. The coefficient size decreases by about one-third from that in column (B), and the coefficient is still statistically significant at the 1 percent level.

With the university fixed effect controlled for in column (D), we find that the estimation results in panel (I) differ only slightly from those in column (C). In panel (II) the coefficient size of the per capita SCI publication coefficients reduces even further, but is still statistically significant at the 1 percent level. The results indicate that, controlling for the departmental characteristics, student quality and the university fixed effect, an increase of the per capita SCI publication by one standard deviation increases the net post-graduate study rate by about 2 percentage points or one-sixth of the standard deviation. It is arguably not a big effect, but the finding indicates that the faculty research activities do have effects on the undergraduate students.

The coefficient estimates of the average SAT score variables in columns (C) and (D) indicate that the score has a U-shaped relationship with the student outcomes. An increase of the score above the sample average increases both rates. It turns out that faculty size has no significant effect on the net regular employment rate once the departmental characteristics and the university fixed effect are controlled for, while the number of graduates still does. On the other hand, faculty size still has positive effects on the net post-graduate study rate in column (D).

Tables 9.7 and 9.8 show the estimation results for humanities and social sciences only. The general pattern of the results across the specifications is similar to that in Tables 9.5 and 9.6. In panel (I) the estimated coefficient of the per

Table 9.7 Estimation results, humanities and social sciences, 2008

	(A)	(B)	(C)	(D)
(I) Dependent variable: net regular employment rate (n = 1,451)				
Per capita SCI publication	49.43 (4.70)	32.37 (3.74)	16.48 (2.79)	14.03 (2.07)
No of male graduates		0.04 (1.53)	0.03 (1.21)	0.02 (0.52)
No of female graduates		−0.04 (1.53)	−0.01 (0.42)	−0.07 (2.20)
No of tenured professors		0.12 (0.65)	−0.31 (1.66)	−0.26 (1.34)
No of untenured professors		0.30 (1.89)	0.05 (0.33)	0.14 (1.02)
Tuition		1.01 (4.13)	1.03 (4.53)	0.40 (1.23)
Average SAT score			−0.71 (7.69)	−0.31 (1.92)
Average SAT score squared			0.002 (8.47)	0.0006 (1.67)
R^2	0.03	0.32	0.38	0.33
(II) Dependent variable: net post-graduate study rate (n = 1,452)				
Per capita SCI publication	9.35 (1.92)	8.34 (2.14)	−0.67 (0.21)	0.56 (0.20)
No of male graduates		−0.04 (3.74)	−0.04 (3.56)	−0.02 (1.15)
No of female graduates		−0.004 (0.32)	−0.004 (0.27)	−0.03 (1.66)
No of tenured professors		0.35 (3.04)	0.08 (0.74)	0.11 (1.08)
No of untenured professors		0.21 (2.28)	0.06 (0.66)	−0.007 (0.10)
Tuition		0.25 (2.09)	0.34 (2.98)	0.04 (0.21)
Average SAT score			−0.17 (3.82)	0.0001 (0.00)
Average SAT score squared			0.0004 (4.82)	−0.00004 (0.33)
R^2	0.005	0.22	0.29	0.20
Department dummies	Not included	Included	Included	Included
University fixed effect	Not controlled	Not controlled	Not controlled	Controlled

Note
The absolute heteroskedasticity-robust t-values are in the parentheses.

capita SCI publication gets smaller as more control variables are added. Unlike the results in Tables 9.5 and 9.6, the coefficient is statistically significant at the 10 percent or the smaller level in column (C), although controlling for student quality reduces the coefficient size substantially. In 2008 we find that the coefficient is still statistically significant at the 5 percent level in the final specification, but in 2009 we find that the coefficient is not significant even at the 10 percent level. The results in panel (II) of Tables 9.7 and 9.8 show that controlling for the departmental characteristics, student quality, and the university characteristics, the faculty research output has no effect on the net post-graduate study rate of the graduates in contrast to the results in Tables 9.5 and 9.6.

The results in Tables 9.7 and 9.8 imply that in humanities and social sciences any relationship between the faculty's research output and the student outcome is explained by their mutual associations with the departmental characteristics, student quality, and the university characteristics. This suggests that the faculty's research activities have little impact on employment or career choice of the undergraduate students in the field.

Tables 9.9 and 9.10 show the estimation results in sciences and engineering. The results in panel (I) indicate that the employment of the graduates has relatively a weak association with the faculty research output in this field. In 2008

Table 9.8 Estimation results, humanities and social sciences, 2009

	(A)	(B)	(C)	(D)
(I) Dependent variable: net regular employment rate (n = 1,174)				
Per capita SCI publication	46.35 (5.33)	31.83 (3.91)	11.36 (1.90)	4.68 (0.89)
No of male graduates		0.03 (1.05)	0.02 (0.77)	0.01 (0.53)
No of female graduates		−0.08 (2.33)	−0.05 (1.65)	−0.05 (1.52)
No of tenured professors		0.83 (4.24)	0.20 (1.07)	0.23 (1.37)
No of untenured professors		0.15 (0.86)	−0.11 (0.77)	−0.18 (1.29)
Tuition		0.92 (3.68)	0.69 (3.10)	0.005 (0.02)
Average SAT score			−0.69 (6.78)	−0.28 (1.57)
Average SAT score squared			0.002 (8.02)	0.0006 (1.81)
R^2	0.03	0.36	0.47	0.40
(II) Dependent variable: net post-graduate study rate (n = 1,174)				
Per capita SCI publication	15.14 (3.43)	14.29 (3.01)	4.22 (0.99)	0.57 (0.21)
No of male graduates		−0.05 (2.55)	−0.05 (3.20)	−0.03 (1.65)
No of female graduates		−0.05 (2.31)	−0.04 (1.91)	−0.03 (1.59)
No of tenured professors		0.67 (4.42)	0.35 (2.60)	0.09 (0.63)
No of untenured professors		0.40 (3.12)	0.27 (2.29)	0.15 (1.52)
Tuition		−0.09 (0.64)	−0.18 (1.37)	−0.46 (2.29)
Average SAT score			−0.27 (4.68)	−0.08 (0.88)
Average SAT score squared			0.0006 (5.70)	0.0002 (0.96)
R^2	0.01	0.33	0.42	0.29
Department dummies	Not included	Included	Included	Included
University fixed effect	Not controlled	Not controlled	Not controlled	Controlled

Note
The absolute heteroskedasticity-robust t-values are in the parentheses.

the per capita SCI publication coefficient is not statistically significant at the 10 percent level under any specification. In 2009 the coefficient is statistically significant at the 5 percent level in columns (A) and (B), but not significant in columns (C) and (D). The results in panel (II) show that the faculty research output has the much stronger association with the net post-graduate study rate than with the net regular employment rate. Furthermore, the coefficient is statistically significant at the 1 percent level under any specification in both years. It implies that the results in panel (II) of Tables 9.5 and 9.6 are mainly driven by the departments in the sciences and engineering field.

We have tested whether the coefficient sizes differ jointly by the field, and the null hypothesis of joint equality is rejected 13 out of 16 times at the 5 percent or the smaller level. The estimation results in this section indicate that the positive association between the faculty research output and the net regular employment rate is mostly, if not entirely, explained by their mutual correlations with the departmental characteristics, the student quality, and the university fixed effect. In particular the student quality, measured by the average SAT score of admitted students in 2003 in this chapter, seems to be the most important factor that determines the outcome.

Table 9.9 Estimation results, sciences and engineering, 2008

	(A)	(B)	(C)	(D)
(I) Dependent variable: net regular employment rate (n = 1,084)				
Per capita SCI publication	0.44 (0.29)	2.61 (1.58)	−0.86 (0.53)	0.29 (0.18)
No of male graduates		0.03 (1.19)	0.04 (1.99)	0.02 (0.77)
No of female graduates		−0.13 (2.84)	−0.12 (2.63)	−0.15 (2.92)
No of tenured professors		0.30 (1.75)	0.06 (0.34)	0.13 (0.55)
No of untenured professors		0.59 (2.43)	0.29 (1.27)	0.34 (1.31)
Tuition		0.21 (1.09)	0.04 (0.22)	−0.35 (0.96)
Average SAT score			−0.30 (3.40)	0.02 (0.12)
Average SAT score squared			0.0007 (4.09)	0.0001 (0.31)
R^2	0.0001	0.44	0.47	0.44
(II) Dependent variable: net post-graduate study rate (n = 1,084)				
Per capita SCI publication	14.40 (12.34)	8.91 (8.27)	4.97 (4.84)	4.72 (4.85)
No of male graduates		−0.07 (3.60)	−0.05 (3.40)	−0.03 (2.47)
No of female graduates		−0.05 (1.80)	−0.06 (2.61)	−0.01 (0.30)
No of tenured professors		0.67 (4.78)	0.41 (3.77)	0.13 (0.97)
No of untenured professors		0.75 (4.20)	0.42 (2.85)	0.49 (3.28)
Tuition		−0.003 (0.02)	−0.15 (1.30)	−0.04 (0.18)
Average SAT score			−0.16 (2.82)	0.10 (1.11)
Average SAT score squared			0.0005 (4.01)	−0.0001 (0.62)
R^2	0.25	0.46	0.54	0.47
Department dummies	Not included	Included	Included	Included
University fixed effect	Not controlled	Not controlled	Not controlled	Controlled

Note
The absolute heteroskedasticity-robust t-values are in the parentheses.

On the other hand, the faculty research output has a significant estimated effect on the net post-graduate study rate of the graduates in the sciences and engineering field, although the departmental characteristics, the student quality, and the university fixed effect still explain about two-thirds of the raw association.

The contrasting results by the field may be partly due to the differences in how research is conducted. Most research in the humanities and social sciences field is carried out by one or at most a few researchers, while most research in the sciences and engineering field is carried out by a team of a much larger size. Thus demand for graduate students by the faculty members in departments with active research programs in the sciences and engineering field is likely to be high, and the faculty members are likely to encourage more students for further study and seek actively for graduates who have been taught by active researchers. However, the demand for and the supply of the graduate students are likely to be much lower in the humanities and social sciences field.

Table 9.10 Estimation results, sciences and engineering, 2009

	(A)	(B)	(C)	(D)
(I) Dependent variable: net regular employment rate (n = 1,010)				
Per capita SCI publication	3.15 (2.03)	4.20 (2.18)	0.15 (0.08)	0.48 (0.35)
No of male graduates		0.01 (0.50)	0.04 (1.65)	0.07 (2.40)
No of female graduates		−0.07 (1.39)	−0.05 (1.02)	−0.04 (0.77)
No of tenured professors		0.41 (1.91)	0.09 (0.42)	−0.08 (0.42)
No of untenured professors		0.92 (3.13)	0.35 (1.27)	−0.24 (0.87)
Tuition		−0.07 (0.36)	−0.16 (0.90)	0.03 (0.08)
Average SAT score			−0.44 (4.77)	−0.005 (0.04)
Average SAT score squared			0.001 (5.66)	0.0001 (0.34)
R^2	0.005	0.46	0.50	0.47
(II) Dependent variable: net post-graduate study rate (n = 1,011)				
Per capita SCI publication	16.01 (11.74)	9.86 (7.30)	6.49 (5.78)	4.69 (4.44)
No of male graduates		−0.11 (5.30)	−0.09 (5.27)	−0.07 (3.89)
No of female graduates		−0.06 (1.83)	−0.07 (2.43)	0.001 (0.04)
No of tenured professors		0.81 (5.27)	0.57 (4.41)	0.27 (2.36)
No of untenured professors		1.33 (7.47)	0.87 (5.96)	0.72 (5.16)
Tuition		−0.31 (2.42)	−0.36 (3.16)	−0.42 (2.04)
Average SAT score			−0.15 (3.16)	−0.04 (0.81)
Average SAT score squared			0.0005 (4.59)	0.0001 (1.19)
R^2	0.31	0.53	0.60	0.43
Department dummies	Not included	Included	Included	Included
University fixed effect	Not controlled	Not controlled	Not controlled	Controlled

Note
The absolute heteroskedasticity-robust t-values are in the parentheses.

V Summary and discussions

In this chapter we find that while the raw association between the faculty research output and the student achievements in the labor market or advance into post-graduate studies is strong and statistically significant, the association is explained mostly by departmental characteristics, student quality, and the university fixed effect. In particular, the association between the research output and the percentage of the graduates who have found regular employment becomes almost zero and statistically insignificant once those factors, especially student quality, are controlled for. On the other hand, the association between the research output and the percentage of the graduates pursuing post-graduate study remains positive and statistically significant in the sciences and engineering sector, even after those factors are controlled for. The findings suggest that the drive by universities and the government to increase the faculty research output and its success are likely to have a limited effect on the students at the undergraduate level at least in the short run. Especially in the humanities and social sciences field, the effect is likely to be very small. In the sciences and engineering field, on the other hand, the effect is likely to be limited to increasing the proportion of graduates who pursue a post-graduate degree.

Notes

1 See website, online, available at: www.academyinfo.go.kr (in Korean only). A separate website is maintained for primary and secondary educational institutions.
2 If more than one, say *n*, authors have co written a published paper, the number of publication added by the paper to an author's research output is computed as follows. If the author is the first or the corresponding author, it is $2/(n+2)$; otherwise, it is $1/(n+2)$. If the number of authors is 15 or more, $n=15$.

References

Hattie, John, and Marsh, Herbert W., "The Relationship between Research and Teaching: A Meta-Analysis," *Review of Educational Research*, 1996, pp. 507–542.
Marsh, Herbert W. and Hattie, John, "The Relation between Research Productivity and Teaching Effectiveness: Complementary, Antagonistic, or Independent Constructs?," *Journal of Higher Education*, 2002, pp. 603–641.

10 Economic crisis and policies on foreign workforce

Kyuyong Lee

I Introduction

In the late 1980s Korea changed from being an emigration country to an immigration country. Korean emigration in the twentieth century started with the movement of workers to Hawaiian sugar cane farms in 1905. Many Koreans emigrated to China, Russia, and Japan in 1910 when Korea lost its national sovereignty. In the 1960s, Koreans went to Germany as mine workers and nurses to help cover the fund for the economic development plan. The guest worker program of mine workers and nurses to Germany was the Korean government's first migration policy. In the 1970s, every year millions of construction workers went to the Middle East oil-producing countries. Also, many students and educated Koreans went to the United States and stayed there. In addition to the United States, Canada and Australia attracted many educated Korean immigrants. By contrast, few foreigners migrated to work in Korea.

This situation changed in the middle and late 1980s as foreign workers flocked to Korea, attracted by job opportunities doing 3D (difficult, dangerous and dirty) work that Koreans shunned. Most of these foreign workers came from China, Southeast Asia, South Asia, and Central Asia as production workers in the manufacturing sector. The number of foreign workers increased quite rapidly from 10,000 in the 1980s, to 200,000 in 1996, to 700,000 in 2010. In the 2000s, the inflow of marriage migrants, foreign students, and overseas Koreans introduced a new dimension of immigration. Indicative of the country's new status, in 2007 the UN declared Korea an immigrant-receiving country.[1]

This chapter analyzes Korean immigration policy, particularly policies dealing with immigrant workers.

II Recent trends in immigration

Table 10.1 shows an increase in the number of foreigners residing in Korea from 492,000 in 2000, to 910,000 in 2006, to 1,168,000 in late 2009.[2] The foreign-born proportion of the population increased from 1.01 percent in 2000, to 1.86 percent in 2006, to 2.35 percent in 2009.

Table 10.1 The increase of foreigners staying in Korea as percentage of population

Year	Total number of foreigners staying in Korea	Whole population	The percentage of foreigners in the total population (%)
2000	481,611	47,732,558	1.01
2001	576,835	48,021,543	1.20
2002	629,006	48,229,948	1.30
2003	678,687	48,386,823	1.40
2004	750,873	48,583,805	1.55
2005	747,467	48,782,274	1.53
2006	910,149	48,991,779	1.86
2007	1,066,273	49,268,928	2.16
2008	1,158,866	49,540,367	2.34
2009	1,168,477	49,773,145	2.35

Source: Korea Immigration Service statistical yearbook, each year, Ministry of Justice.

Nearly half of the immigrants came from China (47.5 percent of all foreigners staying in Korea, with 32.3 percent of the total being Korean Chinese). The next largest flow was from the United States with 127,000 people, Vietnam with 91,000, Japan with 47,000, the Philippines with 46,000, and Thailand with 44,000.

Table 10.2 shows the number of foreigners staying in Korea in terms of their visa status from 2001 to 2009. The number of foreign students did not change much between 2001 (7,428 people) and 2004 (9,708 people) but increased to 24,797 in 2005 and to 80,985 in late 2009. Marriage migrant refers to a person with the right to stay as the spouse of a Korean national. In the 1980s, Japanese women entered Korea by international marriage through religious organizations. In 2001 there were 25,182 marriage migrants. The number increased by

Table 10.2 The trend of foreigners in terms of stay status

Year	Total foreigners	Foreign students	Professional workforce	Low-skilled workforce	Marriage migrants
2001	576,835	7,428	21,710	110,250	25,182
2002	629,006	7,288	21,955	128,229	34,710
2003	678,687	9,708	22,431	291,572	44,416
2004	750,873	9,705	21,729	295,087	57,069
2005	747,467	24,797	24,785	173,549	75,011
2006	910,149	38,649	29,011	231,773	93,786
2007	1,066,273	56,006	33,502	442,677	110,362
2008	1,158,866	71,531	37,304	511,269	122,552
2009	1,168,477	80,985	40,698	511,160	125,087

Source: Korea Immigration Service statistical yearbook, each year, Ministry of Justice.

Note
Figures exclude foreigners who entered Korea with non employment visa and in a state of employment. It is estimated that the entire foreign workforce would reach 700,000 if these people were included.

10,000–20,000 people every year and reached 94,786 in 2006 and 125,087 in the late 2009. As of late 2009, women made up 87.3 percent of marriage migrants. The number of marriage migrants from China and the Philippines grew in the 2000s. Over the same period the nationality of marriage migrants diversified to include migrants from Vietnam, Cambodia, Mongolia, and Thailand as well.

Professional and low-skilled workers came to Korea with different visas. Table 10.2 shows that in 2001 there were 21,710 professional immigrants compared to 110,250 low skilled immigrants. The numbers of both groups increased through 2009 but the increase was much greater among the low-skilled. Since the data exclude the largely low-skilled foreigners who entered Korea without an employment visa and worked, it understates both the total numbers and the number of the low-skilled. If these people are included, the size of the foreign workforce would likely exceed 700,000.

The proportion of immigrant workers who are illegal immigrants is high in Korea compared to other countries. In 1991 when firms could not legally use low-skilled foreign workers, illegal stayers made up about 94.3 percent of all foreign workers. This led the government to introduce the foreign workforce industrial trainee system in November of 1991, which brought in foreign workers who were supposed to be educated for a period and then work for a period. This system reduced the illegal stayer proportion of the foreign workforce to 58.9 percent in 1994. However, there were not enough foreign trainees for firms to fill their demand for foreign workers, so the proportion of the foreign workforce who were illegal stayers rose to 79.8 percent by 2002. The government responded by enacting the foreign workforce work permit system in August of 2003 and by legalizing the existing illegal stay foreign workforce through the supplementary provision Article 2 of the Act on Foreign Workforce Employment. This reduced the proportion of illegal stay foreign workforce to 35.5 percent on December of 2003. As of late 2009, among 1,168,477 (in total) foreign stayers, 177,965 were illegal stayers, producing an illegal stayers rate of 15.2 percent. The visa status of illegal stayers showed that short-term common

Table 10.3 Trend of illegal stayers

Year	Total stayers	Illegal stayers	Illegal stay rate (%)
2000	481,611	184,547	38.3
2001	576,835	255,206	44.2
2002	629,006	289,239	46.0
2003	678,687	154,342	22.7
2004	750,873	207,841	27.7
2005	767,467	204,254	26.6
2006	910,149	211,988	23.3
2007	1,066,293	223,464	21.0
2008	1,158,866	200,489	17.3
2009	1,168,477	177,955	15.2

Source: Korea Immigration Service, statistical yearbook, each year, Ministry of Justice.

use (C-2) and short-term comprehensive (C-3) took up the largest portion with 64,587 people; non professional employment (E-9) with 30,165 people; and visa exemption (B1) and tourist (B2) with 23,812 people.

Korean policies on immigrant workers treat professional workers and non professional workers differently. Professional workers are covered by employment visas from E-1 to E-7 while non-professional workforce policies are covered by the employment permit system and visiting employment system. The basis of this distinction lies in the premise that the professional foreign workforce have a requirement to be college graduates with work experience, while non-professional foreign workers do not require a specific functional level because their work consists of simple tasks. The employment permit system covers non-professional less skilled workers, and there are special provisions for less skilled workers of Korean ancestry resident in other countries who want to work in Korea.

III From training to permit system

The foreign industrial training system did not succeed in providing a well-functioning legal channel for immigration of less skilled workers. Workers who entered Korea under the system frequently left their firm because they could easily find illegal employers willing to pay a higher wage; those who stayed had problems of wage arrears and human rights abuse; many worked without receiving the promised training. Initially the system set a two-year training period and a one-year employment period. Then the government made it more realistic by shifting the terms to one-year training and two-year employment (amendment to the enforcement ordinance (2002.4.18) and enforcement regulations (2002.4.27) of the Immigration Control Law). However, as the foreign immigrants who came in as trainees can gain legal employment, the training employment system had the characteristics of a work permit system in reality. In November 2003 the government passed the law on the employment of foreign workers to turn the system into a full-scale work permit system (this took effect on August 16, 2004). The existing industrial trainee system ran parallel with work permit system by 2006 and was combined with work permit system as of January 1, 2007.

The work permit system allows companies which failed to find the domestic workforce for particular jobs to recruit foreign workers. The permit system operates as follows.[3] Every year the foreign workforce policy committee in the Prime Minister's Office sets the number of entering foreign workers, type of industry, and selection of sending countries. The committee is composed of the deputy ministers of the Ministry of Strategy and Finance, Ministry of Foreign Affairs and Trade, Ministry of Justice, Ministry of Knowledge Economy, and Ministry of Labor, the director of Small Business Administration, and vice ministers of related state administration institutes. The foreign workforce employment committee (chairman: Deputy Minister of Labor) in the Ministry of Labor assists in determining the policies.

The selection and introduction procedure of foreign workers is as follows. Korea makes a memorandum of understanding (MOU) with other countries to regulate the qualifications of job seekers, methods, and mutual rights and obligations. The governments or public institutes of sending countries send a job seekers list based on objective criterion such as Korean language proficiency and work experience. The Employment Support Center of Korea's Ministry of Labor issues a written permission of employment of foreign workers to employers who have searched fruitlessly for domestic workers (3–7 days) and recommends foreign job seekers through an employment management computer network. Employers select qualified people for their business. Immigration support activities on foreign workers are performed by the Human Resource Development Service of Korea and employment education is carried out by the Human Resource Development Service of Korea, private business agency institutes and the Korea International labor Foundation.

The employment period was initially set to three years. In October 2009, the government amended the law to allow the employment period to be voluntarily decided by the agreement of directly involved parties. The new law allowed foreign workers to stay in Korea for a maximum of four years and ten months. Foreign workers were not allowed to change workplaces except in the case of temporary close or shutdown of company or employers' canceling the labor contract. Employers who have illegally employed foreign workers for a specific period (one year or three years) have limited rights to employment of foreign workers under the system. The foreign workers employed by the work permit system are assured of basic rights such as occupational health and safety insurance, the minimum wage system, and are treated equally to domestic workers by applying the National Labor Relations Act. However, by the principle of reciprocity, participation in the Korean National Pension System is exempted unless the foreigner applies for the Korean system. To reduce the risk of unpaid overdue wages to foreign workers, employers not covered by the wage bond assurance law or with fewer than 300 regular employees were obligated to obtain insurances against wage arrears.

IV Visiting employment system and overseas Koreans

Since the 1992 establishment of diplomatic relations between Korea and China, Korea opened the door to overseas Koreans with relatives in Korea to enter the country and work. Overseas Koreans over age of 40 with domestic connections were permitted employment in eight service areas. The door was widened for oversea Koreans in China and the Soviet Union and to 20 industries. However, these workers had to be employed through the employment support center. Overseas Koreans over the age of 25 who had relatives in Korea were provided visiting and co-habitation visas (F-1–4) and permitted to work in low-skilled areas. Enforcement of the visiting employment system in March of 1997 changed the policy toward overseas Koreans. The area for employment for visiting worker immigrants expanded to over 30 industries. Overseas Koreans over the age of 25 in China and the Soviet Union could obtain a multiple year visiting employment visa (H-2) effective for five years which enabled them to freely visit and work. Those with relatives in Korea who had the freedom to move in the past were provided with visas without an annual quota for visa issue, and overseas Koreans who have no relatives in Korea were permitted to enter with an annual quota to protect the domestic labor market.

After completing employment education and applying for employment seeking, job seekers would be helped to find a job or were free to seek a job by themselves. They could change workplace but had to report this. The annual quota for overseas Koreans with no domestic connection was decided by the foreign workforce policy committee. In 1999, the enactment of the Act on Entry and Exit and Legal Status of Overseas Koreans gave overseas Korean in advanced countries like Japan and the United States rights comparable to domestic people such as free entry and exit and guarantee of economic activities. Overseas Koreans with qualifications could be employed freely except in low-skilled labor and speculative activities. The employment management system that provided the qualification of visit and cohabitation for overseas Koreans with foreign nationality and the right to be employed in Korea was combined with the work permit system. The government determines the number of overseas Koreans entering Korea by the visiting employment system, depending on the state of the domestic labor market. For example, in 2009 it reduced the entry quota to 80 percent of the 2008 entry quota, dividing the number admitted equally among overseas Koreans with domestic connection and those without. Decreasing the number of entrants by overseas Koreans with a domestic connection through the invitation of a relative, increased opportunities for those overseas Koreans without a domestic connection who had been waiting for the electronic lottery after passing the Korean language test. The Korean government balanced the re-entry time, strengthened the implementation of employment report, and actively induced foreign workers to be employed in industries with a Korean manpower shortage. A variety of incentives like the right to invite two relatives for two years and an easing of acquisition requirements for permanent residency qualification (from ten years to four years and six months) were provided for overseas Koreans who had worked for long time in such areas as manufacturing and agriculture. The method of priority supply of Koreans without domestic connection was promoted with local manufacturing companies or agriculture and livestock industries where the labor shortage was serious compared to other industries.

Overseas Koreans who have entered with a visiting employment visa (H-2) can conclude a labor contract and be employed by the help of the employment support center or autonomous activities of seeking a job after completing employment education in the Human Resource Development Service of Korea and registering for job seeking in the employment support center. Employers in workplaces which have permission to employ foreign workers by the visiting employment system can apply and be issued with confirmation documentation of special admission of foreign workers from the employment support center after

seven days of efforts searching for domestic workers which is the same procedure under the general work permit system. The employment support center made
the list of candidates three times the total number of required foreign workers
and recommended to employers a list of job seekers with suitable qualifications.
Korean employers who received confirmation documentation of special admission for foreign workers could sign the labor contract with foreign workers who
have been introduced by others rather than the employment support center. The
period of labor contract cannot exceed one year and employers who employ
overseas Koreans should report to the employment support center of the Ministry of Labor within ten days of employment.

V Non-professional immigrant workers

Table 10.4 shows the yearly entry quota of non-professional immigrant workers
determined by the foreign workforce policy committee. The number of foreign
entrants increased to over 100,000 people by 2008 after implementation of the
work permit system. However, the committee reduced this number during the
financial crisis in 2009 and 2010. When the economy recovered, because of the
rising demand of companies for foreign worker, the government introduced the
additional foreign workforce in the second half of 2010. The entering size of the
foreign workforce in 2009[4] was determined by utilizing labor market statistics
adjusted for economic conditions in 2009. Specifically, the demand of the
foreign workforce was assessed in the light of demand changes in the economic
recession and the size of the employment possibility for domestic workers.

The trends of the work permit system and the visiting employment system are
shown in Table 10.5. The number of general foreign workers (E-9) and overseas
Koreans (H-2) increased fourfold in 2000. After the introduction of the visiting
employment system in July of 2007, the number of overseas Koreans grew so
rapidly that they came to outnumber general foreign workers after 2007, reaching a near 2:1 ratio by 2009.

= Which industries and types of firms expanded their employment of nonprofes-
sional foreign workers? Table 10.6 shows huge rises in the proportion of foreign
workers in companies that employed them in construction, manufacturing and
agriculture-livestock, compared to a decline in the proportion in service sector jobs.
The size of firm shows a greater increase in the larger firms that have hired propor-
tionately fewer workers than in the past. Since most of these workers are likely to
be in non-regular jobs in these firms, the spread of foreign workers arguably

Table 10.4 The number of entering immigrants allowed by year

	2006	2007	2008	2009	2010	Addition by second half of 2010
Total	105,000	109,600	132,000	34,000	24,000	10,000
Manufacturing	69,000	69,300	76,800	23,000	19,500	8,600

Source: The Ministry of Labor, press release.

Table 10.5 Non-professional foreign workforce except illegal stayers, general and overseas Korean

Year	2005	2006	2007	2008	2009
Total	104,348 (100)	199,620 (100)	362,460 (100)	454,431 (100)	461,203 (100)
General (E-9)	52,305 (50.1)	115,122 (57.7)	134,012 (37.0)	156,429 (34.4)	158,198 (34.3)
Overseas Koreans (H-2)	52,043 (49.9)	84,498 (42.3)	228,448 (63.0)	298,002 (65.6)	303,005 (65.7)

Source: Ministry of Justice.

Note
Percentages in brackets.

Table 10.6 The proportion of foreign workers in Korean companies employing foreign
workers: non-professional foreign workforce

	2004	2005	2006	2007	2008	2009
Industry						
Construction	9.7	14.9	17.8	19.6	23.4	24.0
Agriculture – livestock	24.5	33.1	32.2	39.4	47.4	47.1
Fishery	–	29.0	37.8	41.2	44.9	48.0
Manufacturing	14.8	22.3	19.5	23.0	28.0	27.8
Service	28.0	31.6	29.6	25.5	25.5	22.7
Size						
Less than 5	69.6	63.4	67.5	68.4	70.3	65.5
5–9	36.0	48.9	53.6	54.2	57.2	51.5
10–29	19.6	30.1	31.8	34.0	39.8	36.8
30–99	12.9	17.8	17.7	21.7	27.6	24.7
100–299	6.3	8.3	8.5	11.3	14.5	12.8
More than 300	1.4	3.9	4.3	5.0	6.5	4.0
All	15.5	22.9	20.1	23.2	27.9	27.5

Source: A connection panel of foreign workers database and employees in the workplace employing
foreign workers database.

Note
Annual man-days criteria.

contributed to the growing division in the Korean workforce between regular
employees with union and other labor protections and the more informal workforce
lacking such protections. Given the concentration of overseas Koreans entering
Korea in the construction and restaurant businesses where domestic day laborers
are plentiful, there is likely to be substantial job competition in these industries.

The mechanism for the protection of the domestic workforce does not function well. Employers prefer foreign workers because of the frequent turnover
and higher employment cost of domestic workers in addition to labor shortages.
As can be seen in Figure 10.1, day laborers have been flexibly adjusted to the

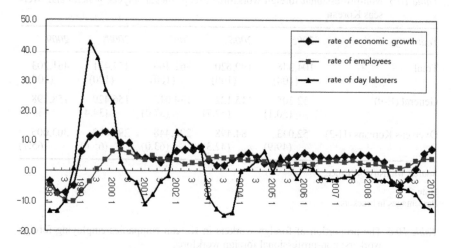

Figure 10.1 Business fluctuations and the trend of employee increase by work status (source: National Statistical Office, *Monthly Economically Active Population Survey*).

change of economic conditions but since late 2006 the number of day laborers has been continuously decreasing without the associated economic change. Among the complex effects of economic conditions behind the trend, the inflow of foreign workers is likely to be large.

VI Professional foreign workforce policy

Korea operates a dual system on the employment of foreign workforce that separates professional and non-professional workforces. In the case of the professional workforce, entrance and stay are permitted if the requirements of the Immigration Control Law were satisfied and the labor contract with the employer was established. Table 10.7 lists the professional workforce governed by the Immigration Control Law: professor (E-1), language teacher (E-2), research (E-3), technical instruction (E-4), professional jobs such as lawyer and accountant (E-5), art and entertainment (E-6), and specific activities (E-7). In addition, there are visas covering workers directly employed and dispatched by foreign companies including: resident employee (D-7), business investment (D-8), and trade management (D-9). A contract with domestic employers is important due to the difficulty of verifying qualifications because there is no systematic verification system for foreign diplomas or licenses yet.

The Korean government continued their efforts to attract outstanding entrants to the professional workforce. The Presidential Council on National Competitiveness on April of 2008 formulated the "Global High-quality Human Resource Attraction Plan." This plan focused on support activities for high-quality human resource – "Contact Korea," visa system reform, and support for employment and stay – to attract outstanding professional foreign workforce. In science and technology, the Ministry of Knowledge Economy, and the Ministry of Education and Science operate Gold Card and Science Card systems. These systems contribute to the utilization of high-quality human resource in developing countries like India and Vietnam, and China by SMEs. The Gold Card provides a longer period of stay (five years) for specific activities than the normally granted length.

The record of attracting outstanding workforce participants is not particularly good.[5] Table 10.8 gives the industrial distribution of entrants with a main professional workforce visa as of September 2008. In research (E-3), manufacturing occupied the largest portion with 38.7 percent, followed by business service (25.1 percent), educational service (25.1 percent), public administration, national defense, and social security (12.0 percent). Manufacturing (53.8 percent) and business service (31.9 percent) occupy the largest portion of technical instruction (E-4) with 85.7 percent. The 98.5 percent of professional jobs (E-5) are employed in the transportation business because most professional job (E-5) visas are for airline pilots. In specific activities (E-7), the food and lodging industry occupied the largest portion with 35.4 percent, followed by manufacturing (16.2 percent), business service (13.8 percent), and educational service (13.3 percent). Most of the workforce in the food and lodging industry are assumed to be employed in cooking related positions.

VII Conclusions and policy recommendations

Korean migration policy is in its infancy, and has been largely directed by the short-term labor market conditions. However, it needs to consider future changes in population and industrial structure, continuing dualities in the labor market, and the fact that migration policy has long-term ripple effects. Also, the country needs to develop comprehensive laws and policies that encompass a wide spectrum of migrant issues such as the education and training policy, visa system, social unification policy, discrimination policy corresponding to the protection of labor market and international rights. Policies regarding short-term stay, workforce development, marriage migrants, the attraction and utilization of foreign students, permanent residency and nationality, and social assimilation of the foreign workforce need to be considered as a whole. In order to accomplish this, Korea needs to create a comprehensive administration structure to unify functions currently fragmented across various departments that pursue often conflicting policy objectives.

Because the change of population structure in the future risks creating labor shortages of non-professional workers, policy should consider diversification of the foreign workforce supply by each skill level. It needs to seek ways to improve the recruitment and selection process to improve the productivity of the foreign workforce entering Korea and to assure a relatively high level of language proficiency and skill. It may be useful to give private employment agencies some roles and responsibility in the screening and recruitment process. The labor market test should be made more effective.

Table 10.7 Activities and stay of professional foreign workforce by stay status

Stay qualifications or range of activities		Upper limit period of one stay	Accompanying documents with visa application
Professor (E-1)	Someone who undertakes education or research direction in professional areas in educational institutes higher than community college or similar institutes as foreigners with qualifications specified by the Higher Education Act	2 years	Career certificates, labor contract or appointment confirmation
Language teacher (E-2)	Someone who undertakes foreign language conversation instruction in foreign language institutes, educational institutes higher than elementary school, affiliated language institutes, broadcasting corporations, company affiliated language institutes, and other institutes as foreigners with qualifications specified by the Minister of Justice	1 year	Diploma or copy of graduation certificate, labor contract, establishment documents of educational institutes, personal reference
Research (E-3)	Someone who undertakes research in the natural science areas or research and development of industrial high technology in laboratories and invited by public–private institutes of Korea (except someone who can be qualified as professor (E-1))	2 years	Establishment documents of invitation institutes, diploma or career certificates, labor contract
Technical instruction (E-4)	Someone who undertakes relevant tasks to provide professional knowledge of natural science or industrial specific knowledge and invited by public–private institutes of Korea	2 years	An order of dispatch or proof of employment, technology introduction contract report receipt, technology introduction contract (or service transaction certificate) or copy of defence industry appointment establishment documents of private–public institutes

Professional jobs (E-5)	Someone who undertakes professional jobs such as law, accounting, and medical treatment permitted by Korean laws as foreign lawyers with qualification by Korean law, accountants, doctors, someone with national vocational qualifications (except someone who can be qualified as professor (E-1))	2 years	Diploma and copy of licenses, employment reference of the head of central administrative institutes with jurisdiction or document conforming employment necessity, labor contract
Art and entertainment (E-6)	Someone who undertakes art activities with profit like music, fine art, literature and entertainment, performance, play, sports, advertisement/fashion model with the purpose of profit or activities commensurate with these activities: art entertainment (E-6-1), hotel adult entertainment (E-6-2), sports (E-6-3)	6 months	1 Shows and entertainment activities in tour hotel, adult entertainment: play reference of Korea Media Ratings Board, play plan, Acquired Immune Deficiency Syndrome (HIV) test certificate, personal reference 2 Others: employment reference of the head of central administrative institutes with jurisdiction or document confirming employment necessity, qualification or career certificates, personal reference
Specific activities (E-7)	Someone who undertakes activities designated by the Minister of Justice by contract with private–public institutes in Korea	2 years	Diploma or copy of licenses, labor contract, employment reference of the head of central administrative institutes with jurisdiction or document confirming employment necessity, establishment documents of private–public institutes, personal reference

Source: Enforcement ordinance of Immigration Control Law (enacted on March 31, 2009), Enforcement regulation of Immigration Control Law (enacted on April 3, 2009).

Table 10.8 The industrial distribution of workplaces employing professional workforce (September 2008)

	E3 (research)		E4 (technical instruction)		E5 (professional jobs)		E7 (specific activities)		Total	
	people	%	people	%	people	%	people	%	people	%
Agriculture and forestry	1	0.1	0	0.0	0	0.0	0	0.0	1	0.0
Fishery	0	0.0	0	0.0	0	0.0	3	0.1	3	0.0
Mining industry	0	0.0	0	0.0	0	0.0	1	0.0	1	0.0
Manufacturing	753	38.7	64	53.8	0	0.0	903	16.2	1,720	21.2
Electricity, gas and water	3	0.2	1	0.8	0	0.0	5	0.1	9	0.1
Construction	24	1.2	8	6.7	0	0.0	357	6.4	389	4.8
Wholesale and retail business	16	0.8	2	1.7	0	0.0	333	6.0	351	4.3
Food and lodging industry	0	0.0	1	0.8	0	0.0	1,970	35.4	1,971	24.3
Transportation	1	0.1	0	0.0	465	98.5	114	2.0	580	7.2
Communication	0	0.0	0	0.0	0	0.0	25	0.4	25	0.3
Finance and insurance	0	0.0	0	0.0	0	0.0	165	3.0	165	2.0
Real estate and leasing service	0	0.0	0	0.0	0	0.0	33	0.6	33	0.4
Business service	488	25.1	38	31.9	0	0.0	769	13.8	1,295	16.0
Public administration, national defence, and ocial security	233	12.0	4	3.4	0	0.0	30	0.5	267	3.3
Educational service	413	21.2	0	0.0	0	0.0	739	13.3	1,152	14.2
Health care and social welfare	6	0.3	0	0.0	7	1.5	6	0.1	19	0.2
Entertainment, culture, and sports service	1	0.1	0	0.0	0	0.0	65	1.2	66	0.8
Other public, repair, and personal service	5	0.3	1	0.8	0	0.0	51	0.9	57	0.7
Total	1,944	100.0	119	100.0	472	100.0	5,569	100.0	8,104	100.0

Source: Kyuyoung Lee et al. 2008b.

Note
Results of the analysis by connecting data of Ministry of Justice and unemployment insurance data.

With regard to low skilled immigrants, one lesson from the experiences of countries with a long history of the utilization of a foreign workforce is that it is not desirable to continuously expand the supply of low-skilled foreign workers. Korea needs a comprehensive consideration of cost–benefit analysis on foreign workforce employment. Foreign workforce supply policy has operated by focusing on the demand of firms without giving adequate attention to either the impact on domestic workers, or the potential long term effects of expanding the size of the foreign workforce on other policies or social goals. The flow of foreign workers to small workplaces in low skilled sectors delays the adjustment of the country's industrial structure adjustment to Korea's new place in a knowledge-based economy.

For overseas Koreans, the key issue is whether policy should reflect the labor market approach or free movement based on overseas Korean policy. The employment policy of overseas Koreans should focus on human resource development policy and employment support policy corresponding to the demand of domestic firms. Employment support for overseas Koreans is weak. Even though overseas Koreans are permitted to look for a job, much of their employment is achieved through illegal employment agencies because looking for work independently is difficult due to practicalities such as the difference of language and living habits. Accordingly, this causes problems such as commission charges and employment and placement in non permissible industries. Overseas Koreans without domestic connection are exposed to job and wage insecurities by the use of an informal employment path. Therefore, labor market support policy for overseas Koreans should be tightened.

For the immigration of professional workers, Korea needs to organize a professional workforce introduction system with appropriate categories for a wider spectrum of skills. One possibility is to provide support for the talent finding and recruitment process corresponding to the future labor shortage. Diversification of countries which provide the professional foreign workforce is needed. Cultivation of a workforce from developing countries should employ a variety of channels such as the establishment of Korean education and training programs and the utilization of the network of professional Koreans abroad.

Notes

1 Kilsang Yoo *et al.*, (2005), pp. 36–42.
2 The distribution of foreigners in Korea in late 2009 showed that the category visiting employment (H-2) has the largest proportion with 26.2 percent, followed by professional employment (E-9) at 16.1 percent, spouse of the national citizen with 10.7 percent, tour and pass (B-2) with 5.9 percent, studying abroad (D-2) with 5.3 percent, comprehensive short period (C-3) with 5.1 percent, and overseas Korean (F-4) with 4.3 percent.
3 Refer to the *Handbook of Work Permit System* (2009), Ministry of Labor.
4 Data of the foreign workforce policy committee.
5 Refer to Kyuyong Lee *et al.* (2008b), Ministry of Justice.

References

Jo, Junmo, "The Direction of Foreign Workforce Attraction Policy for Strengthen of National Competitiveness," Ministry of Justice, 2009.

Lee, Kyuyong and Sungjae Park, "Employment Structure and Effects of Foreign Workforce," *Monthly Labor Review, September*, Korea Labor Institute, 2008.

Lee, Kyuyong, Kilsang Yoo, Haechun Rhee, Donghoon Seol and Sungjae Park, "Analysis of Foreign Workforce Labor Market and Study on the Improvement Direction of long-term Management System," Korea Labor Institute, 2007.

Lee, Kyuyong, Seungyeol Yee, Jayoung Yoon and Sungjae Park, "Analysis of Effects on Domestic Labor Market by the Employment of Overseas Koreans," Ministry of Labor, unpublished, 2009.

Lee, Kyuyong, Seungyeol Yee, Sungjae Park and Yongjin Nho, "Analysis of Foreign Workforce Labor Market," Korea Labor Institute, forthcoming, 2010.

Lee, Kyuyong, Sungjae Park and Kyetaik Oh, "The Study on Improvement Direction of Professional Foreign Workforce Visa System," Ministry of Justice, 2008b.

Lee, Kyuyong, Sungjae Park, Sunwoong Kim, Yongjin Nho and Jaehoon Kim, "Analysis of Professional Foreign Workforce Labor Market," Korea Labor Institute, 2005.

Lee, Kyuyong, Yongjin Nho, Seungyeol Yee, Sungjae Park, Kyetaik Oh and Yongwoo Koh, "Development Direction of Support System of Attracting Foreign Outstanding Workforce," Korea Labor Institute, 2008a.

Yoo, Kilsang and Kyuyong Lee, "Foreign Worker Employment Management Conditions and Policy Issues," Korea Labor Institute, 2001.

Yoo, Kilsang, Junghae Lee and Kyuyong Lee, "International comparison of Foreign Workforce Systems," Korea Labor Institute, 2004.

Yoo, Kilsang, Kyuyong Lee, Haechun Rhee, Joonmo Cho, Yongjin Nho, Hunku Kim and Yoekyoung Park, "Analysis on Low-skilled Foreign Workers Labor Market," Korea Labor Institute, 2004.

11 Economic crisis and Korean vocational training

Chang Kyun Chae

This chapter focuses on the vocational training policies that the Korean government deployed from 1995 to 2009 to deal with the economic crises of 1997 and 2008. Funded by employers through unemployment insurance, Korean vocational training policies are constructed to assist the training of both the unemployed and the employed. Unemployment insurance was first implemented on July 1, 1995. Unemployment insurance funds collected in the form of payroll taxes are divided into two categories: funds for unemployment compensation and funds for employment stabilization and vocational training projects. Workers as well as employers pay a certain proportion of the insurance for unemployment compensation but employers solely fund vocational training projects. The proportion of the unemployment insurance premium paid by employers and employees are summarized in Table 11.1.

All businesses employing more than one worker are required to sign up for unemployment insurance but the actual coverage falls short of this. As of December 2008, the number of the insured is 9.385 million, 40.4 percent of the total number of employees and 58.0 percent of the total number of wage earners. Still, the number covered has continuously risen. As shown in Table 11.2, the number of the insured in 2008 is 2.2 times higher than the 1997 figure of 4.28 million. Moreover, the rate of coverage reached 58.0 percent, in 2008, a 26.0 percent increase from 1997.

Table 11.1 Unemployment insurance premium rate (% of the total wage)

	Employees	Employers
Unemployment compensation	0.45	0.45
Employment stabilization and vocational training projects		
Businesses with less than 150 regular employees	–	0.25
Priority-based businesses with more than 150 regular employees	–	0.45
Non-priority-based businesses with regular employees between 150 and 1,000	–	0.65
Businesses with more than 1,000 regular employees and state-run businesses	–	0.85

Table 11.2 The current application and progress of the unemployment insurance

Year	1997	2008
Number of insured	4,280,430	9,385,239
Applied rate (%)		
among total workers	20.5	40.4
among total wage earners	32.0	58.0
among regular workers	37.1	66.3

For the unemployed without insurance, vocational training is assisted by the government budget instead of unemployment insurance. In response to the rising demand for life-long competency development, government investments here have been steadily increasing. In 2003, the government spent about 806.2 billion won. In 2009 it spent 1,396.6 billion won. The vast majority of the investment came from the unemployed insurance funds, and 256.5 billion won was appropriated for the general account in 2009, 18.4 percent of the total financial investment.

I Training for the unemployed

There are two types of training programs for the unemployed: priority-based training and general employment training. Priority-based training is designed to help the unemployed acquire essential skills for strategic industries that report a shortage of labor or increasing demand in the market. This type of training differs from other forms of employment training in that the government is actively involved in the choice of the occupation types, allocation of the budget, and selection of training institutions. In general employment training allowances for training, transportation, and meals are given to trainees in institutions authorized by the Department of Labor. Once the Department of Labor approves a certain number of trainees and a certain program in a training institution, the authorized institution recruits and trains the assigned number of trainees.

This supplier-oriented aid has several shortcomings in the timing of the training and its potential inconsistency with actual market demand. As a response, the government adopted on a trial basis a new system of vocational training account in 2008. This system expands training options for trainees, lowers the

Table 11.3 Annual financial investment on competency development (billion won)

	2003	2004	2005	2006	2007	2008	2009
Total	806.2	858.4	974.2	1,158.3	1,397.1	1,449.4	1,734.1
Unemployed insurance funds	592.1	642.4	726.8	926.9	1,140.6	1,178.8	1,367.6
General account	214.1	236.1	248.4	231.4	256.5	270.7	366.4

Note
Totals may not sum due to rounding.

entrance barrier, and eases regulations in order to revitalize the training market and consequently improve the quality of training. In addition, this policy applies to all types of employment training from 2011 except for priority-based training.

The result of the training in 2009 is shown in Table 11.4. Approximately 150,000 of the unemployed were trained in the unemployment insurance-funded resource allocation training system, at a cost of 463 billion won, while 90,000 were trained in the General Account system, at a cost of around 57 billion won.

II Training of current employees

The government also offers support for training of current employees, with funds for employers for training and with direct aid to workers to undertake training. Aid to employers uses unemployment insurance funds. When a current or prospective employee completes a vocational training program approved by the Minister of Labor, part of the training expenses are paid out to the employer. Eligible training includes collective training, on-site training, remote training, paid-leave training, and others. In 2009, training expenses of around 450 billion won were provided to around 4.5 million workers.

Conventional training for employees has usually been implemented in this way. But this way of subsidizing training resulted in limited participation of workers in small and medium sized enterprises (SMEs) or temporary employees. As a consequence, there have been significant changes in the system such as promotion of training specialized for SMEs and expansion of direct aid to individual workers. The most representative training program specialized for SMEs is the joint training consortium project. In the joint training consortium, large corporations, association of business owners, universities with state-of-the-art facilities and equipment form a training consortium specifically designed for SME employees. The government subsidizes rent for facilities and equipment, wages, administrative expenses, and program development costs. In 2001 when the project was first implemented, a total of 3.2 billion won was provided to six appointed institutions, and 1,000 SMEs and 4,000 employees participated. In 2009, the number of operating institutions and amount of aid greatly expanded, to 96 and 78.3 billion won respectively. In addition, the number of participating SMEs and employees increased to 111,000 and 231,000, respectively (see Table 11.5). This project is considered to have made a tremendous contribution to the promotion of training for SME workers.

In addition to the joint training consortium, from 2006 the government launched the systemized learning project for SMEs that considers the difficulties for SMEs

Table 11.4 Record of the aids to training for the unemployed

	Number of participants	Expenditure (million won)
Resource allocation training	151,860	463,276
Account training	87,215	57,023

Table 11.5 Record of vocational training provided by employers

	Total	Businesses with less than 300 workers	Businesses with more than 300 workers
Number of assistants	4,516,889	1,575,201	2,941,688
Amount of aid (million won)	448,262	189,406	258,855

Table 11.6 Record of the joint training consortium

	2001	2002	2003	2004	2005	2006	2007	2008	2009
Number of operating institutions	6	8	19	30	47	57	69	83	96
Number of participants (thousand)	4	10	20	38	71	143	295	281	231
Participating SMEs	1	3	8	15	33	63	134	122	111
Amount of aid (billion won)	3.2	6.1	14.1	16.8	39.9	45.0	74.4	70.2	78.3

in participating in training such as procuring temporary substitutes and coordinating work and learning with minimal obstruction to the employees' daily work. The project provides operating expenses for SMEs' learning activities, helps procure the learning space and establishes the foundation of learning networks, offers consulting, and supports the development of on-the-job learning (OJL) programs. In 2009, it supported 307 systemized learning activities for SMEs.

Moreover, the vocational competency improvement project for the employees in SMEs was promoted and provides a quality training curriculum conducive to developing essential skills. In 2009, the project supported around 70,000 SME workers to participate in a cutting-edge training curriculum consisting of nine training areas (business strategy, human resources, marketing, distribution, accounting, HRD, production and quality management, manufacturing technology and R&D) relevant to core work duties. Meanwhile, benchmarking the job rotation system in countries like Denmark, the government is pushing to the forefront paid-leave training and substitute recruitment projects to support substitute recruitment when the core workforce is absent for paid-leave training. Although the project has not shown promising results, it has helped recruit 1,008 substitutes.

Direct support for SMEs and temporary workers is taking place, including the training tuition support system, the vocational skill development card system, and educational loan projects for training. In the training tuition support system, workers must be insured by unemployment insurance to be eligible. Other eligibility requirements are as follows: workers who are expecting to leave for another job; workers who are employed by priority-based enterprises; workers who are over 40; temporary or dispatched workers; self-employed workers who are voluntarily under the umbrella of unemployment insurance; and others. Eligible workers who receive a training program approved by the Minister of Labor at their own expense are paid for in part or for all of the expenses within a limit of one million won per year. In the early stage of the system, the performance was insufficient. With expansion of the eligibility requirements, it was revitalized, and as of 2009, around 56 billion won was provided to 280,000 workers.

The vocational skill development card system issues vocational skill development cards that allow the beneficiaries of unemployment insurance including temporary, part-time, and dispatched workers to register for training programs certified by the Department of Labor. This policy was first implemented on a trial basis in 2006, launched full scale beginning in 2007, and 20 billion won was appropriated for 80,000 workers who applied for the card.

Educational and training loans for the insured workers help employees when they matriculate or enroll in a university at their own expense. The government gives loans for partial or entire tuition or training fees. As of 2009, around 30,000 workers were supported with a total of 99 billion won.

III Training providers

A large proportion of training is provided by designated training facilities, and life-long learning facilities. Still, training provided independently by employers comprises a significant proportion. However, contributions by institutions such as universities appear to be minor. Especially in the case of training for the unemployed, the contribution by universities is virtually nil.

Table 11.7 Record of training

	2002	2003	2004	2005	2006	2007	2008	2009
Number of trainees	35,537	29,177	38,908	70,732	155,620	269,045	287,827	280,667
Budget (million won)	3,434	4,224	5,873	11,688	28,851	52,782	53,508	56,033

Table 11.8 Record of the vocational skill development card

	2007	2008	2009
Number of trainees	11,775	32,200	80,691

Table 11.9 Record of educational and training loan

	2002	2003	2004	2005	2006	2007	2008	2009
Number of trainees	24,443	27,772	30,978	29,150	28,331	25,225	25,507	29,424
Budget (million won)	82,187	63,476	74,799	76,505	81,642	79,851	87,755	99,076

Table 11.10 Training hours by different training providers (thousand hours)

	Employers	Designated training facilities	Life-long learning facilities	Polytechnic	University	Others	Total
Employer training	2,583	561	1,157	131	69	525	5,026
Training tuition support and card system	–	650	2,170	1	6	54	2,881
Re-employment training	–	2,370	224	22	15	53	2,684
Priority-based training	–	673	–	–	–	–	673
Total	2,583	4,256	3,551	154	90	631	11,265

Note
Totals may not sum due to rounding.
Measured by the Department of Labor, authorized training in 2007.

IV Economic downturn and vocational training

A Cyclic changes in vocational training for the unemployed

From the perspective of vocational training, the most common response to the economic downturn is the expansion of vocational training for the unemployed. During a recession, the absolute number of unemployed persons surges. As a result, the participation rate in re-employment training inevitably rises. As Figure 11.1 shows, the unemployment rate and re-employment training are almost perfectly correlated. Immediately following the IMF foreign exchange crisis, the number of re-employment trainees was high, decreasing thereafter. Following the global financial crisis from the second half of 2008, the number of trainees again increased. The correlation coefficient of the two variables is extremely high at 0.945.

In contrast, independent of economic conditions, the training for current employees tends to consistently expand (Figure 11.2). There are some factors that explain this trend. First, the market for unemployment insurance is continuously increasing. For instance, the rising insurance penetration rate is shown in Table 11.11. Furthermore, as there has been a greater emphasis on the importance of life-long competency development, the involvement of business enterprises in employment training has been steadily increasing. Even during the IMF foreign exchange crisis and the global financial crisis after the second half of 2008, there was a notable expansion of the overall number of participants in training programs for employees. As shown in Figure 11.3, the ratio of trainees over unemployment insurance policyholders has been consistently increasing independent of the economic fluctuations. This demonstrates that the continuous growth in the number of trainees is not solely dependent on the expansion of the number of unemployment insurance policyholders.

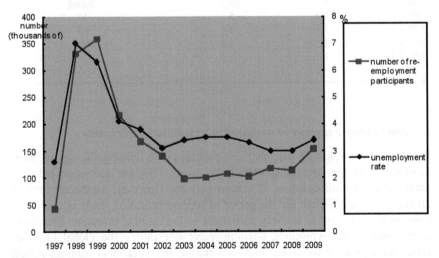

Figure 11.1 Time series of unemployment rate and re-employment training.

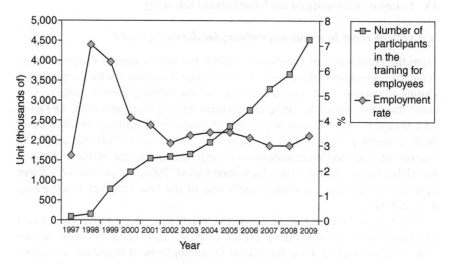

Figure 11.2 Time series of the unemployment rate and employee training participation.

Table 11.11 Expansion of the unemployment insurance penetration rate

Type	Unemployment compensation	Employment stabilization and vocational competency development	Construction industry (million won)
Eligible participants by period			
1995.7.1–12.31	30≥	70≥	4,000
1997.1.1–12.31	30≥	70≥	4,400
1998.1.1–2.28	10≥	50≥	3,400
1998.3.1–6.30	5≥	50≥	3,400
1998.7.1–9.30	5≥	5≥	340
1998.10.–	1≥	1≥	340
2004.1.1.–	1≥	1≥	20
2005.1.1–	1≥	1≥	All licensed construction

B Living expense support of unemployment training participants

Unemployment training participants are provided with training allowances, such as expenses for training, transportation and meals. They are also supported with unemployment compensation in certain periods. However, as the amount of allowances is insufficient and the period of support is limited, many unemployed workers are reluctant to actively participate in the training program. Therefore, in response to the worsening unemployment rate during the global financial crisis, loan policies for living expenses during the vocational training period were first adopted. Loan policies for living expenses during the vocational

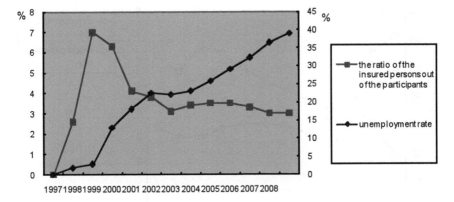

Figure 11.3 Time series of the unemployment rate and the ratio of unemployment insurance policyholders and employee training participation.

training period are designed to help the unemployed and temporary workers receive systematic training and land a better job without concern for living expenses. When the training period exceeds one month, the trainees are eligible to receive a loan proportional to the training period up to one million won a month and 6.4 million won a year. Temporary workers (unemployment insurance policyholders with an annual salary under 24 million won) can receive a loan of up to one million won a month and three million won a year. Especially, the first-time unemployed without an insurance history are eligible for the loan in order to minimize the blind spot of the social safety net. Among the terms of the loan are the interest rate of 1 percent and an equal installment plan for five years after a three-year grace period. In late 2009, 34,013 million won was loaned out to 12,853 unemployed (with 3,203 first-time unemployed), which corresponds to 2.6 to 2.7 million won per person.

C The performance of re-employment training and demography of the participants

The proportion of trainees who are re-employed has improved over time. This fact indicates that the re-employment training has been more effectively

Table 11.12 Loan for living expenses during vocational training (in 2009) (million won)

	Budget	Expenditure	Population	Loan per capita
Unemployment insurance funds (previously unemployed, temporary)	41,393	25,294	9,650	2.62
Labor welfare promotion fund (first-time unemployed)	30,840	8,715	3,203	2.72

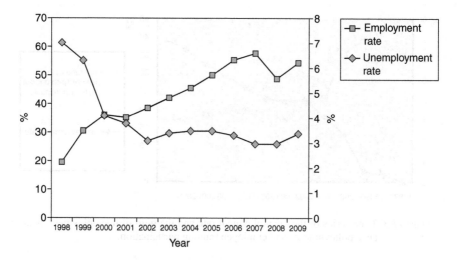

Figure 11.4 Time series of the unemployment rate and the employment rate of the re-
employment training graduates.

implemented than in the past. The influence of various attempts to facilitate the
response to the market demand through the training appears to be significant.
However, as expected, when the economic conditions are not favorable, the
training performance relatively declines in comparison to an economic boom.
The correlation coefficient between the unemployment rate and the training performance based on employment rate is -0.822, indicating that the training performance deteriorates during the economic downturn when the unemployment
rate is high.

The negative effects of recession tend to have the largest impact on disadvantaged groups in the job market, such as women or the less educated or older
workers. This suggests that persons from those groups would be more likely to
participate in training during the economic downturn relative to the economic
boom. The actual results given in Figures 11.5, 11.6, and 11.7 are different in
several aspects. First, during the recession when the unemployment rate is high,
the participation of female workers declines. The correlation coefficient between
the unemployment rate and the participation rate of female workers is -0.388.
The proportion of female among the unemployed rises with the increasing unemployment rate. However, the proportion of female participants among the trainees declines. In addition, the participation rate of workers with lower education
in unemployment training decreases during an economic downturn. The correlation coefficient between the unemployment rate and the training participation
rate of the workers without higher education is -0.635. The same phenomenon
is seen among workers over the age of 50 (with a correlation coefficient of
-0.340). The re-employment training functions as a social safety net as well as
the development of vocational competency during recessions. In Korea, the

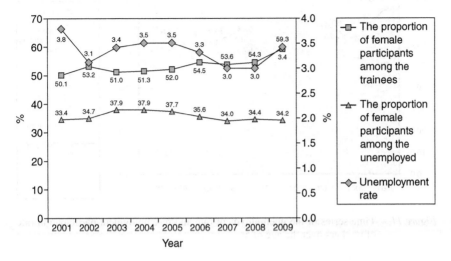

Figure 11.5 Time series of unemployment rate and female re-employment training participation rate.

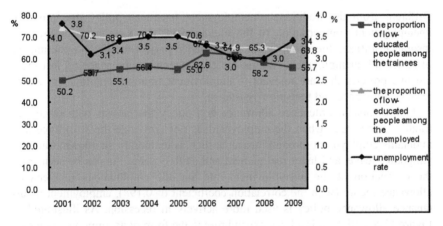

Figure 11.6 Time series of unemployment rate and re-employment participation rate of workers without higher education.

former function is relatively unsatisfactory. Disadvantaged groups are concentrated within the blind spot of the unemployment insurance. This proves that the social safety net is malfunctioning. Excessive emphasis on training performance is causing a so-called "creaming effect." There should be a more concerted government effort to revise re-employment training to support disadvantaged groups.

208   *C.K. Chae*

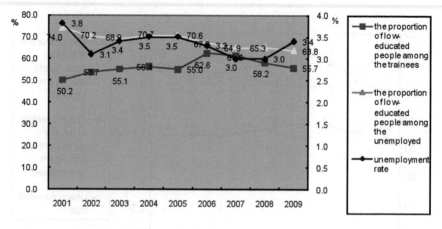

Figure 11.7 Time series of the unemployment rate and re-employment participation rate of workers over the age of 50.

D Supporting unemployed workers through the employment maintenance project

Different from the traditional unemployment insurance policy that provides unemployment compensation to the unemployed, the Korean unemployment insurance initiates the employment maintenance project to alleviate the impact of structural unemployment. Within the employment maintenance project there are two policies that are relevant to employment training: employment maintenance allowance and transition assistance.

Employment maintenance allowance is a policy that assists with wage and training allowances when the employer does not downsize the workforce and maintains employment through measures such as temporary shutdown, training, temporary leave, and labor realignment and shift systems. As can be seen from the correlation of the unemployment rate and the employment maintenance allowance record (with the correlation coefficient of 0.198), employment maintenance allowance policy is used more actively in recession. As illustrated in Figure 11.8, and there is a large expenditure in the form of an employment maintenance allowance when the unemployment rate is high. Especially in 2009, the assistance level of employment maintenance allowance was raised and application requirements for the allowance were eased and the procedure was simplified. This indicates that the practice of the allowance policy has greatly improved.

The transition assistance policy pays the expenses for employers who provide a transition assistance program for employees about to leave the company due to inevitable restructuring. Although this policy is expected to be most useful during a recession, the actual outcome appears to not be the case. The record shows that the unemployment rate is negatively correlated with transition assistance (with the correlation coefficient of −0.376). Fortunately, awareness of this

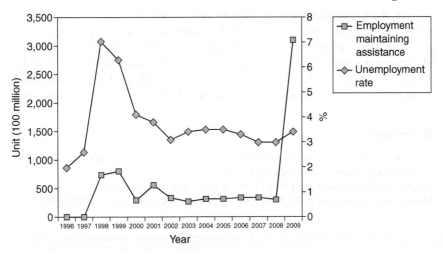

Figure 11.8 Time series of the unemployment rate and employment maintenance
allowance.

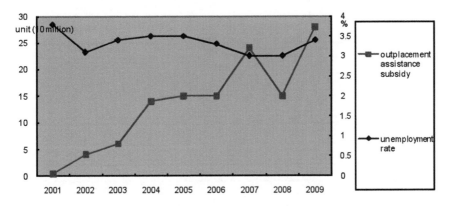

Figure 11.9 Time series of the unemployment rate and transition assistance.

policy appears to be improving within businesses, given that transition assistance
has actively been in use following the recent global financial crisis. In the future,
active use of this policy during a recession seems likely.

V Conclusion

The results of analysis hitherto can be summarized as follows. First, the Korean
government's response to the economic crisis or recession was to expand vocational training and living allowance for trainees. Also, employment maintenance
assistance or transition assistance is also in use in spite of its current limited use.
Second, unemployment training was less successful during a recession than
during an economic boom. Third, the participation of groups of workers such as

women, the less educated, and the elderly appears to be limited. This presumably reflects certain limitations of the current unemployment insurance system in its coverage. Given all the analysis results discussed so far, although the efficiency of training deserves much attention, the role of vocational training as a social safety net should be the most important. The benefits of vocational training should be massively revised and expanded in order to include neglected groups.

References

Korea Research Institute for Vocational Education and Training (2008)' The Twentieth Vocational Education and Training Expertise Forum.
Ministry of Employment and Labor (1996–2010), Labor White Paper.
Ministry of Employment and Labor (1999–2010), Employment Insurance White Paper.

Appendix

Data sets for the study of the Korean labor market

Economically Active Population Survey (EAPS)

경제활동인구조사 (Kyeong Je Hwal Dong In Koo Jo Sa)

National Statistical Office

EAPS started in 1962 in order to provide information for the five-year economic development plans on a quarterly basis. Since July 1982, the Korea National Statistical Office has conducted the survey monthly. Currently it surveys about 30,000 sample households (about 0.2 percent of the Census of Population and Housing) and records information regarding employment and unemployment, such as education, labor force participation, work hours, and job search activities. The contents of the data are similar to those in the *Current Population Survey* by the US Bureau of Labor Statistics. The data are available at the Korea National Statistical Office (online, available at: www.nso.go.kr), Department of Social Statistics.

Korean Labor and Income Panel Study (KLIPS)

한국노동패널조사 (Han Gook No Dong Pae Neol Jo Sa)

Korea Labor Institute

KLIPS is a longitudinal data set of about 5,000 households and their members whose ages are 15 and older. Since its beginning in 1998, the study has been conducted every year by face-to-face interviews. For households, the data include income, assets, housing characteristics, and household structure. For individuals, the data include current employment, work hours, training, education, and work satisfaction. The data structure is very compatible with the Panel Study of Income Dynamics of the United States. The data are publicly available via the Korea Labor Institute (online, available at: www.kli.re.kr), which collects the information.

Monthly Labor Statistics Survey (MLSS)

매월노동통계조사 (Mae Wol No Dong Tong Gye Jo Sa)

Ministry of Labor, Bureau of Labor Statistics

The MLSS started in 1963 to collect basic information on wages and employment. In 1999 the scope expanded from workplaces with ten and more full-time employees to workplaces with five and more full-time employees. It collects information on wages (regular pay, over-pay, and bonus), working hours (total working days, total working hours, regular working hours, and overtime), and employment (current employees, new hires, leavers, and retirements). Since 2006, it also includes a micro survey of about 10,000 work places. The data is available via the Korea Bureau of Labor Statistics (online, available at: http://laborstat.molab.go.kr/.

Basic Statistical Survey of Wage Structure (BSSWS) or Occupational Wage Survey (OWS)

임금구조기본통계조사 (Im Geum Gu Jo Gi Bon Tong Gye Jo Sa)

Ministry of Labor, Bureau of Labor Statistics

The BSSWS is conducted to identify the wages and working hours of workers by types of occupation and industry who are employed by businesses with five or more regular workers. Until 1992 it was called OWS (*Occupational Wage Survey*). Currently it surveys about 6,500 businesses yearly. It contains information about the individual workers as well as businesses. For individuals, it collects general demographic information such as age, sex, marital status, education, and so on and employment related information such as tenure, experience, detailed information regarding compensation and working hours. For businesses, it collects information on employment, personnel policy, wage bills, and general firm characteristics such as firm size, products sold, industrial classification and so on. The data is available via the Korea Bureau of Labor Statistics (online, available at: http://laborstat.molab.go.kr/.

Household Income and Expenditure Survey (HIES)

가계조사 (Ka Kye Jo Sa) or 가계지출조사 (Ka Kye Ji Chul Jo Sa)

National Statistical Office

The HIES has been conducted since 1942 in order to study the revenue and expenditure patterns of urban households. Currently it surveys about 9,000 households (excluding farming and fishing) monthly, sampled throughout the nation. It contains basic information regarding household structure, employment status and housing characteristics, as well as very detailed itemized information of revenue and expenditure of the household. Besides the monthly survey, every five years it collects more detailed information for 27,000 households in the nation. The survey was called the *Urban Household Expenditure Survey* as it used to be restricted to the residents in urban areas. These data are available at the Korea National Statistical Office (online, available at: www.nso.go.kr), Department of Social Statistics.

Youth Panel Survey (YPS)

청년패널조사 (Cheong Nyeon Pae Neol Jo Sa)

Korea Employment Information Service

The YPS is a longitudinal survey to study the transition from school to work of young people. The survey started in 2001 and has been conducted annually. The number of observations in the first year was 8,296. However, the sample size decreased because of attrition. It collects information regarding family, school and work of the young aged between 15 and 29. Besides basic family information (such as family size, residential pattern and income), the survey collects detailed information about schooling, part-time work while at school, job search activities, job training activities, unemployed experience, work experience and the young people's school to work transition. It is benchmarked to the *National Longitudinal Survey of Youth* (NLYS) study of the United States. The survey is provided by the Korea Employment Information Service, and more information can be obtained via their website (online, available at: http://youthpanel.work.go.kr).

Basic Statistical Survey of Business Establishment (BSSBE)

전국사업체기초통계조사 (Jeon Guk Sa Eob Cheo Gi Cho Tong Kye Jo Sa)

National Statistical Office

The BSSBE is a census of business establishments conducted annually since 1994 by the Korea National Statistical Office. It collects basic information such as location, nature of the business, employment, changes in the business on all private businesses except individual farmers and fishermen, military, domestic servants, international agencies and street vendors. As of 2005, there are 3.2 million business establishments employing 15.1 million workers. The information of the survey along with other basic statistical information about Korea can be obtained at the Korean Statistical Portal (online, available at: www.kosis.kr).

Survey on Trends of Labor Demand (STLD)

노동력수요동향조사 (No Dong Ryeok Soo Yo Dong Hyang Jo Sa)

Ministry of Labor, Bureau of Labor Statistics

The STLD is a survey of the 15,000 business establishments with five and more employees, on the current employment and help wanted (positions needed to be filled immediately to satisfy the business demand). The Bureau of Labor Statistics has conducted this survey annually since 1976. The sample is derived from the BSSBE. The business establishments are classified in Korean Standard Industrial Classification. The job data are divided by permanent positions, temporary positions, daily workers and foreign guest workers. The information can be obtained at the bureau (online, available at: http://laborstat.molab.go.kr).

Graduates Occupational Mobility Survey (GOMS)

대졸자 직업이동 경로조사 (Dae Jol Ja Jig Eob Yi Dong Kyeong Ro Jo Sa)

Korea Employment Information Services

GOMS is a longitudinal survey that follows about 25,000 graduates of junior colleges and four-year universities. The sample is the 5 percent stratified sample of about 500,000 graduates who received their degrees in the fall of 2004 or the spring of 2005. The purpose of the study was to study employment and unemployment issues of the highly educated. Key variables include educational programs, job search, experience, vocational and professional training. It started in 2006, but was suspended in 2009. It is modeled after the *Baccalaureate and beyond Longitudinal Study* of the United States and the *National Graduate Study Survey of Canada*. The website for the study is online, available at: http://survey.hrcglobal.com/GOMS/

Index

Page numbers in *italics* denote tables, those in **bold** denote figures.

Verlag GmbH, Kaulbachstraße 24, 80539 München, Germany